The Musical Work

Liverpool Music Symposium 1

The Musical Work: Reality or Invention?

edited by
Michael Talbot

LIVERPOOL UNIVERSITY PRESS

First published 2000 by
LIVERPOOL UNIVERSITY PRESS
4 Cambridge Street, Liverpool L69 7ZU

British Library Cataloguing-in-Publication Data
A British Library CIP record is available.

ISBN 0 85323 825 1 *cased*
ISBN 0 85323 835 9 *paper*

Typeset in Sabon with Gill Sans by
Northern Phototypesetting Co. Ltd, Bolton, Lancs.
Printed and bound in the European Union by
Redwood Books Ltd, Trowbridge, Wilts.

Contents

Notes on Contributors

Lydia Goehr is Professor of Philosophy at Columbia University. She is the author of *The Imaginary Museum of Musical Works: An Essay in the Philosophy of Music* (1992) and *The Quest for Voice: Music, Politics, and the Limits of Philosophy* (1998). She is currently working on modernist opera.

David Horn is Director of the Institute of Popular Music, University of Liverpool. He was a founding editor of *Popular Music* and is currently joint managing editor of the forthcoming *Encyclopedia of Popular Music of the World*.

Serge Lacasse is studying for a PhD at the Institute of Popular Music, University of Liverpool, and also teaches the History of Rock and Rock Music Analysis at Université Laval, Québec. He has written several papers published in Canada, France and Britain. His PhD research concerns what he calls 'the *mise en scène* of the voice in recorded popular music'.

Richard Middleton is Professor of Music at the University of Newcastle upon Tyne. He is a specialist in popular music, and his writings include two books in this field. He is currently working on a study of blues in its world musics context.

Catherine Moore is Clinical Assistant Professor and Director of the Music Business Program at New York University, where she teaches courses in marketing, genre studies and strategic management. Holding a doctorate in Musicology from the University of Liverpool, she has worked in the music industry in Britain, Canada and the United States since 1981. Her research interests include the interaction of culture and industry, international cultural trade and seventeenth-century Italian keyboard and vocal music.

Jim Samson is Stanley Hugh Badock Professor of Music at the University of Bristol. He is noted equally for his work on Polish composers (Chopin, Szymanowski) and for his studies of music of the early twentieth century. His current projects include a book on Liszt's *Transcendental Studies*.

Reinhard Strohm is Heather Professor of Music at the University of Oxford. He has written extensively on eighteenth-century Italian opera, on late medieval and early Renaissance music, and on many other aspects of music history.

Philip Tagg is Reader in Music at the University of Liverpool. A co-founder of the International Association for the Study of Popular Music, he has published extensively on the semiotic analysis of popular music, specialising in music for the moving image.

Michael Talbot is James and Constance Alsop Professor of Music at the University of Liverpool. A specialist in Venetian music of the late Baroque, he has produced books on Vivaldi, Albinoni and Vinaccesi. He has recently completed a book examining the changing nature of the finale in Western instrumental music.

John Williamson is Reader in Music at the University of Liverpool. Among his numerous publications on German music of the period 1850–1950 are books on Hans Pfitzner and Richard Strauss. He is currently preparing a monograph on the stage works of Eugen d'Albert.

James Wishart is Lecturer in Music at the University of Liverpool, where he is Head of Composition and Director of the Electro-Acoustic Studio. His compositions embrace many genres, and he is currently working on a new orchestral work as well as preparing a book-length study of the phenomenon of arrangement and transcription in the nineteenth and twentieth centuries.

Introduction

Michael Talbot

Symposium. Skipping over the first definition of the word in the *Shorter Oxford English Dictionary*, which is 'a drinking-party', one soon arrives at this meaning: 'a meeting or conference for discussion of some subject'. In fact, a typical symposium occupies an intermediate position between what one commonly understands by a 'meeting' and a 'conference'. More ambitious (but also more focused) than the first, less grand (but also less diffuse) than the second, it is an ideal kind of event for the cash-strapped university of today.

The idea of holding a series of Liverpool Music Symposia arose from the coexistence, at this university, of two academic units, the Department of Music and the Institute of Popular Music, which co-operate happily enough in the sphere of undergraduate teaching but rarely find the opportunity to come into direct contact within the scholarly arena. To talk of 'breaking down barriers' is unnecessarily melodramatic. What is needed, rather, is a chance to knock ideas about in a common forum and, by so doing, to reach a clearer understanding of both the similarities and the contrasts that exist between the various musical traditions. It is also useful for students of so-called classical music to learn of (and, if appropriate, adopt or adapt) the concepts and terminology of modern popular music studies, just as the reverse must equally be true.

The theme of the first symposium suggested itself almost by chance. Having read Lydia Goehr's recent book *The Imaginary Museum of Musical Works: An Essay in the Philosophy of Music*, I suddenly realised that the musical work and the varied conception (or, sometimes, non-conception) of it – whether considered diachronically (through history) or synchronically (across the spectrum of musical traditions) – constituted the perfect subject: topical, controversial, multi-faceted and intellectually challenging. From there, the project quickly took wing. In my letter inviting contributions, I described the subject in the following, deliberately provocative terms:

> Within the tradition of what we call, for want of a better term, Western art music, it has seemed axiomatic until quite recently that the basic unit of artistic production and consumption is the 'work' – a hard-edged artefact with a clear identity. One knows – or one thinks that one knows – a musical work as one knows a play, a book or a painting. The prevailing assumption about music that belongs to this tradition is that what composers write, performers play or sing, audiences hear and musicologists discuss are the same things. The objects are fixed and unchangeable, while people's relationship to them varies.
>
> This common-sense, or perhaps naïve, view is increasingly coming under fire from several sides. One philosopher tells us that within Western art music the idea of a work is a historically conditioned construct that crystallised in relatively modern times and may one day be abandoned again. Ethnomusicologists and scholars of popular music show us that our cherished works provide only one possible (and, in a world context, rather rare) solution among many to the question of how to shape a musical culture. Some avant-garde composers seek to give their compositions fuzzy edges or to dissolve their boundaries altogether. Recording offers new ways of encoding and, indeed, generating music that break the monopoly of written notation, which was originally the midwife, and later became the unyielding custodian, of musical works.
>
> Even if, despite these uncertainties, works are here to stay, there is a lot to be gained in not taking them for granted. The more precarious their status, the more interesting and challenging they become, and the more imaginatively we will approach them as composers, performers and commentators.

I was glad when five of my academic colleagues agreed to contribute, and I felt distinctly honoured when five scholars from other institutions, including three from North America, came on board. One of our visitors was Lydia Goehr herself (she is the 'one philosopher' cited in the above blurb); her personal involvement with the symposium, for which I am especially grateful, has enabled her to develop further her original thesis in the light of her continuing work and the differing views and emphases emanating from the other contributors.

The following pages are the proceedings of this symposium, held at the Institute of Popular Music on 21 September 1998. Each essay is based, usually very closely, on a paper circulated to all the participants in advance and discussed *viva voce* at the symposium. No attempt was made to lay down, or even to suggest, which aspect of the theme each participant should cover. In the event, this non-prescriptive policy paid off, for the papers have a liveliness, a sense of close personal engagement with the issues, that a more rigorously programmed approach might have dampened. Naturally, this volume does not have the consistent vision of a single-authored study, but in the wide range of its coverage and the (usually) only mildly dissonant counterpoint of its collective insights it aspires to different virtues.

One problem faced by all the contributors – indeed, the central problem, addressed in the title, from which all the others flowed – was to establish what, exactly, a musical work is, whether from a time-less perspective or in a concrete historical situation. I cannot pretend that a firm consensus was reached, although some common ground was found. There was at least broad agreement among the contribu-tors, as in the world at large, that a musical work, to merit the descrip-tion, has to be discrete, reproducible and attributable (David Horn identifies as many as nine senses), although each of the three men-tioned primary conditions possesses a measure of elasticity, which from the very outset creates immense potential for controversy.

'Discrete' implies the presence of a fixed beginning and end, and the property of being separable from other works. But pieces of music may possess separability at several distinct levels. A Bach prelude can be uncoupled from a Bach fugue, and a prelude-fugue pair from the set of '24', and the '24' from the notional double set of '48'.[1] Simi-larly, a track from The Beatles' 'Sergeant Pepper's Lonely Hearts Club Band' exists, and can be reproduced, separately from the complete album. At which level does the 'real' work reside? Clearly, any theory of 'the work' must accommodate the notion of 'works within works' at a theoretically unlimited number of levels.

'Reproducible' is an equally problematic concept. A musical score and a recording can, each in its own way, be reproduced as perfectly, from a technical standpoint, as a lithograph or a published book, and in so doing ensure the durability necessary for a work to exist. How-ever, the reality of music, for most people, is not a mere artefact (such as a score or a compact disc) but a sound-event, for which the pro-totype, actual or at least conceptual, is a live performance. Live

1. Some languages (not English, however) use their native term for 'work' (*oeuvre*, *Werk*, *opera* etc.) in a special additional sense to refer to a composer's entire output, as if this constituted a single product, a 'super-work', with its own attributes.

performances are intended, in all major musical traditions, to be unique events: total reproducibility runs counter to the basic intention. Even within the one tradition, that of Western art music, which prizes fidelity to a score and therefore, in theory at least, would appear to favour total reproducibility, the factor of 'interpretation' (and the inability of human performers to do exactly the same thing twice even when they strive to do so) subverts any such intention. Reproduction is therefore a highly relative concept: a smooth continuum stretching from perfect mechanical replication, via imperfect human attempts at perfect replication, lightly 'interpreted' but otherwise faithful replication, deliberately or accidentally varied reproduction, paraphrases and so on, all the way to the most distant echoes in the form of jumbled fragments (the so-called *cento* described in Serge Lacasse's essay). Who, then, is able to pronounce, in theoretically cogent terms, on the exact point at which the departure from the source has become so great that a new work arises (or the very existence of a parent work is placed in doubt)? Introducing the concept of 'tune family', as applied to popular music (see Richard Middleton's essay), is one way of coping with the problem.

'Attributability' includes authorship – but only as one of many possibilities. Besides a composer, a performer (or group of performers), a producer, a DJ or a studio technician may legitimately step forward to claim whole or partial credit for a work, as several contributors rightly say. In some cases, the 'property' may lie unclaimed (as in the case of a medieval motet whose composer is not named), but this does not mean that, in the final analysis, it is unowned and therefore ineligible for the status of 'work'. Problems arise, of course, when there are competitors for a work's ownership, with consequences for its identity (and legal status). But these are not arguments about its status as a work *per se*. Where a piece of music may cease to be a work is where its author (or other claimant) is not merely unknown (or disputed) but in principle unknowable. This is perhaps what distinguishes plainsong from traditional folk song. Both pass the tests of discreteness and reproducibility. But a plainsong 'composition', lacking (usually) a named author but notated *ab initio* in fixed, authoritative form, has passed the threshold of attributability, whereas a folk song, which will have evolved in oral transmission via a kind of natural selection, arguably remains – at least, in the form in which it is found by its first transcriber – some way short of this. Even here, a grey area must exist. What if a football chant transmitted purely orally achieves overnight a 'classic', quasi-invariable form? Do we have 'evolving' music (not in any circumstances to be considered as a work) or 'composed' music (potentially a work)? These arguments presuppose, of course, that length and complexity are not in themselves distinguishing criteria. In other words, a signature tune lasting a few seconds can fulfil the necessary conditions for classification as a 'work' as easily as can *Götterdämmerung*.

Proceeding on a purely taxonomic basis, one would not find it easy to exclude any 'composed' and 'closed' musical composition, however trivial or ephemeral. But perhaps more than taxonomy is involved. Lydia Goehr's original argument, while conceding that pre-1800 compositions are taxonomically not always distinguishable from later ones, insists on the necessity of introducing evaluative criteria. A work written according to the 'work-concept' aspires to possess not only objective features (authorship, finiteness, reproducibility) but also some subjective qualities such as status, originality and 'aura' (to delve further into David Horn's list of senses). So the modest album leaves for piano of Wagner (discussed in Reinhard Strohm's essay), even though some of them undoubtedly qualify taxonomically for the label of 'work' – and are accepted as such, alongside the music dramas, into the composer's *Sämtliche Werke* – may arguably fail the test on other grounds. In this perspective, even the famous medieval *Summer Canon*, likewise mentioned by Strohm, may not qualify for 'work' status.[2] Significantly and ironically, as Philip Tagg explains in his essay, the non-receptivity of the world of popular music practice and scholarship to the term 'work' stems from its negative, or at best ambivalent, stance towards the very attributes (status, dignity, durability) that have carried such an unambiguously positive charge for most Western art music of the last two centuries.

There is equally strong disagreement among the contributors over where 'work-ness' resides. For students of popular music (a catch-all term that in reality embraces several more or less autonomous musical traditions), 'work-ness' is a peripheral, not a central, phenomenon. It is an almost fictive concept that enjoys greater currency in the offices of lawyers arguing how much is to be paid to whom than

2. The thought occurs to me that merely to posit a distinction of kind between serious pieces (works) and trivial pieces (non-works) is already to concede Goehr's watershed thesis, since this two-way division is a way of categorising music quite foreign to the discourse before the Romantic era (but not uncommon subsequently).

within the community of musicians and their followers. Hence the precise location of 'work-ness' is, for them, an abstract, even futile, exercise. But for students of Western art music (WECT – the Western European Classical Tradition – in Leo Treitler's formulation), the locus of the work is vitally important, because it determines what one has to aim to be 'faithful' to, in accordance with the demands of *Werktreue*. One school of thought (to which I myself basically subscribe) inclines to the view that, uniquely for this tradition, the work is its score *tout court*; another (closer in this respect to the dominant popular music view) maintains that it is a collection of performances related via one (or more) scores and sufficiently similar to one another to be classed together under a common term. One might liken the argument to a hypothetical debate over what constitutes the 'real' Morris Minor. Is it the designer's plan for the car (including the complete specification of the production processes)? Is it, perhaps, an abstraction based on the features common to all the Morris Minors ever manufactured and driven? Or even a specific car picked as representative, in accordance with some agreed set of criteria? If we transpose these ideas back to the world of music, we see that the first view – the work as score (or any alternative permanent encoding) – is unashamedly composer-centred, and all the clearer for that. The second, practice-centred, is messier, and allows for a variety of different modifying inputs: from performers, instruments and their makers, venues, promoters, producers (for both opera and studio), audiences and so on. The third achieves precision, but at the cost of infinitely multiplying the possible number of works, many would deem absurdly.

This battle over definitions and their application is perhaps, in the final analysis, a battle over priorities and even ideals. It has its counterpart in drama, that other re-creative art. Fidelity to the *Urtext* of a work by Haydn is the precise equivalent of fidelity to Shakespeare's lines as they appear in the *First Folio*. Conversely, the wish to 'bring Handel alive for modern audiences' (equivalent to using non-historical instruments) finds its exact parallel in a theatre director's project that proposes 'a Molière for our times' (using modern dress). The problem of 'work-ness' is therefore not confined to music. Ultimately, perhaps, personal experience, interest and taste all play their part in our choice of definitions. To sum up the situation empirically, but I think accurately: a proponent of the work as 'text' (in Richard Taruskin's apt terminology) is likely to enjoy actively collecting and perusing scores; the advocate of the work as 'act' is likely to go to many concerts (or listen to many recordings).[3] In other words, our concept of the musical work probably correlates closely with our attitude to the written (as opposed to spoken) word; to the relative weight we attach to durability and topicality; and to a raft of other factors that have more to do with educational background, professional activity and social attitudes than with reason and judgement, abstractly considered.

We may choose to harden or soften the edges of works according to whether we propose to deal with them in the mode of literary critics (concerned with text) or drama critics (concerned with act). In the latter sense, a work, in any precise shape or form, is not a given but a construct based on, but rarely limited by, the imagination of its original creator. No sooner does a piece of music acquire its initial identity – in Western art music, via a score; in popular music, via many possible means of preservation including simple memory – than what Jonathan Miller has termed (with special reference to theatre) its 'afterlife' begins.[4] This subsequent existence, a mixture of repetition (which we call 'tradition') and innovatory deviation, can certainly be distinguished, for analytical purposes, from the original textual prescription, but it cannot be discounted altogether if we wish to contemplate a work (or any other kind of piece) in its fullness. Even a musical tradition (WECT) that makes text and work as coextensive as possible cannot altogether close the window of variability opened by performance. A person reading and enjoying a score has to imagine its sound in order to assimilate its content, just as it is impossible to read these present lines without converting the words on the page into a mental sound-picture that is arguably a kind of 'performance' in its own right.[5]

---

3. Taruskin's account of the tensions between notated instructions and performative acts in a series of essays recently published under the apt title of *Text and Act: Essays on Music and Performance* (New York and Oxford, Oxford University Press, 1995) has much relevance for the present discussion.

4. Jonathan Miller, *Subsequent Performances*, London, Faber and Faber, 1986, p. 25.

5. In *Sound and Semblance: Reflections on Musical Representation* (Princeton, Princeton University Press, 1984), Peter Kivy makes the extraordinary claim (p. 102) that reading a playscript text 'does not normally entail the production of mental speech'. I dispute this. Has anyone ever read and understood a word in a play, poem, novel or scholarly article whose sound as spoken was not simultaneously imagined? The parallel between notes in the score and words on the page seems to me very close.

This volume offers eleven different perspectives on what it means to be (or not to be) a work. Some contributions are panoramic in scope; others are case-studies; a few manage to combine long-range and close-up vision. Because the subject of the essays was clearly identified from the start, and, more importantly, because the contributors had the opportunity to enter into dialogue with one another at an early stage, first through the circulation of the initial drafts of the papers and later at the Symposium itself, the cross-references, implicit as well as overt, are very dense.[6] Editors of multi-authored books often take it upon themselves to help the reader by adding footnotes that draw attention to such connections. I have chosen to do this only in very limited measure, believing that readers brave enough to tackle such an thorny subject will be attentive enough to discover the convergences and divergences for themselves. In any case, the contributors have mostly done my work for me.

Although closely connected via their common theme, the essays in this volume form no obvious sequence. Nor is any essay so privileged, by design or by accident, as to rank as a 'keynote' contribution that should lead off by right. My pragmatic solution has been to organise the essays alphabetically by author, which at least gives any reader too impatient to refer to the contents page a better chance of arriving quickly at the intended destination. The exception to this ordering principle is Lydia Goehr's contribution, which, by virtue of being (so to speak) a counterblast to the many reactions to her book, finds its natural place at the end of the volume.

It will be helpful at this point to give a thumbnail sketch of the subject and argument of each essay in turn.

David Horn takes as his starting point the empirical observation that in the discourse around popular music, whether among practitioners, audiences, critics or scholars, the term 'work' is rarely encountered, except (uncomfortably) where legally required for copyright protection. The central reason for the inappropriateness of the word and the concept it embodies resides in the fact that the popular music event is shaped by 'an interactive nexus of performer, per-

6. So dense, in fact, that the present editor had a hard task to verify that phrases and passages quoted from other contributors' papers read at the Symposium had not changed during the course of their revision in preparation for publication. There has, of course, been some unfairness, in that out of any two discussants, only one can have the 'last' word – but such is always the case with a finite debate.

formance and performed'. To privilege a musical text (the 'performed') by giving it a prescribed form would constrain unacceptably the two other components of the triad and weaken this interaction. Horn discerns many 'work-like' elements in popular music, especially in the Broadway musical, but concludes that these are seldom clear-cut or uncontroversial enough to justify using the word.

Serge Lacasse attempts to establish a comprehensive typology of recorded popular music by applying, in adapted form, a set of concepts originally formulated by the literary critic Gérard Genette. This method entails distinguishing hypertexts (texts based on earlier texts) from hypotexts (texts serving as models for later texts). Their intertextual relationship may be either autosonic (reproducing the original sound) or allosonic (imitating the original sound). It may be either syntagmatic (concerned with material) or paradigmatic (concerned with style). The whole of recorded popular music can be located – albeit not always in a simple or unambiguous manner – along the twin axes autosonic/allosonic and syntagmatic/paradigmatic. The multitude of ways in which musical substance is made to migrate from one recorded performance to another would appear to make the notion of 'work' more elusive than ever, although, intriguingly, Lacasse fleetingly raises the possibility of there being some underlying 'ideal' (even when never manifest) form of a popular song – a concept that has its counterpart in the discourse about Western art music (see John Williamson's essay, later).

Richard Middleton brings together two important themes addressed by the first two contributors. Like Horn, he insists that the driving motor of popular music culture is not objects (which is to say: works) but practice. Like Lacasse, he emphasises the density and many-sidedness of the intertextual bonds between musical performances. His detailed analysis of studio 'recompositions' by Bill Laswell of well-known recordings by Miles Davis and Bob Marley throws both arguments into sharp focus. The concept of 'signifyin(g)', on which Middleton lays emphasis, refers to a key element in the African-American musical tradition that has passed into the general practice of Western popular music: the deliberate use of familiar, shared elements as a basis for subsequent transformation.

Catherine Moore shows how the mutations wrought by Laswell are only extreme manifestations of the general tendency of the recording industry to continue to manipulate sounds after the initial performance is over. Commercial pressures and technological wizardry combine to make the recording not merely the reproduction of a musical performance but a carefully crafted 'work' in its own right. Even within the classical sphere, where the integrity of the musical work ought, in theory, to be respected, the latter is in reality broken down, thanks to digitalisation, into a multitude of discrete signals (Michelangelo's 'Day of Judgement' fresco as a jigsaw puzzle, to employ Moore's striking metaphor) capable of being processed into a limitless number of new forms and arrangements. A second tier of 'interpreters' is added to the first in the shape of producers – and above the producers lurks a third tier: the company's A & R department.

Jim Samson examines the pre-recital pianistic culture of the early nineteenth century, as represented by such figures as Chopin and Liszt, discovering in it many features carrying over from the period before the great paradigm shift in Western art music identified by Lydia Goehr, i.e. the establishment of a regulative work-concept in the period around 1800: most notably, the continued, even enhanced, importance of performer, instrument and genre (as opposed to notated text) in determining the nature of the musical event. He stresses the vital rôle of improvisation – a practice that dispenses with works – in this culture and shows how it exerted a modifying influence over other aspects. Samson draws parallels with rock music, showing how, in various ways and at various times, Western art music has come closer to other traditions than one might have suspected.

Reinhard Strohm disputes the historical reality of this great paradigm shift, seeing it as simplistic and far too unilinear in conception. He finds many precedents in Renaissance music for both work-status and the work-concept. Strohm reviews the history of the debate over the nature of the musical work and over the existence (or not) of a watershed in the late eighteenth or early nineteenth century. He insists that the work is a robust, long-established concept within Western art music, and that to question its reality or status goes needlessly over old ground and betrays 'anxiety over the collapse of the value of modernity and the fear of an isolation of the European tradition'.

Philip Tagg begins with a minute examination of the etymological and semantic ramifications of the term 'work'. He goes on to argue that its use, within European music, is bound up with the values of one particular 'community of aesthetic taste', whose central reference point is the bourgeois culture of nineteenth-century Germany. The resistance to the work-concept among practitioners, devotees and scholars of modern popular music is therefore not only because the 'object' is itself taxonomically resistant: it arises equally from a desire to identify with different, autonomous communities of taste. Tagg brings out very forcefully the cultural pluralism within a class-based society, more visible today than ever before.

Michael Talbot accepts the existence of a watershed in Western art music located in the decades around 1800, albeit one not characterised by any major landmark events. He notes, in parallel with the emergence of a modern work-concept, the acceptance by the broad public, for the first time, of a composer-centred (rather than genre-centred or performer-centred) view of music – a perspective that had earlier been more or less confined to practitioners, patrons and connoisseurs. The relevance of composer-centredness to the work-concept is that the 'standard unit' of musical culture becomes the *oeuvre* of a single composer, subdivided into a (usually) heterogeneous body of works that, irrespective of their differences of genre, substance and scale, now always have to be considered in relation to each other by virtue of their common authorship.

John Williamson focuses on a single musician, Ferruccio Busoni (1866–1924), who, in the course of a many-sided career as composer, transcriber, pianist and essayist, adopted a highly individual stance vis-à-vis musical works and their arrangements. Instead of regarding an original and its transcription simply as model and altered copy (hypotext and hypertext, in Genette's parlance), Busoni related both to what he called an 'Ur-Musik': an ideal, latent music awaiting its necessarily incomplete and imperfect realisation by composer and executant. A work is therefore something inherently Protean that cannot be identified exclusively with any one manifestation, whether musical score or performance. As Williamson remarks, Busoni came close to regarding all works as transcriptions (of an ideal prototype), a radical view that plays havoc with conventional attempts to distinguish in a rigorous manner between original, transcription, arrangement, variation and paraphrase, as well as erasing traditional generic boundaries.

James Wishart puts the relationship between hypotexts and hypertexts again under the spotlight. The latter are by a triad of late-twentieth-century composers – Tippett, Berio and Zender – the former all by Schubert. While Wishart does not draw explicit parallels with music from traditions other than the WECT, some emerge very clearly. His positive critical stance vis-à-vis arrangements and re-compositions, which has much more in common with that of commentators on popular music (as Horn, Lacasse, Middleton and Tagg all evidence) than that of many of their confrères in the sphere of classical music, suggests that, as the century and millennium draw to a close, convergence on this issue, at least, is in the air.

Lydia Goehr defends, and at the same time refines, her original proposition in the light of the critique of it offered by Reinhard Strohm. Among the important new points she makes is that the actual emergence of a concept – in this instance, the musical work-concept around 1800 – is distinguishable from what one may retroactively take to be its originating factors, which may indeed lie much further back (one is reminded here of the Marxian idea of the transformation of accumulated quantitative change into qualitative change). Goehr also shows how a historian's or a philosopher's choice of paradigmatic examples, which is never made automatically or innocently, inescapably colours the subsequent discourse. Some element of circular reasoning seems, despite everything, to underlie all our efforts to make conceptual sense of our world.

One thing that comes across clearly in several of these contributions is that a cultural practice such as music cannot exist without commonly accepted units of identification. A work is one kind of unit; examples of others are a theme, a number, a set and an album. Each musical tradition creates or selects the units of identification most appropriate to it (with the important proviso that there can be no certainty that these will remain fixed for all time).[7]

Whether or not there has been a single work-concept governing Western art music of the past millennium (or even of the past two centuries only), the continued existence of a comprehensive and prescriptive notational system has ensured that there have at least always been works. But what if the guiding hand of notation were loosened or withdrawn? Or, conversely, if it were extended, possibly in electronic form, to musical traditions that hitherto have shunned it? In this perspective, the musical work reveals itself to be, in the most literal sense, an **invented reality**: something that, for one musical

---

7.   For evidence that even a high-status canonical art music can exist without works, let alone a work-concept, see Harold Powers, 'A Canonical Museum of Imaginary Music', *Current Musicology*, Vol. 60/61 (1996), pp. 5–25. The tradition in question is that of Indian classical music.

tradition in particular, came into being in historical time, exists now, and may or may not continue in its present form into the future.

In conclusion, I should like to record my thanks: to the contributors, who showed themselves equally adept at fulfilling the demands of *labor* and *opus*; to my colleagues Judith Blezzard, Patricia Fisher and John Williamson for help with editing, organising and chairing, respectively; to the Institute of Popular Music for hosting the Symposium; to Robin Bloxsidge and Liverpool University Press for making the passage to publication so easy; to the Music and Letters Trust and the University of Liverpool for contributing generously towards expenses; to the Research Leave Scheme of the Humanities Research Board and the University of Liverpool for granting me a period of study leave that greatly speeded the preparation of the present volume; to e-mail and its attachments for indispensable, though occasionally wayward, assistance.

I

Some Thoughts on the Work in Popular Music

David Horn

If, as a starting point, we may take a musical work to be a discrete musical object, it is almost a cliché to say that the academic study of popular music is very much in two minds about it. Academic theoretical writing on popular music has frequently borrowed the term 'text' to denote this object: a usage not without its problems, as you will be told by anyone with the experience of teaching 'textual analysis' to students who assume, until instructed to the contrary, that it means the study of lyrics. The tradition of 'textual analysis' is a persistent one, but sociological, ethnographic and economic research has pointed to the need (sometimes seen as overriding) to concentrate attention on the productive and receptive processes and to question the idea that it is possible or desirable to separate a musical object from these processes. At the same time, within text-based approaches themselves, the impact of critical theory has contributed to the challenge posed to the ongoing existence of paradigms based on the idea of a 'work'.

But I would really rather begin elsewhere, in a wider, less rarefied context, where an academic approach is only one among many, and point to the obvious fact that in the everyday language of popular music practice in anglophone countries the term 'work' is rarely, if ever, found. I strongly suspect that its equivalents in other languages – *oeuvre*, *Werk* etc. – make equally rare appearances. This may sound an unpromising opening, but I should add straight away that describing this as an 'obvious fact' is somewhat disingenuous on my part, because I confess that I cannot remember ever consciously considering the matter before. So if it is obvious, I also – naïvely, perhaps – find it surprising, and therefore worth exploring a little further.

By 'popular music practice' I mean the several interconnecting spheres that make up this environment: not only the sphere of music-making but also those of the music industry, of commentators on the phenomenon in their various guises (including academic) and of the audience. In the discourse of this practice a popular musician may speak of 'my music' or 'my songs'; in certain genres, he or she may say, 'Here's a new number'. If a popular musician should introduce a 'new number' with such words as 'And now for my latest work', the audience is almost certain to understand this as ironic. Enthusiasts sometimes discuss a particular 'piece', although they may well prefer to discuss it in its recorded form, and, in that context, to talk about a particular 'track'. Throughout the range of commentary on popular music, from populist to academic-theoretical, whenever it is necessary to pin down for discussion one or more musical objects, the terms 'work' and 'works' are strenuously avoided. A brief search that I carried out on a small sample of popular music monthly journals suggested that the process of identifying individual pieces by a generic name was likewise being avoided, 'songs' being the only, partial exception.[1] The sole occasion when a non-generic collective term was called for came in discussing the totality of items on a CD, and, indeed, the closest this writing comes to referring to 'works' is to talk about 'albums'. For their part, academics, as we have already noted, like to talk about 'texts'.

The ways in which the popular music industry, in particular its publishing and recording arms, refers to musical artefacts in its marketing sometimes give the impression that it would like to use the term 'work' if it could. (When it talks to itself about artefacts, it talks about 'product'.) Here, no doubt, one sees the influence not of popular music practice but of practice in the art music departments of those industries. This can be witnessed even in record and publishing companies with no classical arm. The notion of the 'work' (the term itself occasionally surfaces) commonly relates to notions of completion; so, for example, the Document label's massive reissuing programme of African-American blues and gospel records of the 1920s and 30s features a number of CDs with titles constructed around the phrase 'the complete recorded works of'. Jazz record labels have been using this approach for a considerable time, extending the concept of completion in some instances to the reissue of every known recorded take. Musicians celebrated and revered for their outstanding improvisatory

---

1. The journals in question were 1998 issues of *Select*, *Mojo* and *Vox*.

skills, such as Charlie Parker, have been the most frequent recipients of this honour.

Even so, I am familiar with only one example from popular music publishing where the term 'work' itself appears (with this sense of completion). That is in the title of the two-volume set of the music of Scott Joplin, *The Collected Works of Scott Joplin*, edited by Vera Brodsky Lawrence. This edition was published, in 1971, not by a commercial publisher but by the New York Public Library. It clearly did not set a trend, but I suspect that where the usage will reappear – which it may already be doing – is in the publishing of collected editions of popular and popular-related music of the nineteenth century, such as that of Stephen Foster. This may be because, in commercial publishing eyes, the risk entailed by describing sets of popular music artefacts as 'works' diminishes when those works predate recorded sound, with its ability to encode and distribute actual performance: when, in effect, the mode of encoding and distributing those works was primarily that of printed notation – the form used, and used in the identical way, by art music composers and their publishers (I will return later to the question of the relationship between recorded sound and the notion of the work).

Just because the term itself is so rare in popular music practice does not mean, of course, that the ideas and implications contained in it are also rare. One could point to a number of phenomena that appear to be part of popular music practice, but for which the language of that practice has no term of its own (a situation that sometimes leaves it prey to the attention of new, powerful – and power-seeking – terms nurtured elsewhere) and/or does not generally use the term that does exist. Some technical musical vocabulary would fall into the second of these categories. As an example of the first, one may cite the importation into popular music commentary of terms first used in non-musical circumstances and subsequently applied to music in the expectation that they will fit: such a term, for example (to cite one recent importation), as 'hybridity'. Clearly, there are also areas of practice where language may have struggled to invent and develop as rapidly as practice itself. This is perhaps most apparent in the arena of technology; but we should hesitate before we conclude that the problem is the absence of ideas, or of an ability to respond to ideas by creating an appropriate language. Where technology meets language, as, for example, in the recording studio, linguistic inventiveness is often evident. As Antoine Hennion showed in 1981 through a study of

French recording professionals, the imperative to be able to com-
municate experienced by musicians, producers and engineers in a
pressurised environment leads to the employment of everyday speech
in a practical but imaginative, often metaphorical, way that often
resorts to antitheses and draws in other areas of life in unexpected
ways.[2] Reviewing Hennion's book, Philip Tagg selected and translated
some of his favourite expressions: the producer wanting the Fender
guitar sound to be 'hairier'; a musician's description of a sound as
'majestic with a hangover'. It is a practical solution to a particular
problem, but it is also, as Tagg remarked, in effect an 'aesthetic verbal
vocabulary'.[3]

Tagg saw Hennion's work as providing 'a veritable gold mine of
transmodal expressions for the semiotically and culturally-sociologi-
cally orientated music analyst, offering great potential for expanding
traditional musicology to link the sound event with its social meaning
(which should be the main aim of musicology anyhow)'. However
much I might agree with that formulation (which would go some way
to solving the dilemma noted at the beginning of this essay), discussing the aim of musicology is not among my objectives here. My
point at this juncture is a more basic one, and it has two parts: first,
we should accept the likelihood that, if popular music needed to
denote and connote in one simple term the multifarious strands of
thought that converge around that term, it would have one, whether
it was its own term or was introduced from elsewhere; second, the
fact that, on the one hand, there is no widespread use of the term
'work' and no single equivalent but, on the other hand, there is evidence of 'aesthetic verbal thinking' and a tendency to link the sound-
event and social meaning may mean that popular music prefers to
have the freedom to express related ideas in other ways; and it is these
that we need to investigate.

I have referred to 'multifarious strands of thought that converge
around' a term such as 'work'; I could perhaps have called it poly-
semic. But what are these strands, these shades of meaning? I can think
of nine different senses which are, or can be, attached to the term
'work' when it is used in what we might for convenience call Western
aesthetic discourse. Not all are necessarily present in any one usage,

2. Antoine Hennion, *Les Professionels du disque: une sociologie des variétés*, Paris,
   Métailié, 1981.
3. Philip Tagg, review of Hennion's book in *Popular Music*, Vol. 3 (1983), p. 311.

but none, I suggest, is ever far away. A list of these nine senses follows. I should stress that this list is not the result of sustained scholarship but, rather, of a need to put to good use the accumulated impressions that have been absorbed over the years. I should emphasise in addition that I do not in any way wish to imply that the list is comprehensive. I will focus on the work in discourse about music, but each of the senses – with the partial exception of the last – is present to some degree in discourse about other forms of artistic expression as well.

1 The **piece** of music: the discrete, identifiable musical object. This sense is ever-present. But the term 'piece' carries fewer connotations than 'work'; the latter is not, or is not merely, a synonym for 'piece'.

2 A piece of music with its own **identity**, or, if you prefer, 'character'. One work is distinguishable from another not only by a figurative or actual distance between them as objects, but also because we understand them to be somehow different in nature.

3 An **achievement**, the outcome of endeavour. While the success of that endeavour is not entirely measurable by the amount of effort expended on it, it can play a part in that measurement.

4 The endeavour is that of an identifiable **author**, or of a collaboration between authors (in collaborations it is not unusual for one author to be viewed as the more important). With the idea of authorship come two others: the author has shown **creativity**, and the result of that creativity lends **authority** to both the piece and its author.

5 As the end product of an often individual-centred creative process with its own identity, the work can be said to have **originality**. It possesses this partly because no two pieces produced by this process are ever likely to be identical, but also because it has to exist in an aesthetic environment that sets a high value on music that combines difference with inventiveness and where there is at least a relative absence of imitation.

6 Originality in its turn bequeaths two things. The first is the potential to obtain **status** or rank. Within the Western aesthetic process the potential for status in some form is the birthright of any work, because that process has come to involve a ranking system, and all works can expect to be positioned in relation to others. One feature of the ranking system is the practice of **canonisation**, by which

the status of certain of the works can be expected to rise considerably above that of the rest.

7   Being part of a canon is not the end of the matter, however; the
    second gift of being considered original is that works, especially
    ones which the canonisation process has treated well, may be
    thought to go beyond originality and to exude a hard-to-define
    sense of artistic sanctity, the phenomenon that Walter Benjamin
    termed the **aura**.

8   At the same time, in the everyday world where music is a means of
    making a living, a work is a piece of **property**. To exploit one's
    musical property in as many ways as the law recognises and per-
    mits requires one to signal both its authorship and its individual-
    ity, for the system is founded on the provable claim to authorship
    and the identification and use, in many different contexts, of sep-
    arable musical objects.

9   In order to ensure that the individuality of the musical work, both
    as property and as artistic expression, can always be recognised,
    the work's existence incorporates some form of **blueprint** or tem-
    plate for performance. It is taken for granted in discourse about
    the musical work that it can be brought into existence by people
    other than its originator, and, indeed, that this is a major reason
    for its existence.

We should also note that while usage of the term 'work' may be confined to the function of identification, one of the consequences of the
meanings that converge around the term is that its function seldom
stops there. It plays a major part in establishing and working out
processes of categorisation: for example, by style or genre. It is an
enabling device in the activities of performance, reception and scholarship. It also facilitates evaluation and so contributes to categorisation by status. By means of these functions, it acquires another: that
of aiding in processes of control and regulation.

We can all, I am sure, think of compositions in Western art music
in the discourse for which all nine of my senses might well be present,
and where the usage of the term might well involve the different
processes summarised a moment ago. But my purpose is to think
about popular music: I have suggested that the term 'work' is rare in
this context; but is the same true of all these shades of meaning?

Perhaps because of an intermittent envy of those disciplines that
encourage the compilation and presentation of information in neatly

tabulated form, complete with statistics where necessary, it occurred to me that it would be an interesting exercise to try to plot the appearance of my nine senses of the 'work' in popular music discourse: to come up with columns of ticks to mark their presence or absence, and to add in ratings for each according to a level of (in)dispensability. I imagine the exercise as being based on an examination of as many types of source as possible, verbal and written, and being organised mainly by genre, from, say, late-nineteenth-century popular song to contemporary dance music, including such sets as ragtime, music hall, 1920s Tin Pan Alley, big band, swing, country blues, Broadway, bebop, film music, rock and roll, rock, country music, chart pop, hip hop, dance music and so on. This would clearly be a mammoth task, and I have not attempted it, although I continue to believe in its possible merits.[4] But merely proceeding on the basis of my own knowledge, sketching out how the exercise might proceed and filling in some selected columns by way of experiment revealed some interesting things. These are presented below. Because the investigation is partial and unscientific, I have not offered any tables or columns and ask you to indulge me, in a spirit of furthering scholarly enquiry, by imagining them for the purpose of the exercise.

Before we proceed to test for the presence in popular music discourse of the individual senses that can be attached to the term 'work', as enumerated above, we need a column for the totality of meanings. In the case of popular music, however, having created the column, we have to leave it largely empty. Indeed, the only examples familiar to me where popular music discourse can begin to embrace the range of meanings that cluster around a great many art music compositions belong to the genres of the stage and film musical; and even here, the presence of one particular sense, that of authorship, is not guaranteed.

---

4. That the compilation of information in tabulated form about matters musical, i.e. not only contextual, can be a very important part of popular music research is demonstrated by Garry Tamlyn's recently completed dissertation on the origins of the snare backbeat in rock and roll (*The Big Beat: Origins and Development of Snare Backbeat and Other Accompanimental Rhythms in Rock 'n' Roll*, unpublished PhD dissertation, University of Liverpool, 1998). Tamlyn's presentation includes a large number of charts that display the results of analysing over 2,500 individual recordings for the presence of backbeats and other accompanimental rhythms.

1   A column for **piece** is ticked for every one of the selected genres, but rating the importance of this in each case is difficult, because the degree to which a piece can be isolated from other factors is variable. In the case of many genres – especially after the advent of commercially issued sound recordings – the idea of a piece is incomplete without the idea of its performance.

2   The notion that individual pieces of popular music may be distinguishable by their own **identity** or character is common across popular music genres. But, as with 'piece', this notion is not necessarily established by virtue of the composed element alone. Performance, whether live or recorded, and technical production in the recording studio are major sites of the elements that enable identity distinctions to be drawn between pieces. Indeed, identity can sometimes be seen to reside in the activity of performance *tout court*, without particular concern for the end product, a phenomenon reminding us of the space that frequently exists in popular music between 'text' and 'interpretation'. Yet, at the same time, it would be wrong to ignore the powerful influence that the record, as the end result of a combination of activities, exerts over the notion of identity.

   If one plausible conclusion to draw from these observations is that the notion of identity in popular music discourse points to the complex relationship within that discourse between the activity of production, especially its performative aspects, and the end product, they also reveal how strongly that notion is informed by a keen awareness of the many ways in which similarity and difference interweave. Unlike Theodor Adorno, whose denial of a valid relationship between similarity and difference in popular music seems, with hindsight, perhaps the most perverse of his judgements, popular music discourse accepts that identity can – and frequently does – arise out of the subtle possibilities for interplay here: out of difference contained by similarity (as, for example, in a cover version, of which more later); out of difference created out of similarity (as in a jazz improvisation); or out of similarity extended by difference (as in an 'interpretation' of a song).

3   A tendency to recognise and talk about an individual popular song or record, or a body of such songs or records, as an **achievement** is similarly common across a range of genres. To cite some very obvious examples: one thinks of the characteristic discourse around a single recording such as The Beach Boys' *Good*

Vibrations (1966); or The Beatles' LP 'Sergeant Pepper's Lonely Hearts Club Band' (1967); or the apparently finite corpus of music from musicians as disparate as, say, George Gershwin, Violeta Parra and Bernard Herrmann. Again, however, a caveat is needed because of the importance attached in many generic contexts to the act of performing, and to the implied corollary that finding a single, preferred outcome to a musical task, one that could be regarded in some way as definitive, is not essential to the aesthetic value of the genre in question. Jazz provides an obvious example of this: the numerous takes of Charlie Parker records referred to earlier as evidence for the music industry's desire to sell the idea of completion are also evidence that for Parker himself there was unlikely ever to be one single preferred outcome of soloing one more time on the chords of *I Got Rhythm*. But jazz is not the only example. What attracts audiences time and again to popular music concerts, when the music itself is well known, is the pleasure to be taken in watching the details – and the variables – of performance and (often, also) in being part of the event.

4   The idea of **authorship** is present to some degree in the discourse of most popular music genres but carries weight in only a few. One thinks, for example, of some subgenres of rock music (especially, perhaps, the singer-songwriter tradition); of certain areas of the musical theatre (musicals as varied as Rodgers and Hammerstein evergreens and the convention-breaking shows of Sondheim are identified with their authors, but far more have entered public consciousness by their titles alone); of a small number of jazz bandleaders such as Duke Ellington who were also known for their origination of material. Ellington is an interesting case in this context in that, although he is well known both as a songwriter and as a creator of pieces for jazz orchestra, it is not so much the pieces themselves that carry the authority of ownership as the arrangements. Countless other musicians have performed their own versions of his 1931 melody *Mood Indigo*, for instance, and have done so in the tried and trusted jazz manner of using, and placing their stamp on, whatever available material was found appealing. Put another way, they have added their voices to the ongoing, many-voiced dialogue with the piece. But the moment they attempt to reproduce the unusual voicings which gave the first performances and recordings of *Mood Indigo* their particular character, they enter into an entirely different relationship,

one that recognises – and, often, reveres – the presence of the author.[5]

In the case of film music, authorship is important within the film-making industry and within academic writing, but, with a very few exceptions, is almost entirely absent from the language of the audience.[6] In the discourse of a wide range of genres, from nineteenth-century popular song through country blues to rhythm and blues, most jazz, rock and roll and dance music, the author or authors of the music, in terms of 'credited' authorship, are minor players.

5   With (again) the partial exception of the musical theatre, the idea – and, with it, the importance – of **originality** is a comparatively late arrival. It is found in much rock music. It is likewise central to discourse about most postwar jazz, but only rarely in the context of a piece of music; originality and bebop, for example, come together around performance and, especially, improvisational processes. When the word appears in discourse about earlier genres, it is very often being applied retrospectively. There is no evidence, for example, that the contemporary audience for country or vaudeville blues thought in terms of originality. Moreover, when the marketing of these musics played on an element of difference, it did so with an equal pinch of familiarity.

6   A column for **canonisation** in relation to pieces of popular music displays similar differences between genres, but the divergence of attitude among different groups is particularly marked. Many popular music scholars tend to see any expression that implies the presence of a canon as evidence of the shadow of the thought police, but there is no evidence that the more general audience is as hostile to, or suspicious of, the idea that certain pieces could be elevated far above others. What is interesting for our purposes is that the desire to create a canon (as opposed to the advisability of

5. As Ellington scholars and biographers have often reported, the actual melody of *Mood Indigo*, like a number of others credited to the Duke, may well have been the invention of one of his musicians. The issue has considerable importance because of the way copyright law recognises musical property (and Ellington's musicians were known to make finger-rubbing gestures to him from their stands in order to remind him of the debt he owed them for property of theirs that he had appropriated), but it seems unlikely that *Mood Indigo* would have acquired its status by virtue of its melody alone.

6. This parallels what Michael Talbot says later (pp. 172–74) about composer-centredness in earlier art music.

doing so) is doubtless present in the discourse of any one popular music genre, but its actual establishment is always subject to intense debate, because there are no agreed criteria. One of the reasons for the absence of those criteria is that a concept of the work, which might provide an agreed basis, does not dominate. The closest popular music comes to art music canons in relation to the work is probably, once again, in the musical theatre, where the existence of a notated blueprint, a set of agreed theatrical conventions (borrowed, to some degree, from opera) regarding the 'integration' of music and drama, and another set of criteria derived from the study of classical song, have permitted, perhaps encouraged, the idea of the 'Broadway masters'. In many other areas, arguments about a canon may take ideas of the work into account in varying degree, but a great many of them tend to revolve ultimately around a complex of ideas involving the relationship between performance and creation.

7   As it appeared in Benjamin's celebrated formulation, the **aura** of a work of art belonged to the world before mechanical reproduction. The various features that it subsumed (uniqueness, authority – the 'most sensitive nucleus' of a work of art – quality of presence, and location within 'the fabric of tradition') were all threatened by mechanical reproduction's ability to lift the work of art out of its own time and space.[7] Popular music's long and frequently inseparable relationship with the means of mechanical reproduction suggests that aura, in this premechanical sense, would be rare in popular music discourse; and such does, indeed, appear to be the case. What is not rare, however, is the presence of these various characteristics of the auratic in new guises.[8] One such guise was noted in (4) above: the particular sound-quality of Duke Ellington's arrangement of his *Mood Indigo* identifies it to such an extent that however many versions of the tune are performed, in however many arrangements, this particular arrangement inhabits its own time and its own territory above the hurly-burly, preserving its own quality of presence. What this fact suggests is that the challenge posed by the task of filling the space which, as we noted earlier, often exists between the popular music 'text' and its

7. Walter Benjamin, 'The Work of Art in the Age of Mechanical Reproduction', in *Illuminations*, ed. Hannah Arendt, London, Fontana, 1973, pp. 223 and 225.
8. As Richard Middleton notes in his essay in this volume (p. 80), 'New forms of aura rush to fill the vacuum'.

'interpretation', and which ensures a fluidity in the notion of identity, can also result in the partial closing down of that space; and that we may look here for the 'aura of the popular'. But important though this aspect undoubtedly is, it does not tell the whole story, for it omits any rôle for mechanical reproduction. If we look closely, we see that, far from acting destructively, mechanical reproduction is central to the creation of this new-style aura. For whereas the principal source of that aura might be said to reside in the notated score of Ellington's arrangement, in the place where the voicings were laid out, the reason that the sound obtained by those voicings became so central to the identity of this *Mood Indigo* and set it apart from all others lay in the circulation and influence of the first recordings – within the very world of mechanical reproduction, therefore, that Benjamin claimed to have been so destructive of the auratic in its original form.

As we move through popular music history into the era in which the particular sound-character of any popular music record is attributable, at least in part (and often in substantial measure), to processes of technical production in the recording studio, records themselves can be seen as auratic in character, especially in retrospect. Let us, by way of example, take an everyday situation in which a radio listener hears a record not broadcast for many years and responds with pleasure (or distaste, since there seems to be no reason why aura should always be attractive) to reacquaintance with an object which he or she recognises as not just different but uniquely so, and which seems now to 'have its own existence in the place where it happens to be'.[9] The listener may be responding to melody or rhythm or vocal timbre, or to any combination of these and other parameters, but the first – and, in all probability, last – point of recognition is the particular sound-character of the record, in which the processes of technical production have played a crucial part.

By its nature, as our investigation has implied, the record cannot be considered strictly auratic in Benjamin's sense: in the (not entirely improbable) event of finding yourself viewing a framed seven-inch vinyl recording of, say, The Beach Boys' *Good Vibrations* on a gallery or museum wall, you are unlikely to be aware of a unique quality of presence; you may have one just like

9. Benjamin (1973), p. 223.

it yourself, albeit unframed, in a box of records at home. In this sense, it could be argued that the use of the term 'aura' to convey a new type of sanctity around recorded music is not entirely appropriate. But what the record on the gallery wall does is to suggest a challenge to conventional ideas of the auratic, not their demise. In the same spirit, considering the auratic in the context of popular music serves to reveal that its characteristics have been reinterpreted, by a strange irony, in the very context of mass reproduction technology that Benjamin identified as their destroyer. Further, what has happened in this process of reinterpretation is that auratic status is being acquired not so much through composed music as through a combination of practices: compositional, performance-related and technological.

8   In the discourse of musicians and the industry, but not, or not so much, of commentary, the question of a piece of music as **property** is important in virtually every generic area. But here, too, the issue is problematical and becomes a subject of debate. Even those genres that rate the musical work very low in their hierarchies of importance are obliged to recognise its importance in legal terms, thus illustrating the impact on popular music of the dominant position occupied by the idea of the work in the legal system's understanding of how music functions. In many areas, popular music practice does not concede priority to the work, but in the area of copyright it is forced to do so. Two brief examples will illustrate how this basic contradiction can translate into an actual problem:

(i) In the case of many African-American recordings up to the end of the 1940s, copyright in the pieces of music recorded was held by record companies through the device of naming a producer as author or citing the piece as 'traditional'. This practice often deprived the real authors of the pieces, who were also the performers, of their royalty rights. These artists were not schooled in the ways of the copyright law; nor did they reify the music they performed. The rare exceptions were those African-American songwriters who understood from white-dominated Tin Pan Alley practice the primary position, in the eyes of the law, of an identifiable piece of music with its own identifiable authors, and they succeeded in influencing an oral/aural tradition of music-making sufficiently to get their music recorded. In bebop, of course, musicians, by now more aware, increasingly took advantage of the limited opportunity within an improvisatory genre to establish legal ownership of a piece. As a result, they based far fewer performances on the existing jazz 'standards' (often Tin Pan Alley or Broadway tunes owned by Tin Pan Alley or Broadway songwriters and publishers), preferring to invent their own, even if these new pieces were sometimes no more than melodies using the chords of those same standards (it was to the melody, significantly, that the law paid most attention).

(ii) In much rock and pop music the final 'outcome' – the piece of music as it becomes recognised by the audience – often owes a lot to the contribution of individual members of the ensemble, who, because they are not credited with the melody or the lyrics, have no claim on ownership. Drummers, in particular, fall into this category and have sometimes expressed grievances about the matter in ways that have led to the demise of the ensemble.

The principle of collective work as a basic creative procedure has been enhanced by the enormous developments in technology, which have led to the involvement of producers and engineers as well as musicians. Although the resulting disparities, in terms of ownership and reward, have been recognised on some occasions, and although the law itself moves slightly, from time to time, in response to changing circumstances, the basic position remains the same: forms of popular music expression are controlled legally by concepts based on an idea of the work that, if not alien to them, at least skew their practice. The whole issue of 'sampling' – the importation into a piece, via technology, of musical ideas expressed elsewhere – is another good example of the tensions that can exist between artistic practice and the law of property.

9   The idea that one form of existence for an individual piece is as a guide, indicating the parameters of performance, is not uncommon in popular music; but that the guide should become a **blueprint**, and the indications strict directions, most certainly is. Even in those genres where notation is vital, it is far from being the case that popular music accepts it as having controlling power. That scholars can slip up here is demonstrated by Allen Forte's recent study of American popular song, which, although it contributes richly to our understanding of the songs' harmonic, melodic, rhythmic and structural character, at the same time impoverishes

the genre, since the author omits to include evidence of the way in which performers – not just one or two of them but the vast majority – have seen performing the songs as a kind of partnership.[10] Although he sometimes points to interesting moments in jazz performance, Forte is generally rather impatient with performers, especially singers, drawing attention to those instances where they fail to live up to the demands of the score.[11]

It would be possible to continue in this vein, but I believe I may have said enough to support the proposition that although the ideas connected to the concept of the work appear in popular music with great regularity, they are rarely unchallenged and unproblematised; indeed, in debate they often emerge as highly ambiguous. In seeking a way to begin to understand this, I want to direct our attention towards two key phenomena that emerge from this exercise, almost by default. The first is what I propose to call the 'popular music event'. The second is what could, from one perspective, be seen as an objectification of the event, i.e. the popular music record.

The popular music event is the sum of a number of smaller occurrences, which might include any or all of the following: the origination or the borrowing of a musical idea; the development of the idea; the conversion or arrangement of the idea into a performable piece; the participation of those (musicians, producers, technicians) whose task is to produce musical sound; the execution or performance of this task; the transmission of the resulting sounds; the hearing of those sounds. Sometimes these occurrences appear to link together and proceed as a sequence: for example, an individual provides an original idea, which an arranger then arranges for a known set of performers; at other times, they do not, or do not all: for example, it might be impossible to distinguish the gestation point of an idea in a context of impromptu participation of a number of executants.

But if logical sequentiality were in control of the popular music event, it would be likely that the earliest occurrences in the sequence would be dominant; and if the breaking of that sequentiality were the driving motivation of those involved, those occurrences which challenged that control most effectively would be themselves dominant.

10. Allen Forte, *The American Popular Music Ballad of the Golden Era, 1924–1950*, Princeton, Princeton University Press, 1995.
11. There are examples of both on p. 23.

Clearly, both of these situations can and do occur in the context of particular popular music events. For instance, a tune and its first arrangement may come to be seen as 'definitive' (cf. *Mood Indigo*, once again), while in some jazz contexts the importance attached to the way in which the execution of the set task – the performance – is carried out not only reduces the significance and influence of the original 'idea' but also strikes a blow against the subordination of the performer to the piece. In most popular music events, however, such hegemony is always challengeable, because the relationships between the various individual occurrences that make up the event are not preset. Rather than speak of logical sequences or of hegemonic practices, it would be sensible to think of the popular music event as structured around an interactive nexus of performer, performance and performed.

By 'performer' I mean here anyone involved in the execution of a piece of music: musicians, chiefly, but also others involved in decisions that lead to the production of sound. By 'performance' I mean the carrying out of the performer's tasks. By 'performed' I mean the material on which performer and performance work, and which works on them (I do not mean the resulting sounds, the end product). I have avoided such terms as 'piece', 'item' or 'number' here, because they suggest an object, and it seems to me that what popular music performers see in their material – invented or given, or half-and-half – is not an object but a potential event. That may be why, as I indicated earlier, even generic terms denoting objects, such as 'song', are used less often than one might expect.

The potential event is one in which much is negotiable, according to a variety of conventions, generic and otherwise. This can be clearly seen, for instance, when the performed material has a prior existence. Take the practice known as 'covering'.[12] In essence, 'covering' involves performing your own version of a piece of music that others have also performed. To this basic meaning others are sometimes added, implicitly or explicitly: the piece of music being 'covered' is associated with another performer or performers, perhaps because they made the first recording, or because they have forged a relationship with it (although the relationship can sometimes be too close for a 'cover' to be comfortable: it is probably almost impossible to

12. Serge Lacasse discusses the nature of 'covering' at length (pp. 45–47) in his essay in this volume.

perform *My Way* without slipping into parody of Frank Sinatra, or into somewhat oleaginous homage to him).[13] Another possible implication is that there is a difference between 'covering' and 'interpreting': 'covering' generally requires some kind of close approximation to an original; interpreting may possibly involve that, but does not have to. In some quarters, the phrase 'cover version' is often used to convey derogation; a believer in the need for originality might say: 'There are eight covers in the Top Twenty at the moment', and give you to understand that the current scene is low on creativity, hence low on interest. In historical terms, 'covering' is also associated, in one reading of popular music history, with 'cutting one's teeth'. The Beatles were probably the most famous example of popular musicians whose 'cover versions' of African-American records have been seen with hindsight as a necessary prelude to the breaking through of their own creativity. For still others, including many musicians, 'covering' is an opportunity to engage in a dialogue with music other than their 'own' and with other performers who have been involved in 'covering' that or similar music.

I have (once again!) referred to shades of meaning. This is not, I hope, out of pedantry; nor does it indicate merely a vagueness in the use of language in popular music practice. It strikes me that what we have in 'covering' is evidence of flexibility around the whole area where origination meets imitation; or, in terms of my earlier formulation, it indicates that there is movement within the nexus of performer-performance-performed that permits many alternatives. We can point to uncertainties of meaning; we can point to tendencies, in some quarters, towards certain preferences and qualitative judgements, and to their absence elsewhere. But what this suggests to me is not indecision or a want of appropriate values; nor the mess you can get into if you do not have 'works' in the first place. When we point to these tendencies, we are indicating that the relationships within this nexus are not simple or predictable. Nor are they agreed: they frequently express themselves in tensions that can be constructive in some cases, destructive in others.

13. The original of *My Way* was a French song (*Comme d'habitude*, by Claude François and Jacques Revaux, 1967) that was unknown to most of the audience for Sinatra's recording. As with many white 'covers' of black songs made during the 1950s, therefore, the status of Sinatra's recording as a 'cover' (if such it was) was not recognised by most of his audience – another interesting aspect of this phenomenon.

In recent years, some scholarship in the area of African-American cultural history and practice has raised one particular example of cultural activity centred around the elevation of pre-existing cultural data to a place of eminence. I am referring to the concept of 'signifying', by which is meant a set of rhetorical interpretative strategies that play in different ways on pre-existing material or information.[14] Although especially apparent in jazz, 'signifying' has been seen at work in a range of contexts, from slave fiddle players to hip-hop.[15] The concept has become important in rethinking arguments about the survival of African cultural tendencies in the New World and in debates within African-American cultural politics.[16] We have no space or reason to deal with either of these aspects in any detail, fascinating though they are, but I would like to make a point that is connected to them. If it is correct to say that, in the New World environment in which enslaved people and their descendants found themselves faced with an aggressive dominant culture, this one feature of their cultural practice (which they doubtless shared with other cultures) acquired a previously unknown importance; and if it is correct to say that in subsequent periods, whether of hope or more often disillusion, it was used with increasing sophistication as both survival mechanism and creative response; then it is also correct to say that musical practice which actively interprets one thing through the filter of another has the potential to carry social and political, as well as musical, meaning. And what I have identified as the flexibility of the nexus of performer-performance-performed permits this to happen, perhaps in ways that would not be available, were the world of popular music constrained by the idea of the work (it is, of course, potentially affected by other concepts, for example, the commercial market, but that is another topic altogether).

The second of my key phenomena, and my final subject, is that of the popular music record.

In the early years of its development, the recording (the cylinder, then the flat disc) was seen by the public, listening through primitive

14. Or, to give it in the format suggested by Henry Louis Gates, the scholar whose work laid the foundation for subsequent study: 'Signifyin(g)' (Henry Louis Gates, Jr, *The Signifying Monkey: A Theory of Afro-American Literary Criticism*, New York, Oxford University Press, 1988).
15. Samuel Floyd, in particular, has applied Gates's theory to African-American music (Samuel A. Floyd, *The Power of Black Music: Interpreting its History from Africa to the United States*, New York, Oxford University Press, 1995).
16. Richard Middleton elaborates further on 'signifying' in his essay in this volume.

headphones at fairgrounds and exhibitions, mainly as a novelty, while the publisher-dominated music industry saw it mainly as another means of promoting the sale of printed music. During the first two decades of the twentieth century, as equipment manufacturers put more affordable means of reproduction into more homes and sales increased, the industry recognised that the record possessed a dual capability: to be a powerful promotional tool for the sale of music in other forms, and to achieve sales in its own right. In the first capacity, its existence as a tangible artefact was incidental, but in its second capacity, it was central. As people began to own records, they realised that an experience of music in performance captured inside a small physical object was an irresistible combination.

The experience of music that the record provided to the listener – as became more apparent when recording technology improved and the illusion of an actual performance was easier to believe – was a new one for several reasons: it could be released when the owner wished, thus taking control partially out of the hands of entrepreneurs and/or performers; since it captured sound without vision, it threw attention more on to sound (vision now being present in the realm of the imagination, or not at all); and it meant that one could bypass the blueprint function of printed musical scores and 'make music' in a different way. In all this, of course, we should note the importance of the victory, in the early stages of commercial recording history, of playback-only over reproduction-and-playback. Had Edison's original idea of making recording and reproduction simultaneously available to the public (as later occurred with tape recorders) been successful, it is at least conceivable that printed music would have retained its primary position, in public perception, as the necessary 'source' of music.

That it is possible, evidently, to entrap sound within physical material and release it repeatedly in an identical form still strikes my simple mind as a wonder. Perhaps the wonder of it is also produced by a sense that what we have entrapped or encoded in a record is not a piece, or even a work, as previously conceived. 'In 1877 music became a thing', wrote Evan Eisenberg, half sorrowfully – meaning that whereas notation enabled music-making, recording had a tendency to complete it.[17] But it is not the musical score or music-making

17. Evan Eisenberg, *The Recording Angel: Music, Records and Culture from Aristotle to Zappa*, New York, McGraw-Hill, 1987.

that a popular music record turns into a thing; a record is one particular result of the interaction and dialogue of which we have just been
speaking: between performance, performer and performed. As such,
it is not a completion, an end product, but another part of that
process. It is true that the idea of the record as end product or completion is present in popular music practice; indeed, it is common.
Frequently, the source of the idea is its rôle in the marketplace, which
needs the buying and selling of units. But the status of the record as
end product or completion is never totally secure and can itself be a
source of dialogue or confrontation – often with commercial impera-
tives – within the conventions of a genre. In jazz, for example (as
noted earlier), the music's aesthetics tend to emphasise the ultimate
value of the performing process, the acts of musical discovery that, as
Ralph Ellison memorably remarked, 'serve to remind us that the
world is ever unexplored',[18] and to be uncomfortable with the tendency of the record to be used to give certain end results definitive
status. One consequence of this is that, because a jazz performance
that is heard repeatedly on record cannot endlessly recapture or
repeat its sense of discovery, the record acquires value for reasons different from those applicable to a live performance, setting up a
dichotomy. The popular music charts, by contrast, seem to be part of
a set of conventions that lives by the idea of the record as end product, and the industry certainly does all it can to support the notion
that the claims of the end product do not conflict with the idea of the
musicians as actual performers in 'live' contexts. But the two ideas do,
in fact, often conflict.

   If, finally, we return to our checklist of properties of the term
'work' and look for them in the way the record functions in popular
music, we can find many of them apparently present. A popular
record is a musical artefact which, if not itself a piece, is the bearer of
one, and, as a consequence, can

- possess identity;
- be seen as a completed achievement;
- become part of a canon;
- acquire auratic qualities; and
- certainly, be exploited as property.

18. Ralph Ellison, 'What America would be like without Blacks', *Time*, 6 April
    1970.

Even if a record does not act like a blueprint, new interactive technology can turn it into a template of a different kind. These factors, added to the sheer prominence of the record in the practice of popular music, might lead us to think, at the end of this particular journey of investigation, that in popular music the record is the work in a twentieth-century guise. But to follow this line of thought is to start from the wrong place. I have noted already that when topics that we have identified as aspects of the work – the piece, identity, originality and so on – appear in popular music, they do so in ways that subject them to debate; they are rarely clear-cut. I suggest that this is because popular music practice involving these issues is generated not by a work-concept but by a different set of precepts arising from the interactive nexus of performer-performance-performed. This nexus is capable of generating debate about the concept of the work – not the other way round.

2

Intertextuality and Hypertextuality in Recorded Popular Music

Serge Lacasse

Presentation

In 1994 the late Lucien Poirier (to whom this essay is dedicated) held a postgraduate musicology seminar at Université Laval (Québec) entitled *La Musique au second degré*. The seminar's title referred to Gérard Genette's book *Palimpsestes: la littérature au second degré*.[1] In this study Genette develops a theory of 'hypertextuality', which studies and characterises particular relationships that occur between different works of literature. The goal of Poirier's seminar was, therefore, to explore the possibility of applying this theory to music.[2] The present essay is an attempt to apply the process, in part, to recorded popular music, which means that I will be considering the recording as the main object of my inquiry. By no means, however, is the process intended to be exhaustive; it aims simply to provide some new ways of looking at recorded popular songs, especially when one is

---

1. Gérard Genette, *Palimpsestes: la littérature au second degré*, Paris, Seuil, 1982. All quotations and references are taken from Gérard Genette, *Palimpsests: Literature in the Second Degree*, translated by Channa Newman and Claude Doubinsky, Lincoln and London, University of Nebraska Press, 1997.
2. Of course, since this was a 'traditional' musicology seminar, the works examined came mainly from the 'classical' repertoire. Following the seminar, an article has been published by Vincent Brauer, Serge Lacasse and Renée Villemaire: 'Analyse d'une oeuvre hypertextuelle: *Las Meninas, vingt et une variations transformelles sur les* Kinderszenen *de Robert Schumann*, de John Rea', *Les Cahiers de l'ARMuQ*, Vol. 17, May 1996, pp. 35–44. For other examples of intertextual relationships found in the classical repertoire, see Robert S. Hatten, 'The Place of Intertextuality in Music Studies', *American Journal of Semiotics*, Vol. 3 no. 4, 1985, pp. 69–82.

considering the relationships occurring between a number of them.[3]

Gérard Genette's *Palimpsests*

Genette's 'hypertextuality' should be regarded as a subcategory of what a large number of theorists, following Kristeva's definition,[4] have come to know as 'intertextuality'.[5] In his introduction Genette uses the term 'transtextuality' when referring to the ensemble of any type of relation, explicit or not, that may link a text with others – which is how most theorists seem to use and understand the term 'intertextuality'.[6] Actually, Genette considers intertextuality as a subcategory of transtextuality along with four others: paratextuality, metatextuality, architextuality and, of course, hypertextuality. 'Intertextuality' is defined by Genette in a more restrictive sense, and is used to identify 'a relationship of copresence between two texts or among several texts: that is to say, eidetically and typically as the actual presence of one text within another' (quoting, allusion and plagiarism being its most important, if not only, manifestations).[7] It is in reference to these definitions that I will be using the terms 'intertextuality' and 'transtextuality' in the pages that follow.

Again according to Genette's nomenclature, 'paratextuality' refers to the ensemble of relationships between a particular text and some of its accompanying features, such as the general title, chapter titles,

---

3. For intertextual analyses of some rock songs, see John R. Covach, 'The Rutles and the Use of Specific Models in Musical Satire', *Indiana Theory Review*, Vol. 11 (1990), pp. 119–44; also id., 'Stylistic Competencies, Musical Humor, and *This is Spinal Tap*', in *Concert Music, Rock, and Jazz since 1945: Essays and Analytical Studies*, ed. Elizabeth West Marvin and Richard Hermann, Rochester, N.Y., University of Rochester Press, 1995, pp. 172–228. Although Covach's analyses are quite enlightening, it seems to me that more attention should have been paid to technological musical parameters; indeed, the discussion focuses mainly on melody and harmony, making little reference to recording techniques.
4. Julia Kristeva, *Sèméiôtikè: recherches pour une sémanalyse*, Paris, Seuil, 1969.
5. For a quite comprehensive account of the evolution of the notion of intertextuality (especially in literature), see Donald Bruce, *De l'intertextualité à l'interdiscursivité: histoire d'une double émergence*, Toronto, Paratexte, 1995.
6. Judith Still and Michael Worton, 'Introduction', in *Intertextuality: Theories and Practices*, ed. Judith Still and Michael Worton, Manchester, Manchester University Press, 1990, p. 22.
7. Genette (1997), pp. 1–2.

foreword, illustrations and cover. Similarly, Genette defines 'metatextuality' as a commentarial relation which links one text with another, the most important examples being reviews and critiques. Another subcategory of transtextuality is named 'architextuality' by Genette and denotes a more abstract relationship between texts by virtue of their belonging to the same particular genre (novel, poem, essay, etc.).[8]

Finally, Genette considers the last type of transtextual relation, 'hypertextuality', which is the subject of the remainder of his book and is defined as 'any relationship uniting a text B [the 'hypertext'] to an earlier text A [the 'hypotext'], upon which it is grafted in a manner that is not that of commentary'.[9] In other words, a hypertext is a result of some kind of transformation or imitation of a hypotext, two practices which lie at the centre of Genette's theory. I will thus be considering relations between songs in terms of practices: first, practices that aim at including some elements of a previous text within the present text (intertextuality); second, practices which aim at producing a new text out of a previous one (hypertextuality).

II

In this section we will study some examples of intertextuality and hypertextuality in recorded popular music. As a matter of fact, we will be looking very briefly at intertextual practices, focusing mainly on hypertextuality, for which Genette has provided a much more comprehensive paradigm. The main reason why I still wish to discuss certain aspects of intertextual practices is that some of them are closely bound up with recording techniques – in particular, with sampling, which constitutes the foundation of a large number of today's recorded popular songs.

Intertextual Practices

As mentioned in the introduction, intertextuality is defined by Genette as 'the actual presence of a text within another'. Genette gives the examples of quotation and allusion as illustrations of inter-

8. Ibid., pp. 3–5.
9. Ibid., p. 5.

textuality.[10] We will thus be describing as 'intertext' the text in which one finds elements from a previous text. I would like, first, to look at some cases of quotation in recorded popular music.

Quotation

A quotation is characterised by the actual insertion of an excerpt from a given text within another. In literature, for example, it is possible to transcribe part of a given text and insert it directly into another. This inclusion is usually acknowledged by quotation marks (a form of indication that is obviously not possible in music). According to this definition of a quotation, it seems to me that there are two kinds of quotation when one is dealing with recorded music. I would like to term them 'allosonic' quotation and 'autosonic' quotation, respectively.[11]

Allosonic quotation can be illustrated by the following example. It is quite common in jazz that a musician performing a solo decides to 'quote' a snatch from another tune. Here, the melodic line he is quoting is of an abstract nature and could have been performed in any number of ways, by any musician and with any (melodic) instrument. In other words, what is shared between the original text and the intertext consists of an abstract structure. Although allosonic quotation is interesting from a general point of view, it is not especially typical of recording techniques and will therefore not be studied at length here.[12] But I wished to use this example to introduce the 'autosonic' and 'allosonic' pair of concepts, to which we will constantly return in the present essay.

Conversely, autosonic quotation is intimately linked with recording techniques. Its nature can be illustrated by a practice commonly used nowadays: sampling. When we import a sample taken directly from a recording into another (for example, a drum loop), what is common

10. Plagiarism as such will not be studied here, but we will later examine a practice involving copying.
11. I am of course partly and freely drawing from Nelson Goodman's terminology ('allographic' and 'autographic') as introduced in *Languages of Art: An Approach to a Theory of Symbols*, New York, Bobbs-Merrill, 1968. I would like to thank Lydia Goehr for pointing out to me that an unmodified use of Goodman's terminology would not have been appropriate in the context of this essay.
12. It is naturally possible to find allosonic quotations within recordings; what I mean is that we do not need recording techniques in order to produce allosonic quotations.

to both recordings is of a physical nature. What is shared is not so much a 'sameness of spelling' (to borrow an expression used by Goodman when characterising allographicity) as a 'sameness of sounding'. The technique of sampling is usually associated with autosonic quotation. Note, however, that digital sampling is not the only way of doing this, for one can still use analogue techniques (rerecording, splicing, collage, etc.) – but, of course, digital technology is much easier to manipulate.

It is important to realise that, most of the time, autosonic quotations are altered in one way or another: one can speed them up or slow them down, loop them, modify their spectral content (through equalisation), add reverb, echo or flanging to them, etc. It is likewise rare to hear an autosonic quotation that has not been immersed, so to speak, within the overall sonic texture, mostly by juxtaposing other sounds with it (for example, drum loops are often mixed with other rhythmic programming, as in Peter Gabriel's *Digging in the Dirt*).[13] Both manipulations can make it difficult to identify the recording from which the quotation has been extracted (as is sometimes made evident in legal disputes concerning copyright infringement).[14] Most of the time, however, identification is fairly easy, since quotation is usually used in order to relate the intertext to some previous recording(s). For example, when listening to Puff Daddy's *Been Around the World*, we can hear very clearly a sample taken from David Bowie's *Let's Dance*.[15] The sample has been looped and slowed down, and some rhythmic programming added to it; nevertheless, it remains easily recognisable. Such practice is very common and typical of rap and other related musical styles.

Another song by Puff Daddy employs quotation in a quite different manner. Indeed, in the song *Come With Me* there is a very obvious quo-

---

13. Peter Gabriel, *Digging in the Dirt*, 'Us' Geffen GEFSD 24473. For an extensive analysis of this song, see Serge Lacasse, 'Une analyse des rapports texte-musique dans "Digging in the Dirt" de Peter Gabriel', M.A. dissertation, Québec, Université Laval, 1995.
14. D. M. Howard and others, 'Acoustic Techniques to Trace the Origins of a Musical Recording', *Journal of the Forensic Science Society*, Vol. 33 (1993), pp. 33–37.
15. Puff Daddy and The Family, *Been Around the World*, 'No Way Out', Bad Boy 78612-73012-2, 1997; David Bowie, *Let's Dance*, 'Let's Dance', EMI SO 517093, 1983.

tation of Led Zeppelin's *Kashmir*.[16] But what could be taken as samples from the original Led Zeppelin recording are actually not this: Jimmy Page (formerly Led Zeppelin's guitarist), and a number of musicians and arrangers, have reperformed the whole musical track for Puff Daddy's *Come With Me*. Interestingly enough, most musical elements stay very close to the original recording of *Kashmir*. For example, not only are the drums played in a very similar fashion, but the sound is also quite similar (although the sound quality is now much better). In fact, one feels as if Puff Daddy's song is **pretending** to have used sampled excerpts from Led Zeppelin's original recording —which I find quite interesting, and which may reveal some new trend.[17] It is thus possible to have allosonic quotations that mimic the autosonic. We are entering here the domain of pastiche and copy, which are examined in the next section; but just before, a word about allusion.

Allusion

Some other forms of intertextual practice may be found in recorded popular music. For example, the lyrics of The Beatles' *Glass Onion* contain many allusions to other songs of theirs, mostly by reference to their titles. The songs evoked in *Glass Onion* include *Strawberry Fields Forever*, *The Fool on the Hill*, *Lady Madonna*, *Fixing a Hole*, and *I am the Walrus*. I do not believe, however, that it is possible to have autosonic allusions, for the very fact of being autosonic would imply that a direct quotation was entailed (unless one were to consider a very much altered sampling as an autosonic allusion rather than a quotation). It is, of course, possible to find many other occurrences of allusion (and of intertextual practices in general) in recorded popular music, but I would like now to move on to the main topic for consideration: hypertextual practices in recorded popular music.

Hypertextual Practices

As we have seen earlier, hypertextuality is defined as the production of a new text (hypertext) from a previous one (hypotext). Genette is well aware of the fact that it would be possible, according to this def-

16. Puff Daddy, *Come With Me*, 'Come With Me', Epic/Sony 34K 78954, 1998; Led Zeppelin, *Kashmir*, 'Physical Graffiti', Swan Song CD 92442, 1975.
17. Of course, even a superficial comparison between the two songs suffices to confirm that Puff Daddy's song contains no direct sampling from Led Zeppelin's original recording.

inition, to relate, in some shape or form, any text to any other text. For this reason, he claims that we need to find some kind of 'agreement' linking the hypertext to its hypotext.[18] Such agreement could simply appear in the title, or in any other paratextual element (the liner notes of a recording, for example). It may also be less explicit (such as a short allusion somewhere), but it should be there in some guise or other in order to restrict the corpus. As we shall see from the following examples, it is usually quite easy to find some form of agreement either in the recordings themselves or in some paratextual declaration. I will therefore begin with cases that I find easier to describe and which are related to the idea of parody.

Parody

The first example to be considered is Weird Al Yancovick's *Smells Like Nirvana*, a parody of Nirvana's *Smells Like Teen Spirit*.[19] Already in the title we can find part of the agreement we are looking for: it is very clear from which hypotext the hypertext originates. Genette writes apropos of parody that it 'gravitates to short texts (and, it goes without saying, to texts that are sufficiently well known for the effect to be noticeable)'.[20] Indeed, when hearing Yancovick's parody, a listener familiar with Nirvana's original version (and there are many) will find it very easy to identify the hypotext.[21] But, most importantly, Genette characterises a parody as retaining the **stylistic** properties of the original text while diverting its **subject**. The example thus conforms exactly to this definition of parody: the overall song sounds very close to the hypotext (similar style), but with new lyrics (different subject). Even within the new lyrics some important structural properties are preserved, such as most of the rhyme patterns and the prevalence of the vowel 'o' in the chorus. Further, Yancovick's singing is quite similar to Cobain's, which can be regarded as another common stylistic feature. In this instance, the relation between the hypertext and its hypotext could be described as occurring in an

18. Genette (1997), pp. 8–10.
19. Weird Al Yancovick, *Smells Like Nirvana*, 'Off the Deep End', Scotti 72392 75256-2, 1992; Nirvana, *Smells Like Teen Spirit*, 'Nevermind', Geffen DGCD 24425, 1991.
20. Genette (1997), p. 31.
21. A very good discussion of listeners' competencies can be found in Covach (1990, *passim*), where the author analyses cases of intertextual practice that seem to correspond to Genette's *chimera* (pp. 47–48 in Genette's *Palimpsests*).

allosonic mode, because the elements subject to transformation are of an abstract nature (melodic line, musical style, singing style, etc.). In other words, there is no **direct** manipulation of the hypotext (viewed as a recording) in order to produce the hypertext (which distinguishes this example from some others that we shall encounter).

Travesty

I should like now to turn to another example, which could be considered very similar: Mike Flowers's version of Oasis's *Wonderwall*.[22] Again, this is a humorous version of an earlier song (at least, it should be perceived as such by a large number of rock music listeners; we will return to this point later). But, unlike the previous example, Flowers's version does not transform the subject (in this case, the lyrics) of Oasis's song so much as its musical style. Even if some lyrics are removed,[23] there is no mistaking that the whole point is to serve up a well-known song in a completely different style: the melody and lyrics are the same, but they now have a new orchestration and vocal style, which is very close to that cultivated by American crooners of the 1960s.[24]

This type of transformation looks very much like Genette's category of 'travesty', defined as the rewriting of some 'noble' text as a new text that retains the fundamental content but presents it in another style in order to 'debase' it.[25] Another example of this kind of transformation would be *A Fifth of Beethoven* (1976) by Walter Murphy and the Big Apple Band, a travesty of Beethoven's *Fifth Symphony* that turns the great master's theme into a disco tune.[26] We are

22. The Mike Flowers Pops, *Wonderwall*, 'A Groovy Place', London 828 743.2, 1996; Oasis, *Wonderwall*, '(What's the Story) Morning Glory?', Epic CEK 67351 928366T, 1995.
23. For example, Flowers sings only the first verse.
24. I would like to thank Mike Brocken at the Institute of Popular Music (University of Liverpool), who has brought to my attention a couple of recordings that could be considered as sources for Mike Flowers's style: Jack Jones, *Follow Me*, RCA 1703, 1968; Andy Williams, *The Face I Love*, CBS 2675, 1966.
25. Genette (1997), p. 58.
26. For some time now, lounge music has been exploiting travesty. One example would be the version by Zacharias of the Doors' *Light My Fire*, which can be found on 'Rock 'n' Roll Hits: On the Rocks Part One', Capitol 7243 8 65161 2 2, 1997. Although this is an instrumental, I believe it can still can be regarded as a travesty; there is no doubt that the contrast between this version and the original is more a matter of style than content. We will come later to the case of instrumental versions.

once again in the realm of the allosonic, for the same reasons given when discussing parody.

Such forms of travesty that aim to 'debase' the hypotext are described as 'burlesque' by Genette. But there is one interesting point about travesty (and any type of transformation or imitation that aims to provoke a given effect in the listener): its power to evoke humour depends largely on the listener's own point of view and socio-cultural background. A disco fan may find Murphy's version of Beethoven's piece interesting (or simply entertaining), while a classical music lover might find it funny or (most probably) outrageous.[27] Further, we can find other forms of travesty which aim (by inversion, as it were) to 'ennoble' a quite 'vulgar' song. There are plenty of examples of Beatles songs turned into 'classical' pieces. There is even a string quartet version of Jimi Hendrix's *Purple Haze* performed by the Kronos Quartet.[28] Here again, depending on the listener's personal standpoint, the new versions may be considered either 'nice' or 'ridiculous'. Of course, Genette pays more attention to the author's intentions than to the work's reception, for which reason I would prefer simply to use the single term 'travesty' without regard to the practice's intended function (debasement or ennoblement).[29]

Pastiche

As we mentioned earlier, hypertextuality comprises a set of practices implying transformation or imitation. So far, we have been dealing with typical (allosonic) transformations of hypotexts in order to produce new hypertexts. However, things become a little different with pastiche, defined by Genette as the imitation of a particular style applied to a brand new text. In other words, an author of a pastiche identifies and assimilates a particular set of stylistic features in order

27. Of course, the same thing could be said, up to a point, of parody. It is quite possible to find rock music listeners who will find Yancovick's treatment of *Smells Like Teen Spirit* really funny, whereas some Kurt Cobain fanatics will detest it.
28. Kronos Quartet, *Purple Haze*, 'Kronos Quartet', Nonesuch 79111, 1995. An interesting thing about this recording is that the entire mix has been treated with flanging, which somehow recalls Hendrix's electric guitar sound.
29. This 'omission' by Genette (his failure to confront the factor of reception) has been criticised by some theorists of intertextuality, notably by Donald Bruce, in *De l'intertextualité à l'interdiscursivité*. Genette has partly revised his position, or at least explored the point of view of reception, in his *L'Oeuvre de l'art: les relations esthétiques*, Vol. 2, Paris, Seuil, 1997.

to create an entirely new text displaying the stylistic configuration in question. This means, then, that the hypertext has no precise hypotext. There is a difference here from travesty, in that the hypertext is entirely new: that is, there is no content common to the hypertext and its presumed hypotext, only a stylistic similarity. It is possible, for example, to imagine a band that would record a new song in the style of (say) The Beatles with such success that some listeners who were not very familiar with The Beatles' *oeuvre* believed that they were actually listening to a new Beatles song. We might therefore consider that such a hypertext has not one but many hypotexts, consisting of the ensemble of texts sharing similar stylistic properties and thus belonging to a common generic corpus (for example, the whole of The Beatles' songs). It is from this ensemble of hypotexts that the author of a pastiche will 'extract' the stylistic features characterising his or her new song.

In the previous section we encountered an example of travesty by Mike Flowers. On the same album Flowers has written three original songs that are neither travesties nor parodies,[30] but which could be considered pastiches of 1960s-vintage crooners' pop songs.[31] Genette sums up this situation when he writes:

> The parodist or the travesty writer gets hold of a text and transforms it according to this or that formal constraint or semantic intention, or transposes it uniformly and as if mechanically into another style. The pastiche writer gets hold of a style [...] and this style dictates the text.[32]

Pastiche, then, can be considered only from an allosonic point of view, since its very nature relies on a purely abstract feature: style.

We will now move to a series of practices for which there are (presumably) no equivalents in literature. This forces us sometimes to depart from Genette's nomenclature and to try to find terms that are acceptable in a popular music context. Naturally, I do not claim to be 'inventing' anything, since most terms that I will be using already exist within the vocabulary of popular music. My main intention in this discussion is to interpret these 'new' expressions in terms of Genette's hypertextuality.

---

30. *A Groovy Place*, *Crusty Girl* and *Freebase*, in The Mike Flowers Pops, 'A Groovy Place'.
31. See note 22.
32. Genette (1997), p. 82.

Copy

When talking about practices of imitation (such as pastiche), Genette writes: 'It is impossible to imitate a text **directly**; it can be imitated only indirectly, by practicing its style in another text'.[33] This claim is certainly true for literature, since an exact imitation of a particular text (viewed allosonically) would result in a mere copy, which would obviously be of no aesthetic value. In popular music, however, copying might possibly assume an aesthetic value, as when a cover band playing in pubs tries to be as faithful as possible to the original recording of the song being covered,[34] or, as Richard Middleton points out, 'when bands focus their live performances on accurate reproduction of their **own** recording – or when audiences complain that they have not succeeded'.[35] An exact (autosonic) copy, though – as in a digital rerecording of a song appearing on an album – would be of no aesthetic interest, being the equivalent of a new edition (from standing type) of a given written text.

In the context of popular music, I will therefore define a copy as a performance that aims at being the closest possible imitation of a pre-existent, usually recorded, performance.[36] The aesthetic value here resides in the ability of a particular artist to reperform as faithfully as possible what has been already performed. So it is possible to regard copying (in the sense of 'copying a performance') as a hypertextual practice in popular music, although such a practice applies more frequently to live performance, which lies beyond the scope of this essay.

Covering

The next hypertextual practice that I would like to examine is covering. In this essay 'covering' has a different meaning from 'copying'

---

33. Ibid., pp. 83–84.
34. For some years now, there has existed a new fashion for 'tribute' bands. Only last year (1997) in Québec, there have been, apart from the usual Beatles and Elvis imitations, tributes to Genesis, Deep Purple, Yes, Led Zeppelin, Pink Floyd and Red Hot Chili Peppers, to mention just a few.
35. See chapter 3, p. 77 (my emphasis).
36. For obvious reasons, it is much easier to imitate a performance by listening to a recording than by attending one or more live performances. See H. Stith Bennett, 'The Realities of Practices', in *On Records: Rock, Pop, and the Written Word*, ed. Simon Frith and Andrew Goodwin, New York, Pantheon Books, 1990, pp. 221–37.

and is associated with the idea of interpretation or reading.[37] Covering, then, should be conceived as a rendering of a previously recorded song that displays the usual stylistic configuration of the covering artist. In other words, a 'cover' is an (allosonic) hypertext consisting of a rendering of a hypotext that reveals no intention to be either a travesty or a copy.[38] I am well aware of the vagueness of such a definition, but let us look at some examples in order to clarify the concept.

A simple example would be Elvis Presley's cover of Arthur 'Big Boy' Crudup's *That's All Right*.[39] It is assumed that this cover was not intended to make fun of Crudup's song, nor to ennoble it (although some might argue so). This is therefore not a travesty as we understand the term here (the style is somewhat different but shows no clear intention to 'debase' or 'ennoble' the original version); and we are certainly not dealing with a parody (the subject is clearly the same) or a copy. It is simply a rendering of Crudup's song by Elvis, which means a performance displaying a set of stylistic features peculiar to Elvis Presley's 'sound'.

Many artists themselves cover some of their older songs. The 'unplugged versions' that are so popular nowadays are good examples of such 'auto-covers'.[40] Another interesting example would be the auto-cover of Led Zeppelin's *Kashmir* (again!) by Jimmy Page and Robert Plant, two former prominent members of Led Zeppelin.[41] Without going into detail about this version, it is worth noting, first,

37. For an interesting discussion of covering see Chapter 1, pp. 29–30.
38. There is naturally no clear demarcation between travesty, cover, copy and even parody. The point here is simply to try to outline a number of practices in conformity with Genette's theory. In any case, this point will be discussed again later.
39. Elvis Presley, *That's All Right* (1954), 'The Sun Sessions', RCA 6414-2-R, 1987; Arthur 'Big Boy' Crudup, *That's All Right* (1943), 'Arthur 'Big Boy' Crudup: Complete Recorded Works, Volume 2', Document DOCD-5202. Presley has recorded two other songs by Crudup: *My Baby Left Me* and *So Glad You're Mine*, both in 1956.
40. Just think of 'unplugged versions' by Nirvana and Eagles, to mention only the two most popular. Sting and Phil Collins, among others, made unplugged versions (probably before this expression had been coined) of a couple of their earlier hits during the 1981 Amnesty International Gala in London: *Roxanne* and *Message in the Bottle* by Sting, and *In the Air Tonight* by Collins. The recordings can be found on 'The Secret Policeman's Other Ball', Island XILP 9698, 1982.
41. Led Zeppelin, *Kashmir*, 'Physical Graffiti'; Jimmy Page and Robert Plant, *Kashmir*, 'No Quarter', Atlantic CD 82706, 1994.

that this hypertext results from a live recorded performance, and, second, that it includes new arrangements (such as the inclusion of a traditional Egyptian band, to which a whole section of the new version is devoted). Nevertheless, it is quite clear that we are still hearing the song *Kashmir*, albeit presented in a different manner. Thousands, probably millions, of covers exist; it would need very detailed stylistic analysis to provide us with a clear picture of how we arrived at a given hypertext from a given hypotext. Such a process would certainly lead us to formulate subcategories of covering, which might be useful for a consideration of certain social behaviours related to music.[42]

Translation

The translation of lyrics into another language is another hypertextual practice. But here again, there is a wide range of possible ways of doing it. For example, some translations imply remixes and even new arrangements, as is the case for the song *Fernando* by Abba, which has been recorded in English, Swedish and Spanish, each version displaying particular characteristics.[43] We thus find ourselves oscillating between the allosonic and the autosonic, depending on the amount and kind of change which is at issue.[44]

Instrumental Cover

It is quite common to find, in the popular music repertoire, instrumental versions of well-known songs (for example, a 'muzak' instrumental version of The Beatles' *Yesterday*, with the string section playing the melody in straight eight notes). An 'instrumental cover', as I understand the term here, is an instrumental (and allosonic) rendering of a previously recorded song where the main vocal line has

---

42. For example, what musical stylistic configuration is proper to Paul Anka's cover of *Tutti-Frutti* and Little Richard's original version respectively? And how, when listening to it, could we relate each version to the corresponding social group according to this stylistic analysis? Of course, such an examination would inevitably deal with racial issues, but I believe that an analysis of musical style would cast extra light on the whole problem.
43. For a detailed examination of the three versions and their relationships with each corresponding audience, see Philip Tagg, *Fernando the Flute*, Liverpool, Institute of Popular Music, 1991.
44. A possible way of circumventing the problem would be to consider lyrics and music separately.

been replaced by an instrumental melodic line (which has, of course, to follow the original melody in some way or another). It therefore has to be distinguished from a 'remix' of a song from which the voice track has simply been removed (we will come to remix in a moment). Again, there is no clear-cut boundary between a cover and an instrumental version, for it is possible to find covers in which sung lines have been partly (but incompletely) retained. Usually, however, it is possible to distinguish one from the other. I would now like to move to a quite recent practice which is peculiar to some styles of recorded popular music and has risen greatly in importance: the remix.

Remix

There are so many kinds of remix practice that it will not be possible here to describe them all. However, I would like to examine what appear to be the most important or usual ones. Remix practices range from simple edited versions to complex remixes entailing a large number of new performances. Once again, human practices resist becoming entirely conceptually distinct, remix being no exception.

Edited version

I call an 'edited version' a hypertext that is shorter or longer in length than the hypotext but otherwise shows no apparent change in the overall sound. In other words, an edited version sounds as if someone has cut out some part of the master tape (for shorter edited versions) or has inserted some additional material, again by cutting and pasting. An edited version can also entail some reordering of sonic information. It could, on that basis, be considered autosonic in relation to its hypotext, since its transformations deal directly with the hypotext. There are many edited versions of songs to be found in albums intended for air play. One example would be *While the Earth Sleeps* by Peter Gabriel and Deep Forest (written for the motion picture *Strange Days*).[45] It is worth noting that the expressions 'album version' and 'long version' are added in the respective cases to the

45. Deep Forest and Peter Gabriel, *While the Earth Sleeps (Album version)* and *While the Earth Sleeps (Long version)*,'While the Earth Sleeps', Columbia COL 662821-2, 1995. Attentive listening will reveal that there are some tiny diffrences in the mixes of the two versions (for example, the dynamic level and stereophonic behaviour of some background sounds), but I believe that these differences should be viewed as negligible in the perspective of the overall sound.

common title *While the Earth Sleeps*, which would constitute our hypertextual agreement.[46]

Instrumental remix

An 'instrumental remix' is different from an 'instrumental cover' in that it consists of a remix of the original song from which the leading voice has simply been removed. Instrumental remixes are often used for TV shows in which the artist sings live over the instrumental remix.[47] Obviously, it may happen that an instrumental remix is edited as well; when one deals with remixes, all kinds of hybrid manifestation can occur.

Remix

Remixing is a practice directly related to the technology of multitrack recording. Strictly speaking, a 'mix' denotes a particular configuration (in time) of a number of parameters of previously recorded material.[48] A pure 'remix' would thus consist of a new configuration of the original prerecorded elements. But the term encompasses a much larger number of related practices. For example, it is possible to make drastic changes during a remix process simply by removing important parts (such as the leading voice). It is also possible to add new material (most of the time, through synchronised MIDI programming). Further, most remixes are edited in some way (a remix is usually much longer than its hypotext). It thus becomes difficult to give a comprehensive account of the large range of possibilities that we can obtain.

46. What is not so clear, however, when one considers edited versions, is which one is to be regarded as the hypotext. People will usually agree that the album version should be considered as the hypotext, even though this may not necessarily be the case.
47. This could be regarded as similar to karaoke, except that, most of the time, karaoke instrumental versions are entirely reconstructed through MIDI programming (which would make them instrumental, and allosonic, covers without the principal melodic line). At any rate, karaoke is becoming a very common practice in popular music, but it is not directly related to recorded popular music, since it is a kind of live performance. However, one specific element of karaoke, interaction between the listener and the song, will be discussed later, when I consider a couple of CD-ROMs.
48. Such parameters would include loudness, stereophonic position, spatial environment and timbral characteristics. For a very good book on the subject, see William Moylan, *The Art of Recording: The Creative Resources of Music Production and Audio*, New York, Van Nostrand Reinhold, 1992.

Actually, a whole paper (if not a book) should be devoted to the question. Therefore, we will look at just a couple of examples.

Some remixes (such as the instrumental remix mentioned earlier) are still quite easily related to their hypotext by listeners. But it is also possible to produce remixes that are very remote from their hypotexts – remote enough to be considered almost as separate pieces. For example, Peter Gabriel's *Digging in the Dirt* has been remixed by David Bottrill in such a way that the song is hardly recognisable, except for such elements as guitar riffs and short vocal lines (which are heavily processed).[49] Because of these few common (autosonic) elements, we can still relate the remix to its hypotext. An even more complex form of remixing of Miles Davis's and Bob Marley's music by Bill Laswell has been illuminatingly discussed by Richard Middleton.[50] Such a hypertext is very distant from its hypotext and could even be considered as a work in its own right (although someone conversant with Davis's or Marley's music would still be able to recognise the hypertextual filiation).

There are even forms of 'interactive' remix: that is, remixes that are intended to be performed by the listener. I have in mind the CD-ROMs *Xplora 1* and *Eve* by Peter Gabriel, which allow the 'listener' to remix (and edit) for himself or herself particular songs (in the case of *Xplora 1*, the song is our familiar *Digging in the Dirt*).[51] Of course, the CD-ROMs do not allow the listener a totally free hand. It is a matter of a limited number of 'premixed' tracks that the listener can manipulate to a certain extent.[52] Nevertheless, since the sounds evolve over time, control over even that small number of parameters can still lead to an infinite number of possible 'remixes'. This kind of interaction (of which Gabriel's attempt constitutes, I believe, just the timid beginning) undoubtedly places the question of artistic 'authorship' in a new perspective.

More usually, though, remixes aim to present a given song in a different style ('dance' versions for clubs offer one example). In such cases they could be considered, in part, as a form of 'autosonic

---

49. Peter Gabriel, *Digging in the Dirt* (instrumental), 'Digging in the Dirt', Geffen GEFDM 21816, 1992.
50. Chapter 3, especially pp. 62–71.
51. Peter Gabriel, *Xplora 1*, CD-ROM, Real World, 1994; *Eve: The Music and Art Adventure*, CD-ROM, Real World, 1996.
52. In the case of *Eve*, we are dealing more with editing than with remix, but manipulations still have to be carried out by the user.

travesty'. I say 'in part' because most remixes include some new material added in order to render the desired style (rhythmic programming, new bass line, etc.). The autosonic 'portion' of the remix would constitute the material that appears in both the hypotext and the hypertext (in a fairly similar guise, as in the case of autosonic quotation).[53] Indeed, if a remix exhibits no autosonic elements (or only very few, of minor importance) in relation to its hypotext, it becomes, by definition, a cover. I therefore regard remixing as an essentially autosonic practice, even if it rarely displays its autosonic aspect in its purest form.[54]

John Oswald
The Canadian composer John Oswald has developed some quite interesting practices that entail the transformation of recorded popular songs. I would like to end this incomplete exploration of hypertextual practices by examining some of his 'works'.

Plunderphonics
David Mandl writes the following about a piece by John Oswald:

> In 1989, Oswald released *Plunderphonic*, a CD containing manipulations of music by The Beatles, Dolly Parton, Public Enemy, Michael Jackson, and others ... Sources were scrupulously credited, with catalogue numbers etc. provided. One thousand copies were produced, with Oswald footing the bill himself and giving them away for free (and specifically stipulating that no copies should be bought or sold). In February 1990, the Canadian Recording Industry Association demanded that Oswald cease distribution and destroy the three hundred remain-

53. A good example of a typical remix would be War's *Low Rider* (Remix), remixed by Arthur Baker in 1987, the hypotext being *Low Rider* (1975). Both versions appear on War, 'The Best of War, and More', Priority CDL9467, 1991. As one can hear, the original voice is still present in Baker's remix, but has been edited so it appears in different places (in relation to the original version). Moreover, a lot of rhythmic programming has replaced the original rhythmic section. Many other alterations makes the remix both different and interesting.
54. In other words, there have to be some significant autosonic elements in the hypertext for it to be considered a remix. An example of a hypertext that is presented as a remix, but which I regard as an auto-cover, is Peter Gabriel, *Blood of Eden* (Special mix for Wim Wenders's 'Until the End of the World'), Real World PGSCD9, 1993. Indeed, even the lead vocal track is entirely new.

ing copies. Not wanting to fight a potentially costly lawsuit, Oswald complied.[55]

The reason for this strong reaction from the Canadian Recording Industry Association was that Oswald had used commercially released recordings as his basic material. On his *Plunderphonic* each track presents a well-known recorded piece with an entirely new sonic configuration. Such a practice (which is autosonic, by the way) could be viewed as a 'mega-editing' process; but I would like to draw a distinction between plunderphonics and edited versions, because the former clearly aim to denature the hypotext. Moreover, the amount of manipulation is much greater than in the case of a simple edited version. Because of its singularity, I would like to coin the expression 'plunderphonics' to denote this practice, which, incidentally, is not new. Oswald himself cites Jim Tenney's *Collage 1* (1961) as an early example of such a practice applied to popular music, in which, as Oswald explains:

> Elvis Presley's hit record 'Blue Suede Shoes' (itself borrowed from Carl Perkins) is transformed by means of multi-speed tape recorders and razor blade. In the same way that Pierre Schaeffer found musical potential in his *objet sonore*, which could be (for instance) a footstep, Tenney took an everyday music and allowed us to hear it differently. At the same time, all that was inherently Elvis radically influenced our perception of Jim's piece.[56]

From this last sentence, one can start reflecting on the impact of hypertextuality on listeners. To what extent does the knowledge of hypotexts affect our listening of hypertexts? Or, to pose the question in a better form suggested by Oswald: to what extent does our 'reading' of a given hypertext influence our perception of the corresponding revisited hypotext? I believe that such questions, which can obviously be applied to intertextuality as well, should be investigated

55. Note by David Mandl in John Oswald, 'Plunderphonics, or Audio Piracy as a Compositional Prerogative', Internet document, http://www.halcyon.com/robinja/mythos/Plunderphonics.
56. John Oswald, 'Plunderphonics, or Audio Piracy as a Compositional Prerogative' (see n. 55). Looking at practices commented on earlier, one can see that Oswald's practice differs from Laswell's: Oswald's basic material is not a master tape that he remixes but the final mixes themselves, which he directly manipulates. He is therefore not remixing but patching.

in some depth. We need a better understanding of the 'social' inter-action of listeners with music.

Cento

In a more recent work Oswald has even merged together very short samples from about 5,000 recordings of popular songs.[57] Is this inter-textuality (quotations) or hypertextuality? Since the whole thing is made up of excerpts from other recordings, I would argue that it con-sists of a hypertext that has an unusually large number of hypotexts. Indeed, Genette identifies a fairly similar practice in literature which he calls *cento* and defines as a blending technique 'which consists in taking from here and there a line of poetry in order to constitute a whole poem that should be as coherent as possible'.[58] To draw out lines 'here and there' sounds similar to drawing out quotations 'here and there'; since, in the case of Oswald's piece, the (very) short quo-tations are autosonic, I would coin the expression 'autosonic *cento*' for this final hypertextual practice.[59]

III

As I have said throughout this essay, the list of intertextual and hyper-textual practices in recorded popular music could be lengthened con-siderably. I have tried here to identify some of them with reference to Genette's terminology. In this section, I would like to propose a pre-liminary categorisation of transtextual practices. The main criterion I have chosen for this suggested categorisation is the allosonic/autosonic dichotomy. But before this preliminary categorisation is presented, we need to return to a couple of concepts encountered ear-lier in this essay.

Preliminary Considerations

First, I would like to discuss travesty again. I have a problem with the

57. John Oswald, *Plexure*, Japan, Avant AVAN 016, 1993.
58. Genette (1997), p. 46.
59. The corresponding allosonic practice would be the medley, I suppose. However, it might be difficult to reproduce allosonically what Oswald is doing autosoni-cally with recording techniques, since the longest of the samples he uses for *Plex-ure* lasts about two seconds (most of the other samples having durations that should be measured in milliseconds).

idea of considering travesty as a 'transformational practice' as such. Indeed, travesty is more of an effect following some transformation than an actual transformational process. I would therefore like to attempt to identify its underlying procedure. A first step would be to consider travesty as a subcategory of covering (an author of a travesty produces a new rendering of the hypotext which is, presumably, humorous). I would therefore propose as a term for their common underlying procedure 'transtylisation'. This would denote the process of altering specifically the stylistic features of a given song in order to obtain a new version of it.[60] Such a version could subsequently be examined in relation to its intended effect. A travesty would then result from a transtylisation procedure that aimed to denature a given piece in some way. Conversely, a cover would presumably have no such intention, though resulting equally from a process of transtylisation (the new stylistic configuration being the covering artist's own).[61]

According to the preceding reasoning, a copy would result from a minimal transtylisation. Indeed, the cover band strives for a performance that exhibits, in as exact a form as possible, the stylistic configuration of the original recording (same sound, same instrumental playing, same voice – and often same looks!). In other words, the cover band aims at a *degré zéro* of transtylisation. I would therefore regard all the following practices as forms of allosonic transtylisation: copy, cover (including instrumental cover) and travesty.

I would prefer to classify allosonic parody as a category on its own because of its possible autosonic counterpart. Indeed, parody has been regarded as a practice characterised by the alteration of the subject of a song without changing its style. Plunderphonics, then, seems to be one possible example of autosonic parody: the style is somewhat the same, since we retain the sonic structure; however, the content is altered through a number of manipulations which, in my opinion, modify the song's 'subject'. In any case, plunderphonics appears to be more closely related to parody than to travesty. A lot has to do with the sonic content: plunderphonics still sounds like the hypotext but

60. Genette uses the term 'transtylisation' to denote another practice peculiar to literature, and which is not so far removed from what I am proposing here; see Genette (1997), pp. 226–28.
61. As we have seen earlier, transtylisation may present some minor changes in content (formal structure, lyrics, chord progression, etc.); but most of the fundamental elements are usually still present; if this were not the case, the hypotext would obviously not be recognisable.

displays a different linear content. In other words, travesty (along with any transtylisation practice) transforms its hypotext paradigmatically, while parody (allosonic **and** autosonic) acts syntagmatically on its hypotext.

This paradigmatic/syntagmatic dichotomy can help us to classify some other practices. Translation, for example, could be considered as related to transtylisation, since it acts paradigmatically on its hypotext (we still say the same thing but use a different system). As one can see, most of these categories (and the following ones) are not mutually exclusive. For example, it is quite easy to imagine a song that would be both a translation and a parody of a given hypotext.[62] For their part, both *cento* and medley, which are respectively autosonic and allosonic, are practices that join their hypotexts syntagmatically.

Finally, pastiche is an interesting case in that it is the ultimate paradigmatic and allosonic practice: paradigmatic because the hypertext is constructed from scratch according to a given stylistic configuration; and, of course, entirely allosonic, because the hypertext is not produced by any autosonic transformation of a given hypotext (in fact, there is no precise hypotext but merely some abstract common features belonging to a group of songs).

Summary Table of Transtextual Practices in Recorded Popular Music

I would now like to present a summary table of transtextual practices employed in the recording of popular music. As I have argued in the preceding section, the main criterion for categorisation is the allosonic/autosonic dichotomy. The table displays, however, an additional column based on a paradigmatic/syntagmatic dichotomy (the

62. I have two examples in mind. The first is taken from the music heard in Québec during the 1960s, when there was a fashion called *yé-yé* that consisted mostly of translated covers of hits originally sung in English. But most of the translations were so terrible that many of them were (and still are) regarded as parodies. My second example, which concerns cinema, occurred during an Academy Awards presentation that I was watching on TV. At a certain point during the show, some excerpts from a number of originally English-language movies were projected in different languages (for example, we could see and hear Humphrey Bogart saying something like 'Je t'aime, ma chérie!'). I was quite surprised when, after a short while, the audience started laughing very loudly. As a French-speaking person, I did not realise until then that even an entirely faithful translation could, in the right circumstances, become hilariously funny.

syntagmatic column displaying practices dealing mostly with subject or content, and the paradigmatic column showing practices involving transformation or imitation of a style or system). Further, I have tried to arrange the elements in the table according to an increasing order of abstraction. First, along the autosonic/allosonic axis; second, along the syntagmatic/paradigmatic axis. I have also tried to order elements contained within the cells according to the same principle wherever possible. Naturally, the table is incomplete, and I hope that others will try to add practices and – why not? – extra lines and columns.

Table 1: Summary Table of Transtextual Practices in Recorded Popular Music

	Syntagmatic *(Subject/Content)*	*Paradigmatic* *(Style/System)*
Autosonic	Autosonic Quotation Autosonic Parody *Plunderphonics* Cento Instrumental Remix	Remix
Allosonic	Allosonic Quotation Allusion Allosonic Parody	Transtylisation *Copy* *Cover* *Travesty* Translation Pastiche

As one can see, remix stands alone in its cell, which does not wholly reflect reality, since remix ought to stand somewhere in between 'autosonic' and 'allosonic', and between 'paradigmatic' and 'syntagmatic'. On a general level, though, remix is paradigmatic in that, most of the time, it aims at presenting a song in a different style for a number of purposes (such as dancing); it is autosonic to the extent that most of the time we will hear autosonic material from the hypotext. However, as we have seen, there are a very large number of remixing possibilities. Accordingly, in a more complex analysis remix would be broken down into a large number of subcategories distributed throughout the table.

Similarly, allosonic parody appears as the only hypertextual practice within its cell (allosonic quotation and allusion being intertextual
practices); it is possible, however, to think of a couple of other hypertextual practices that I have not discussed and which could fit in there.
For example: relyricisation, which would consist of writing new lyrics
to an existing song. This looks very much like translation but is significantly different because translation acts paradigmatically on its
hypotext (same subject using a different system), whereas a relyricisation would transform its hypotext syntagmatically (different sub-
ject/content). A number of additional practices could appear there
(such as remusicalisation), but we will end our discussion here for the
moment.

IV

In this essay I have been exploring the possibility of applying Gérard
Genette's theory of hypertextuality to recorded popular music. To try
to apply literary theory to music is always a difficult task (ask semi-
oticians!), but I believe it can be very fruitful. Hypertextuality (and
transtextuality as a whole) can offer us a new perspective when looking at, and listening to, music: different pieces of music are linked in
a number of ways; they thus share certain features. Among other
things, a knowledge of this network of interaction enables us to
'understand' a given piece better.

But as well as being explored in much greater depth, transtextual
practices should also be studied from the listener's point of view. It
should then become evident that the listening process is a very complex and refined social practice. Of course, each listener has his or her
own, unique transtextual network; but it should be possible also to
look at an entire group's transtextual network, which would obviously be more intricate but might contain a number of identifiable
common paths and milestones. On a more general level, it would be
useful to extend the whole process to the whole of musical styles and
practices, including non-Western ones.

During Lucien Poirier's seminar, in which we mostly dealt with
classical music, much time was spent discussing important issues that
arose automatically when one examined the relations existing
between different pieces of music: the status of notation vis-à-vis the
sonic nature of music; the performed version of a work in relation to
its (presumably) ideal condition; and many other questions leading

invariably to the problem of the ontological status of music. It would be interesting to observe how some conceptions of the 'Work of Art' might relate to the above table of hypertextual practice. For instance, if we consider the allosonic/autosonic division attempted here, we can see that the autosonic practices deal, by definition, with concrete manifestations of music (that is, actual sound events), whereas allosonic practices relate to a more abstract conception of music. This sends us back to a conceptualistic versus nominalistic debate around the question of the ontological status of the work of art. I am not sure who is right in the dispute between nominalists and conceptualists (although I find the conceptualistic view, paradoxically, more 'practical'), but transtextual practices show that it is possible to act both on the abstract elements of music (melody, lyrics, form, style, etc.) and on its concrete aspects (sound, performance, etc.). This calls, in turn, for a dual conception of the recorded popular song: (a) the song viewed abstractly in some 'ideal' form, and (b) its recorded incarnation viewed as a concrete manifestation of the same song.[63]

The musical work: reality or invention? I do not think it is possible to answer the question directly. What I believe, though, is that the very fact that we are able to trace back transtextual links means that we are able to link some 'things' together. But, in any circumstances, the decision to name these things 'works', 'pieces', 'songs', 'manifestations' or 'performances' becomes relevant only if it forms part of a more important project: to describe and understand the intricate interactions of music with human beings, along with other human activities. Transtextuality might provide us with a (quite) new interesting tool for doing so, since it already contains within itself the very idea of interactivity.

63. See Gérard Genette, *L'Oeuvre de l'art: immanence et transcendance*, Vol. 1, Paris, Seuil, 1994. This volume is available in English as Gérard Genette, *The Work of Art: Immanence and Transcendence*, trans. Gary M. Goshgarian, Ithaca and London, Cornell University Press, 1997.

3

Work-in(g)-Practice: Configurations of the Popular Music Intertext

Richard Middleton

There is scope for debate over the exact historical period when the concept of the musical work was established, still more over the moment when musicians started to produce works, but we shall surely agree on the central defining characteristics of this category: a work, as Lydia Goehr puts it, is 'a complex structure of sounds related in some important way to a composer, a score, and a given class of performances'.[1] There is a suspicion that this type of musical production is peculiar, at least in its origins, to that system, with all its associated social, aesthetic and discursive apparatuses, which Leo Treitler has termed the WECT: the West European Classical Tradition.[2] (Acronyms can serve the reificatory function, useful on occasions, of displaying the object for the fascinated scrutiny characteristic of the museum visitor.) As the authority of this system apparently implodes in the late twentieth century – at the same time, ironically, as it completes its dissemination to the last corner of the globe – it seems natural to question the sustainability of the work-concept. The contemporaneous rise in prominence of pop music provides a particular and pressing context for this question, since popular music, as Goehr points out, seems generally to be uncomfortable with 'work' thinking. It is not surprising, then, that a key theme in popular music studies since its beginnings some thirty years ago has been a concern to place a politics of pop **practice** in opposition to the apparently quasi-religious inventory of iconic classical **objects**.

The pop critique, explicit in much of the scholarship, implicit

1. Lydia Goehr, *The Imaginary Museum of Musical Works: An Essay in the Philosophy of Music*, Oxford, Clarendon Press, 1992, p. 20.
2. Leo Treitler, 'Towards a Desegregated Music Historiography', *Black Music Research Journal*, V.l. 16 (1996), pp. 3–10.

(arguably) in the music, is three-pronged. Popular music pieces can only rarely and in heavily qualified ways be attributed to a single author: a composer. More commonly, their production is a collaborative process, which may involve lyricists, songwriters, singers, instrumentalists, arrangers, orchestrators, producers, engineers, set designers, video directors and more. Transmission of these pieces between musicians is as much – and often more – through aural and oral channels as it is through scores; notation is rare today, and even when used is, and has been, generally no more than a sketch, an outline, a starting-point, or else an attempt to approximate what has already been achieved, in performance or recording studio, through non-literate methods. There is little sense, finally, that performances going under the same title make up a distinct class of events related in a consistent way to a pre-existing ideal form; rather, they comprise a potentially infinite series of events, related through family resemblances, which may move variable distances from siblings and from any notated 'parent'. Moreover, the extensive use in popular music of **borrowing** – the importance of 'tune families', the reliance on common-stock models, formulae, grooves and riffs, the privileging of variation over originality – compound this effect, which amounts to a thorough blurring (or non-recognition) of the boundary between 'performance' and 'composition'. Even when, in the nineteenth century, an older focus on public domain material began to give way to the publication of newly produced sheet music, identified and protected in due course by copyright legislation, songs were identified as often as not with their most celebrated performers rather than with their composers; if *Champagne Charlie* 'belonged' to anyone, it was to singer George Leybourne, not its writer, Alfred Lee. With the coming of records, this order of priorities could assume more luxuriant expression, the resulting proliferation of song versions acquiring the term 'covers'. In the second half of the twentieth century, the centrality to song dissemination and identity of the 'star quality' of performers *qua* performers renders ever more porous the boundaries around the singular work. At the same time, the radical changes to a song that can result from performance in different contexts – concert, club, disco, drive-time radio with talkover DJ, supermarket muzak – point in a similar direction.

From a historical point of view, the fact that this difference between vernacular music and the WECT could emerge so strongly is not too surprising. Just at the time, around 1800, when 'popular music' as we understand it was emerging as a distinct category so, too, were developing all the ideological and institutional accoutrements of the work-concept: the autonomy aesthetic, the 'serious' listener, the canon, music academies, 'great man' music history, and so on. Popular music, defined with a new intensity as 'different' – in fact, as 'low' and 'trivial' – could to a large extent continue to operate differently precisely because of this placing in the hierarchy. Pop was saved from complete assimilation to work-thinking by its vulgarity.[3]

The best umbrella term for the popular music practices I have been describing is probably **intertextuality**. A key feature of intertextuality (a rather modish term since the heyday of post-structuralists such as Julia Kristeva) – the idea that all texts make sense only through their relationships, explicit or implicit, with other texts – can be found earlier in the century, in theories as diverse as Peirce's 'infinite semiosis' and Bakhtin's 'dialogics' (to which I shall return). Indeed, this notion can no doubt be traced back still further (all theories of borrowing, parody, quotation, allusion, glossing, punning, etc. are germane), just as intertextual types of practice are rampant even in pre-1800 European art music (as Goehr points out). 'Intertextuality' is a good term for our purposes because it can cover such a range of techniques, requiring only that a text refer to other texts; but in exactly this respect, of course, it pushes against the tendential self-sufficiency of 'works'.

The popularity of post-structuralist perspectives, including the much-trumpeted 'death of the author', fed a loudly celebratory strand in cultural theorising, keen to trample on the élitist claims of art-objects in the interests of a supposedly postmodern politics of difference. And this theoretical move coincided with what appeared to be a significant shift in the practice. The dethroning of modernism, the rise of 'pop culture', and a quantum leap in the mass reproduction of the classics all pulled at the terms of the debate. The end of 'aura', foreseen by Walter Benjamin, was welcomed in the name of Baudrillard's 'simulacra' – copies without an original. Right across the culture, but particularly clearly in the sphere of music, there was a distinct technological factor to this shift. Digital technology – easily controlled sound-synthesis and signal processing, samplers and computer-controlled mixing equipment – offered a radically new

3. For the *vulgus*, it might be said, is 'common' (in more than one sense) rather than individualistic.

compositional setting, one that seemed to signal that works were now always works-in-progress, and that music was just material for reuse. Particularly in the sphere of electro-dance music, the ubiquity of sampling and multiple mixes appeared to some to go so far as to threaten the legal status of musical works and the identifiability of their producers – a development which, for many activists and left-leaning theorists, was entirely to be celebrated.[4]

Into the Mix

Remix culture, then, is seen by some iconoclasts as the final nail in the coffin of work-thinking. As critic Richard Williams puts it:

> One thing that seems to have disappeared from popular music in the last few years is the idea of a unanimously approved masterpiece, the single fully achieved and inviolable piece of work which achieves the status of a classic text. Re-mix culture more or less did away with it, with some help from new playback formats and the availability of such a vast quantity of music that the notion of consensus began to seem futile. In exchange we get the new idea of music as a continuing process, permanently open to radical revision. In the future, perhaps, all music will be effectively 'unfinished'; and the idea of authorial attribution may become as obsolete as the 32-bar Broadway ballad.[5]

Williams is discussing two CDs by the American bass-guitarist and producer, Bill Laswell, the first a 'reconstruction and mix translation' of pieces by jazz trumpeter Miles Davis, the second a set of 'ambient translations' of songs by reggae singer Bob Marley.[6] In both cases, Laswell (quoted by Williams as believing that 'tape memory has replaced composition')[7] got hold of the original master tapes and used them to produce new music which, in the range of its reconstructive

---

4. The best exploration of the implications of digital technology for musical practice and thought is Paul Théberge, *Any Sound You Can Imagine: Making Music/Consuming Technology*, Hanover, Wesleyan University Press, 1997.
5. Richard Williams, 'Fixing It in the Mix', *The Guardian,* 23 January 1998, G2 section, pp. 16–17, at p. 16. (In the year that saw Tony Bennett headlining at the Glastonbury Festival, the idea that the Broadway ballad is obsolete might be thought somewhat tendentious!)
6. Bill Laswell, 'Panthalassa: The Music of Miles Davis 1969–1974', Columbia CK 67909 (1998); Bill Laswell, 'Bob Marley Dreams of Freedom', Island 524 419-2 (1997).
7. Williams (1998), p. 16.

practices, casts fascinating light on the status of the work-concept at the end of the twentieth century.

There is a poignancy in choosing Davis for a remix project, for, having previously created instantly sanctified masterpieces for the emergent jazz canon, the great trumpet soloist found his late sixties and early seventies recordings (the ones that Laswell uses) attacked by jazz aestheticists for withdrawing from the challenges of authorial responsibility and retreating behind the open-ended anonymous vulgarities of funk-rock groove. Apparently, Davis showed little interest in what appeared on the albums. The dominant rôle in the mixing, choice of takes and formatting of the LPs was that of producer Ted Macero, and large quantities of material were left unused. Davis, despite his notorious prickliness over his own creative status, was already challenging the masterpiece aesthetic.

His 'In a Silent Way' LP tailors its form to the album format.[8] The first side is devoted to a single piece, *Shhh/Peaceful*, although at the end its hypnotic tonic-chord groove simply fades out: the performance could evidently have been prolonged indefinitely. Side 2, by contrast, encases a lengthy funk-styled improvisation, with solos for guitar, trumpet and tenor sax (*It's About that Time*), between two statements of *In a Silent Way*, a much slower, lyrical theme in unmeasured rhythm: a conventional ABA structure, then, though apparently rather arbitrary in its conjunctions of material. Two compositional modes are evident, both of which avoid the jazz conventions of periodic structure: the first consists of simple, 'out of time' thematic statement (*In a Silent Way*), the second of open-ended modal improvising over drones and riffs (*Shhh/Peaceful* and *It's About that Time*).

Initially, the most striking features of Laswell's reworking lie in the sphere of sound. Digital technology enables him to separate out the various instrumental parts with marvellous clarity, bringing many of them further up in the mix, but without cluttering the texture. Overall, the sound becomes much 'fuller', with much greater 'depth' (soloists right in the listener's face, for example). Sound quality is altered, too. In line with changing aesthetic norms, drums and (especially) bass become more prominent, altering the focus of the texture and, through the use of prolonged sustain on the bass, increasing the force of the drones. The guitar becomes more plangent, often with

8. CD reissue: Miles Davis, 'In a Silent Way', CBS 450982 2 (originally issued in 1969).

heavy reverb. Electric piano and organ sounds are filtered and 'eq-ed' to alter their timbres (and may also be sampled and modified to produce 'new' sounds). A good example of how such processes can change the whole effect can be found in the initial trumpet statement of the *In a Silent Way* theme. Davis's trumpet (with added digital delay) becomes much 'larger', more 'outdoors', its original halting breathiness expunged in favour of something more 'panoramic'. Similarly, the delicate filigree accompaniment is boosted into more enveloping washes of sound, while the continuous deep bass drone resonates around the listener's body. Here, and throughout, Laswell's soundscapes could not have been imagined before the experience of ambient music, electro-funk and dub.

At least as interesting, though, is what Laswell does to the form (see Tables 2 and 3). He makes one coherently organised piece, tightly cut from 38 to just over 15 minutes, out of what had been two (or possibly three). The sections are reordered, so that *In a Silent Way* (B) opens and closes the piece, and Laswell drastically shortens both *Shhh/Peaceful* (A) and *It's About that Time* (C) – by contrast, B acquires a new introduction and a new codetta – so that the balance of material is altered. By drawing on the pauses in Davis's A, extending them and adding to them from elsewhere, he creates links between sections that help to produce an effect of seamless flow. Naturally, Davis's sequence of tonal centres gets changed as well, from D-E-F-E (with modal implications) to E-D-E-F-E (still modal, but now beginning and ending on the same tonic, and, because of the adjustment of section lengths, laying much more stress on E). Moreover, Laswell uses the 'modulations' in subtle ways, shifting from E to F and then back from F to E through passages of bitonality; there is a particularly beautiful effect in the course of the latter when a trumpet A flat in F-oriented material from Section C (over a bass drone E) is then treated as a G sharp in the *In a Silent Way* tune (over the same bass drone).

Overall, Laswell exposes the family resemblances between the various materials and makes them live together; at the same time, he makes the performer Davis much more dominant (most of the guitar and sax solos are cut), and it is a particular Davis: the elegiac, lyrical soloist (he is excised from the funky Section C, which in any case is drastically shortened; note also that the first bass riff in this section, which in the original gives it much of its funk character, is mixed so low as to be almost inaudible). But in showcasing Davis, making him

Table 2: Miles Davis *In a Silent Way*

Section	Time	Tonal Centre	Description
A	0.00	D	organ chords, el. pno tinkles, gtr noodles, A–D bass riff, hi-hat groove, all over D tonality
	1.30		pause
	1.35		resume + tpt solo (1.45)
	5.20		tpt out – 'background' groove only
	6.00		gtr solo
	9.15		tenor sax solo
	10.45		sax out – 'background' groove only
	11.55		pause
	12.00		resume – 'background' groove only
	13.25		pause
	13.30		resume + tpt solo
	17.15		tpt out – 'background' groove continues, to fade
B	0.00	E	bowed bass drone (E), gtr tune (x2), el. pno tinkles – unmeasured
	2.12		tpt repeats tune (x2), with similar backing
C	4.15	F	quicker, funk texture, snare drum 4 (or 8) to bar, bass riff I (♫ ♪), + tpt solo
	5.00		bass/drums continue, el. pno interlude with important chordal motif
	5.45		gtr solo over similar backing
	8.25		gtr out – bass riff II (jazz-rock style)
	9.15		bass riff I, tenor sax solo
	10.35		tenor solo continues, with bass riff II
	11.40		tpt solo, with bass riff I
	12.45		tpt solo continues, with bass riff II
	13.15		continuation, but with bigger drum part
	13.55		continues, but with bass riff I
	14.45		continues, but with bass riff II
	15.20		tpt out
	15.40		riff out
B	15.45	E	recap of B tune, on gtr (x2)
	17.50		tpt repeats tune (x2)
	20.00		end

Table 3: Miles Davis: *In a Silent Way/Shhh/Peaceful/It's About that Time*
(realised by Bill Laswell)

Section	Time	Tonal Centre	Description
B	0.00	E	bowed bass drone (E), with 'electronic' sounds
	1.15		gtr tune (x2) over bass drone, el. pno, 'sounds'
	3.20		tpt tune (x2) over similar backing (but plus guitar)
Link	5.20	E	new gtr solo, over bowed bass drone, followed by tpt solo over 'ambient' sounds
A	6.45	D	tpt solo, over A–D bass riff, organ chords, el. pno figures, hi-hat groove (7.00)
Link	10.05	?	pause on organ chords (+ el. pno tinkles)
	10.20		continues – but held bass E enters
	10.40		chordal el. pno motif from Section C enters, in F (still over bass E)
	10.55		bass E out
C	11.15	F	tenor sax solo, over snare 8-to-the-bar plus el. pno chords (plus bass riff I – but this almost inaudible)
	12.10		tenor solo continues, over bass riff II
Link	13.20	?	bass riff out, sax out – chordal el. pno motif (in F)
	13.35		tpt solo (from Section C), in F but over held bass E
B	14.15	E	tune on tpt (x1)
	15.20		end

if anything more of an *auteur* than he originally was, Laswell also thrusts himself forward. When an individual takes so much trouble to produce both a particular emotional effect and a coherent formal shape, we are surely tempted to think of him not only as a remixer but also as a **composer**. (At the same time, we are reminded of dance-club DJs, with their love of seamless segues and control of mood-flow.)

When Laswell turns to Bob Marley, his approach is in one sense the exact opposite, for one of his first decisions was to remove completely Marley's singing voice from the music. While Marley stamped the personality of a global superstar on what had previously been largely a collectively produced style (and Laswell's refusal to tamper with his voice might be read as a mark of untouchability), this move would seem to open the way to radical possibilities of restructuring. Moreover, reggae itself had always been a remix-sympathetic music, especially since the rise and influence of its 'dub' variant from the 1970s onwards; from this point of view, reggae was an obvious choice for a 'translation' project.[9] Yet Laswell prepared by immersing himself in Marley's biography and background, and, according to Williams, 'we are invited to use our imaginations, and to feel his spirit suffusing these carefully textured reconstructions'; if, then, the result is that Laswell 'makes the music sound more like itself', the question is raised again, as it is in the case of the Davis remixes, of exactly how this musical 'self' is being conceived and where it is located.[10]

Marley's original version of the soul-ballad *One Love (People Get Ready)* is dominated by his vocal.[11] The straightforward verse–chorus form, built on conventional triadic chord-sequences and a simple reggae groove from the rhythm section, would be nothing – it would seem – without it, even though there is an important rôle, too, for backing vocal harmonies, especially in the choruses. What Laswell does with this material is extraordinary. The instrumental timbres are comprehensively remodelled and the textures clarified, as we expect by now (for instance, the foregrounded piano of the original disappears); more striking, though, is the addition of great washes of electronic sound, including many wind, water and birdsong-like noises. In effect, Laswell has invented a new genre – 'ambient-gospel' – since

9. Dub, beginning in the late 1960s with the work of such artists as King Tubby and Lee 'Scratch' Perry, is a form of reggae in which vocal (and often other) solos are excised, leaving just the rhythm tracks. The dub version, often issued on the 'B' side of a record and usually subjected to remixing and electronic sound-processing, can be used just as dance music or as backing for MC 'talkover' and 'toasting' (improvisatory rapping).
10. Williams (1998), p. 17.
11. Both Marley tracks discussed here can be found on 'Exodus', Tuff Gong TGLCD 6 (originally issued in 1977).

the other side of his reconstruction is the spotlight that removing the lead vocal throws on the backing singers, whose gospel-styled harmonies are mixed right up and forward, and given structural centrality. The piece starts with ambient sounds, and the basic reggae groove gradually emerges from within this; at this point the texture is so thematically empty that we are expected, it would seem, to be referring to the original recording, to hear Marley's singing in our inner ears. As the 'backing' singers emerge and come to the front acoustically, their harmonies become the focus; and then their backing (the rhythm section) fades out, and we are left with an a cappella gospel hymn (this is what the backing harmonies were, latently, all along), surrounded by electronic ambient sounds, which fade out to conclude the piece.

By turning the texture inside out, Laswell has in one sense certainly discovered elements that were embryonically present and put them in the centre; and in doing that, he has reconnected the material to an older musical and religious tradition which had been important in its formation but which had been 'modernised', as gospel song was secularised into soul music. At the same time, this process shifts the original recording from its specific cultural setting, an African-American axis weighted towards black Jamaica, into a more 'global' one, with the ambient soundscapes in particular appearing to place this cultural tradition within 'modernity', and to connect the song's spiritual message (the 'one love' suffusing righteous human nature) with the image of a mediatised universal Nature.

Marley's *Exodus* is a longer and more loosely structured piece than his *One Love*. Quasi-improvised verses, of variable length, alternate with chanted choral refrains and with extended instrumental passages, telling the story of the long journey of the 'Jah people' (God's chosen people in the Rastafarian religion). But the music possesses a striking density. This applies both to texture (a clattering network of highly active voices – bass, drums, guitar, keyboard and horns – all positioned in a low-to-middle register) and to structure: once the groove is established, around a virtually unchanging A minor drone harmony, most change is small-scale, and there is a good deal of quasi-improvisatory riffing around a variety of similar figures, drawing on minor-pentatonic G-A-C-D-E scale-material). The style is very funky, an effect created especially by Marley's singing, wah-wah from guitar and keyboard, and driving, percussive horn parts similar to those employed by James Brown.

Losing Marley's vocal has a less dramatic impact than in the case of

One Love: so much more is going on, and in any case, it does not carry much of a tune. But, as with *One Love*, Laswell seizes upon the new prominence of the vocal group, extends the structural weight of their refrains, and blows them up enormously in the texture. Their voicing is widened, through octave doubling and mixing up the parallel harmonies (see Ex. 1), and they are given massive reverb and echo. At the same time, the range of instrumental sounds is expanded (for example, acoustic piano takes on an important role), the bass, drums, guitar and keyboard lines are clarified (often with altered timbres), the entire middle of the texture is opened out, and the overall range is extended upwards (through extra harmonics and the addition of often high-register electronic sounds, not to mention the added higher vocal parts). Laswell does not recompose the form in the obvious way seen in his work on Davis, but he does organise the essentially open-ended process through different means: Marley's principle is largely thematic (via the verse/chorus alternation), but, deprived of this possibility, Laswell relies more on changes in dynamic level and in texture (for instance, several times the bass drops out and then returns).

As with *One Love*, Laswell's *Exodus* seems to be removed, at least in part, from its previous specific cultural space. It is noticeable that the funky horns do not feature until near the end, and the blown-up vocal chants leave behind the personal inflections typical of soul singing to become the voice of a choral collective. The dramatic, 'wide-screen' textures suggest, once again, a more global vision, and the ambient sounds are those of electronic modernity. Guitar lines

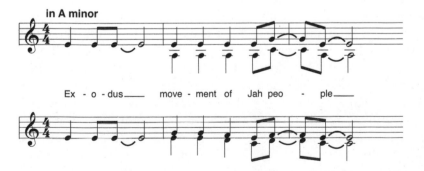

Example 1   For each continuation, the upper part gives Marley's lead voice, while the lower part shows some of the harmonies made more prominent in Laswell's version.

often have the larger-than-life 'twanginess' found in the soundtracks of Hollywood Westerns, and a particular keyboard phrase (Ex. 2) half-buried in Marley's recording but foregrounded in piano octaves by Laswell suggests the same provenance; we realise at this point that the minor-pentatonic melodic material of the piece is congruent with this particular movie sound-world, and cannot help wondering if, perhaps, Laswell has a Hollywood 'Exodus' in his mind.

Example 2

The shift from cultural specificity to a more panoramic vision can, once again, be justified in terms of pointers in Marley's own music (emphasising groove and chant might be seen as a neo-Africanist move with which he would probably have sympathised, and the potential is readily available in his own *Exodus*); and there is, perhaps, a strange logic (albeit containing an ethnic inversion) to a link between reggae Rastafarianism and the black-and-white morality of the American Western. At the same time, Laswell's route to this achievement is surely stamped through-and-through with the mark of a quite personal perspective, an imagined world that is equally specific both to him and to a late-twentieth-century, globally-construed moment. Whose is the music, then?

Laswell has (according to Williams) deliberately chosen music to work on from 'the beginning of the era that came after' the age of masterworks, 'the beginning of the language that we're speaking now'. For Williams, he has 'helped us towards an understanding of that new language's grammar and syntax'.[12] Yet categorising these recordings by Laswell does not seem to be quite this easy, as we have seen. How might they be classified? At times, when the relationship to the original is close, they feel quite like covers – or remixes. At other times, when the connection is less tight, the more flexible Jamaican music term 'version' seems more suitable. Sometimes, we are reminded more of categories familiar to us from Western art music history: the 'arrangement', the 'transcription', the 'parody'

12. Williams (1998), p. 17.

(which, in its fifteenth- and sixteenth-century version, seems technically not too far removed from Laswell's approach), or even the 'fantasia on a theme'. Are we in new times, or old? Is there an author in this work-house, and if so, who is it?

A fairly cursory survey suggests that record shops are filing Laswell's CDs not under his name but those of Davis and Marley; and, indeed, on the CD sleeves Laswell's name is presented in tastefully smaller type than theirs. On both recordings, however, he credits (as is common) a range of engineers and production assistants. To this he adds, on 'Dreams of Freedom', thanks to the Marley family, to The Wailers (Bob's original band), to other musicians who participated in the original recordings, and to three more who contributed new material for the remix (though not for the tracks discussed in this paper), not to mention Chris Blackwell (of Island Records) for 'creative direction and concept'; on 'Panthalassa', again, all the musicians from the original Davis recordings are listed. On both, also, the composers of the original pieces are credited – mostly Davis or Marley, but including, for example, keyboardist Joe Zawinul for *In a Silent Way*, and various others for some of the Marley tracks. Consulting CD reissues of the original albums, we find that producer Ted Macero's name features on 'In a Silent Way' as well; and production on 'Exodus' is credited to 'Bob Marley and the Wailers'. There is an extra intertextual interest concerning *One Love (People Get Ready)* in that composition is credited jointly to Bob Marley and African-American soul singer Curtis Mayfield, who, indeed, wrote a song called *People Get Ready*, which was a hit for his group, The Impressions, in 1965. It turns out that the verses of Marley's song function as a very loose cover of Mayfield's tune: Marley uses freely varied but recognisable versions of Mayfield's melody and its repeating three-chord harmonic progression, but with completely different lyrics (at the same time, there is certainly a thematic allusion to Mayfield's 'people get ready' sentiment).

Signs of Practice

It is too easy, then, to present the relationship between contemporary popular music and the work-concept in black and white, and over-radical, terms. My argument, in fact, is that (i) today's intertextual practices are to some extent the latest chapter in an old story, and are thoroughly embedded in long-lasting vernacular habits; and (ii) at the same time, their relationship with work thinking and its musical habitat is not one that can be defined in terms of a pure opposition: rather, the musical world we have to deal with here is singular, albeit one whose structure is warrened with ever-mutating networks of variants and divergences.

Some aspects of typical popular music compositional practices have already been described, but the ramifications of intertextuality can be pursued deeper into the textures and processes of vernacular forms. I have written elsewhere about the importance and nature of repetition in popular music.[13] Although repetition as such is plainly a privileged semiotic marker for music, as compared with other semiotic systems, it seems clear that iterative processes – repeating tunes, phrases, sections, rhythmic patterns, riffs, chord-sequences – are especially favoured in most sorts of popular music. Offering an element of the (so to speak) preformed, and standing over against the demands of painfully thought-through invention, such processes spurn the sort of uniqueness generally associated with 'works' (which is no doubt why, since Kant, music aestheticians have often been troubled by them). They generate the potential for infinitely extensible structures – a strophic song can have as many verses as can be made up, a West African 'timeline' or Cuban dance rhythm can be looped indefinitely, and a call-and-response dialogue can be repeated for as long as the musicians have stamina – and it is therefore no surprise to find recorded popular pieces often either ending at an arbitrary point or fading out, as if endless. Generative repetition can energise a repertory as well as an individual performance. If you can construct a song over a single riff, or a repeating 12-bar blues chord-sequence, then you can use the same riff or sequence to create a somewhat different song tomorrow; so can someone else. There is a seamless shift from this technique into the *maqam* principle on the one hand and the reproduction of standard generic formulae on the other. Within this whole range of contexts, repetition processes can be taken to signal the imprimatur of the collective, and point towards the anonymity not of 'the masses' (as élitist cultural critique would have it) but that

13. Richard Middleton, *Studying Popular Music*, Milton Keynes, Open University Press, 1990, Ch. 7; id., 'Repeat Performance', in *Music on Show: Issues of Performance*, ed. Tarja Hautamäki and Helmi Järviluoma, Tampere, University of Tampere Department of Folk Tradition, 1998, pp. 209–13; id., '"Over and Over": Appunti verso una politica della ripetizione', *Musica/Realtà*, Vol. 55 (1998), pp. 135–50.

which comes from standing in the interstices of social and generational exchange.

It is this understanding of repetition which has been theorised by African-American literary scholars as 'Signifyin(g)'. Signifyin(g), as found right across African and Afro-diasporic culture, is defined as the continual paradigmatic transformation, inter- or intra-textual, of given material, the repetition and varying of stock elements, the aesthetic of a 'changing same' (to use a phrase invented by Amiri Baraka). In its musical forms – constant variation of common-ownership material, intertextual reference, building performance on known frameworks, structural models and standard tunes – Signifyin(g) looks askance at the goal-directed drive for coherence typical of the mainstream WECT culture. It is worth noting, however, that Signifyin(g) is not only different, it also Signifies on the mainstream culture, for example, on the standard processes of signifying, with their syntagmatic chains always searching for closure: 'the absent *g* is a figure for the Signifyin(g) black difference'.[14] So there is not only otherness but also relation. And we notice the extraordinary coincidence whereby the gradual transformation of the popular musics of the Western world through African-American influence, beginning in the early nineteenth century with American minstrelsy and the spiritual songs of the 'Second Awakening', takes place over exactly the same period as the newly regulative work-concept makes its bid for hegemony – and does so not only elsewhere in the musical system, but also in relation to popular genres (the nineteenth century is, after all, when large-scale publishing of notated popular music pieces, with identified composers, begins). The two historical forces dance on together, like positive and negative electrodes defining the dynamics of the musico-magnetic field.

A common feature of the African-American tradition, though not confined to it, is the sense that there is more than one 'voice' in the texture (call-and-response, lead voice varying underlying framework, etc.). By contrast (at least in the paradigm case), the performers of a **work** must bend themselves to 'the composer's voice' (to quote the

14. Henry Louis Gates, Jr, *The Signifying Monkey: A Theory of Afro-American Literary Criticism*, New York, Oxford University Press, 1988, p. 46. Similarly, the optionally present *g* in the title of this paper, 'Work-in(g)-practice', is a figure for the Signifyin(g) pop difference, which also marks my debt to, and Signifyin(g) upon, Gates's theory.

title of Edward Cone's book).[15] Even if, in a certain sense, polyphonic music in itself says 'we', as Adorno suggests, in the WECT tradition the parts are felt to be subsumed into a single controlling authorial vision. And, anyway, as genuine polyphony declines in importance in WECT music over the nineteenth century, the effect of this mono-logic authority, suppressing all threat of the mess that dialogue might introduce, grows ever heavier.[16] Call-and-response, with its built-in ambivalence over both textural focus and start/end point, is a key technique in African-American music, directing us outside the con-fines of monologic closure. The 'vocalised tone' often applied to instruments, giving them a definite persona, and the personalisation of instruments (the guitar as lover, for example), tend in a similar direction. Right across the range of popular genres, the sense of a net-work of complementary voices – guitar comments, horn riffs, backing singers, active bass-lines, drum fills – playing off the vocal lead, which itself may well be 'conversing' with the voices of previous performers of the song, not to mention those of composer, songwriter, arranger and producer, is palpable. Who is speaking here, we are forever being driven to ask, and to whom?

Perhaps the most useful conceptualisation of intertextuality is the 'dialogical' theory of semiotics associated with Mikhail Bakhtin. For Bakhtin, the key moment in the communication process is not any of the pre-existing large categories (the language-system, the code, the message) but the **utterance** (the performance-event, we might say). And an utterance is always structured dialogically: an awareness of context, of addressees, of possible responses and of a whole history of previous usages of its terms, themes and intonations is built into its mode of operation. Thus

> Utterances are not indifferent to one another, and are not self-suffi-cient; they are aware of and mutually reflect one another ... The living utterance ... cannot fail to brush up against thousands of dialogic threads, woven by socio-ideological consciousness around the given

15. Edward T. Cone, *The Composer's Voice*, Berkeley, University of California Press, 1982.

16. Just as post-structuralist thought turned works into texts and announced the death of the author, so, too, it has sought to uncover the diversity of figures sup-pressed in this repertory by the composer's monologic voice: see Carolyn Abbate, *Unsung Voices: Opera and Musical Narrative in the Nineteenth Century*, Princeton, Princeton University Press, 1991.

object of an utterance, it cannot fail to become an active participant in social dialogue.[17]

There is in the utterance a 'double-voiced' quality – an allusion to other perspectives, subject-positions, moments, that is manifested also at higher levels as 'polyphony' (in texts) and 'heteroglossia' (in language) – which produces, and also originates in, the equally multi-faceted structure of subjectivity itself.

Bakhtin's argument is wide-ranging. But two aspects are of particular relevance here. Firstly, although the dialogic quality of human communication might be considered ubiquitous (and an unfettered 'polyphony', if not exactly the 'natural' condition of culture, at least an inspiring utopic trope), in practice its extent, forms and effects vary in line with both the conventions of genre and the impositions of social power. Class inequality means that dominant forces always try to reduce dialogue in favour of a centralised, monologic mode of discourse, and therefore cultivate genres which facilitate this; for Bakhtin, comparisons between, on the one hand, the closed single-point-of-view logic of legal, religious and academic (!) texts, the epic and the romance, and, on the other hand, the 'polyphonic' quality of the novel (especially as developed by Dostoevsky) and the 'carnivalesque' excess and ambivalence of many 'low' vernacular genres furnish classic examples. This emphasis on the historical and social mediation of semiosis readily offers a persuasive explanatory framework for the emergent hegemony of the post-1800 WECT work-culture, and of its multifaceted relationship thereafter with popular (and especially African-American) genres.

At the same time, the alert reader will notice an apparent historical mismatch, since this rise to hegemony of the (monologic) musical work coincides with the golden age of the (supposedly 'polyphonic') novel. Novels vary in the extent of their 'polyphony', of course. Further (and paradoxically), the potential for critique opened by the very autonomy principle associated with the work-concept creates the possibility that the social turbulence of nineteenth-century bourgeois society could be represented in the forms and styles of musical works. Presumably, this would be why Abbate and others can uncover diversity beneath the apparent closures of this repertory. In fact, the most

17. Much of Bakhtin's work is now available in English; for a good, accessible selection, see *The Bakhtin Reader*, ed. Pam Morris, London, Edward Arnold, 1994. My quotations are taken from pp. 76 and 85 of this text.

unqualified manifestations of the spirit of monologic closure in this period are probably to be found less in the output of a Schumann or a Mahler and more in the broad 'middlebrow' repertory, with a balancing extreme at the other pole located in the multi-authored, mixed-genre, performatively messy excesses of music hall and minstrelsy. To put this point in another way (and recall an earlier remark): there is in this nineteenth-century music culture no rigid demarcation between sites of work thinking on the one hand and practice thinking on the other; rather, all the forces interact, in a variety of ways, across the full topography.

The second point of particular interest lies in Bakhtin's concept of creativity. Authorship for him is less a singular originary intention, more a space in which the interrelationships of the dialogic voices, at once characters in the text and fragments of subjectivity, are played out; the construct of the unitary author (or composer), who speaks **through** his characters, is regarded as an ideological imposition on this space. Nevertheless, Bakhtin does not (with Foucault) see 'the author' simply as a figure at large in certain forms of text and discourse, still less (with Barthes) as a fabrication to be destroyed in favour of empowering the reader; rather, there is a definite relation between the activity of authoring (and indeed the whole spectrum of activities that we might describe as 'uttering') and real human beings, living within real social relations. Even in the furthest flights of intertextual dialogue, the author (composer, performer, etc.) retains the rights and responsibilities of **agency** – a key point for the politics of popular music, and one to return to.

Still Work-ing ...

Bakhtin's sense of historical and cultural specificity can come to our help when, swimming in the heady outpourings of the popular music intertext (its repetitions, its Signifyin(g)s, its multiple voices), we are suddenly brought up short by a thought in a different mood: surely this intertext is the very same category whose individual products have, especially in recent years, acquired such an insistent sense of their individual identifiability and attributability as to require defence through legal action when these are threatened. The several cases hinging on unauthorised sampling stand in a longer tradition where alleged plagiarism has been at issue. The circumscribing of popular music as property, a process marked most clearly by the development of music copyright law from the nineteenth century onwards, may have its peculiarities – the complexities and variabilities of contracts, of production systems and of dissemination modes mean that a host of parties, including composers, performers, publishers, record companies, managers and agents, may or may not get paid, in varying amounts, in different situations – yet it directs our attention to the fact that the absorption of the musical practice into commodity status has generated an administrative iron cage whose operation is absolutely predicated on the existence of a (financially rewarding) relationship between 'a composer, a score, and a given class of performances': not surprisingly, the usual definitional term in copyright law is 'the musical work'.[18]

In this situation, it is hard to ignore the significance of the composer's name on the record label or sheet music, or the extent to which the record form itself (by the 1950s taking over from printed music as the principal dissemination medium for popular music) has contributed to the 'fixing' of pieces in apparently definitive versions. When bands focus their live performances on accurate reproduction of their own recording, or when audiences complain that they have not succeeded, it seems as if we are watching an extension to the *Werktreue* ideal. Rock, blues and jazz critics assemble their 'classic' records into authoritative canons; CD reissues of 'complete works' (even of relatively minor performers), often including variant sources (alternate and unreleased takes) and extensive scholarly notes, match WECT collected editions for pedantic exactitude; discographers argue over the exact dates, personnel and outputs of recording sessions, like so many musicologists in search of the source history of even forgotten works. Obsessive listings ('The 100 Greatest Albums in the Universe' etc.) litter the specialist magazines, and late-twentieth-century 'trainspotters' mimic the reifying impulse of the eighteenth-century aristocrat or the nineteenth-century bourgeois, with their 'unique collections', at once fetishistic and marketable. In one sense, 'the shudder and ring of the [cash] register is the true music; later I will play the record, but that will be redundant. My money has already heard it.', but, although 'records make music cheap ... the

---

18. 'A musical work ... acquires copyright protection immediately it is committed to paper or fixed in some other material form, such as recording' (British Copyright Act, 1956, quoted in Simon Frith, 'Copyright and the Music Business', *Popular Music*, Vol. 7 (1988), p. 63).

disc too has its magic', and the collector's worship of the 'perfect' hi-fi sound is complemented by the way that records can turn performances into icons ('with records ... we experience the immortality of others'), recording into a search for the 'perfect' performance, and studio composition into the realisation of that ideal which score notations could previously only approximate.[19]

There is considerable ambivalence here, though. Assembling alternate takes on record not only documents a work's history but also lays before us a slice of that intertextual world of practice which gave it birth, enabling the listener to follow the Signifyin(g) dialogue between variants. Similarly, although recordings do in one sense freeze process into product, in another they do exactly what their name suggests – **record** a moment, a memory of a moment: and the aesthetic of the 'live recording' is only the extreme manifestation of a widespread approach that tries to give even the most laboriously and technologically constructed 'final mix' the effect of being a 'real performance' (this can extend to programming into the sequencing software signs of imperfection such as rhythmic unevenness). Recordings do take the emphasis on performed nuances so characteristic of the African-American tradition in particular and fix them for ever, as if in the glass-case of a museum, but at the same time, by capturing nuance which notation could only hint at,[20] they push the listener's attention squarely on to the focus favoured by that tradition; the endemic critical activity of comparing versions, the importance of covers, the enhanced status of performer-composers, all follow naturally from this, as (once the technology allows) does the practice of making multiple mixes aimed at different contexts (this appears to start with soul/funk star James Brown in the 1960s), and indeed the whole 'remix culture'. From here, it is a short step to using recordings as raw material; through sampling, scratching, talkover and live mixing techniques the record becomes an instrument of performance. While there is mileage still in Walter Benjamin's much-disputed argument that mechanical reproduction technologies such as records would dethrone the 'aura' of the traditional art-work, for they do democratise access and provide the ubiquitous furniture for a quite new

---

19. Evan Eisenberg, *The Recording Angel: Music, Records and Culture from Aristotle to Zappa*, London, Picador, 1987, pp. 20, 45, 46.
20. Or try to control, as WECT composers, from Rossini to Stravinsky and beyond, have notoriously attempted to make it do.

soundscape, located in some sense outside history, it is arguably his views on the potential of the new technologies to transform cultural **production** that are the more radical. 'Jungle' musician Goldie connects this potential explicitly to the possibilities of threatening the structures of cultural and social capital surrounding the old WECT system:

> The barbarians are breaking everything down. Conventional education has no status – that old passport isn't needed in the nineties, which are decaying through youth culture ever going forward, and the technology allowing us to shrink time. Youth culture has forced the hand of tradition, it's forced aristocracy to retreat. Aristocracy says, 'You can't do that with these machines,' but youth culture finds a loophole. There are no rules! The barbarians are taking over.[21]

Yet there is ambivalence here, too. Goldie has been described as a 'genius'; undoubtedly, he has 'aura' (and his private life is probed as much as Tchaikovsky's). Andrew Goodwin has suggested that the postmodern celebration of D-I-Y digital music technology tends to ignore the fact that in this culture, often, the producer (using the term broadly, to cover everything from studio composers through remixers to club DJs) picks up the charismatic mantle dropped by song-writers and singers.[22] The 'classic' 1981 collage by hip-hop pioneer Grandmaster Flash, *The Adventures of Grandmaster Flash on the Wheels of Steel*, draws virtuosically on material from six existing records: Chic's disco hit *Good Times* (1979), two numbers by pop/rock groups – Queen's *Another One Bites the Dust* (1980) and Blondie's *Rapture* (1981) – and three recent hip-hop records (Flash's own *Birthday Party*, *8th Wonder* by the Sugarhill Gang, and Spoonie Gee's *Monster Jam*).[23] The core of Flash's collage is the basic *Good Times* riff (a characteristic bass figure, together with a two-chord harmonic progression), and because both *Rapture* and *Another One Bites the Dust*

21. The *Guardian*, 23 January 1998, pp. 2–3.
22. Andrew Goodwin, 'Sample and Hold: Pop Music in the Digital Age of Reproduction', in *On Record: Rock, Pop, and the Written Word*, ed. Simon Frith and Andrew Goodwin, London, Routledge, 1990, pp. 258–73.
23. Grandmaster Flash, *The Adventures of Grandmaster Flash on the Wheels of Steel*, 'Jam! Jam! Jam! Sugarhill – the Legendary Label', Music Collections MUSCD 016; Chic, *Good Times*, Atlantic 3584; Queen, *Another One Bites the Dust*, EMI 5102; Blondie, *Rapture*, Chrysalis CHS 2485; Grandmaster Flash, *Birthday Party*, The Sugarhill Gang, *8th Wonder*, and Spoonie Gee and the Sequence, *Monster Jam*, all on 'Greatest Rap Hits, Vol. 2', Sugarhill SHLP 1002.

themselves make use of variations of this riff, while all the hip-hop numbers originate from the same Sugarhill stable that Flash himself belonged to, it is not difficult for him to find 'family resemblances' between his various materials.[24] The result is an entertaining inter-textual exercise in which the Signifyin(g) relations traditionally connecting performances are transferred into the operations of 'tape memory'. Yet there is no doubt that the shape of *The Adventures* is unique and is the work of one man, Grandmaster Flash; and since he self-referentially cuts into his piece such rapped phrases (taken from his source records) as 'Flash is bad', 'Grandmaster cuts faster', and 'Say Flash, one time ... two times ... three times', he seems to accept in advance the adulation due to a composer. Bill Laswell's reputation, similarly, arises not so much from his bass-playing, which is unexceptional, but from his ability to bring together musicians from a variety of backgrounds (pop, avant-garde music, free jazz, African and Asian musics), work as a producer with them and create a characteristic sound-world. This is in a tradition going back at least as far as 1960s producer Phil Spector, whose grandiose studio arrangements for a range of pop singers and vocal groups were aimed, he said, at producing 'little symphonies for the kids'.

It is as if, with both vernacular traditions of musical practice and new technological potentials offering tools with which to undermine the foundations of WECT-style pantheons, new forms of aura rush in to fill the vacuum. The pop *auteur* has become a familiar figure since the rise of the singer-songwriter in the sixties. Bob Dylan, for example, despite his continued touring, despite the plethora of covers of his songs by other singers (and 'bootleg' recordings by himself), despite his frequent insistence that the essence of his work lies in performance, and despite the way he has drawn on pre-existing repertory and conventions in a range of genres, sits securely astride an *oeuvre* of classic recordings, obsessively linked by critics and fans to his own biography and to what they take to be the *Zeitgeist*. For all the obvious differences, comparison with a figure such as Handel seems as much in order as with, say, rural bluesmen.

Singers, too, have taken over aspects of the composer's auratic rôle,

24. Sugarhill Records (formed 1979): one of the first record companies specialising in hip-hop. The 'Good Times' riff was used in many other hip-hop and rap records around this time, functioning as one of many points of intertextual reference.

the star performers wrapping themselves in iconic allure and offering us at one and the same time privileged access to their innermost feelings (it would seem) and 'definitive' versions of the songs they perform. And this goes along with a history in which the appeal of dialogic textural voices, at some moments, in some contexts, has been matched by the attractions of lead and backing in others: a key pop texture, this, unmistakable when Celine Dion soars above the orchestra or Bruce Springsteen scythes through the electric guitars, and one that has been persuasively theorised by Philip Tagg in terms of the figure/ground (inner/outer, subject/object, individual/social) dichotomies so characteristic of a lengthy Western intellectual and cultural history. Soloism arguably takes on new meanings and a new intensity in modern society, in the context of a novel kind of mass individualism fed by market economics, the pursuit of individual pleasures fed by social mobility, consumerism and advertising, and a cult of the self fed by the collapse of religious belief and of social authority. These social processes mesh historically with the rise of the spectacular star performer since the nineteenth century. But there is ambivalence here, too, especially if we consider carefully what terms such as lead and solo have come to cover. What happens sociologically to a 'solo' guitar line, for example, when it is treated with heavy phasing and reverb effects, or when a vocal is double-tracked and 'chorused'? Who is it who speaks through the robotic-sounding vocoder-driven lead voice in Laurie Anderson's 1982 hit *O Superman*? Or the 'fattened' sound of the synth-bass's quasi-lead rôle in Berlin's *Take My Breath Away* (a big hit in 1986), played partly (though not quite completely) in octaves with the echoey lead vocal? To the extent that collaborative and technologised sound production processes (and even, in live performance, amplification and sound mixing) have 'socialised' voices, attenuating and even cutting the direct link between the 'persons' we see (or imagine) and those we hear, a space is opened up within which the question of who is speaking here becomes malleable. We realise that, traditionally in musical performance, a musical voice and a social voice are, so to speak, forced together. What happens now is that this monologic grip is at least potentially cracked open. The relationship between the social dynamics of the performance-event (real or virtual) and those of our broader experience which the former might be taken to represent (or at least to connect to) takes on a certain elasticity. At one extreme are 'works' heard as 'solos', even if performed by large polyphonic ensembles; they speak in the composer's (or perhaps the conductor's) voice. At the other are solo lines heard as speaking for a collectivity; Springsteen, for instance, as a working-class Everyman. While we have certainly not witnessed the death of the author, then, the electronic mask which this figure has taken on has facilitated not only new routes of creativity but also a new politics of listening.

Such masking or 'impersonation' is prefigured by the technique of covering already recorded songs, for whom do we hear in this situation, the new performer or earlier ones, or both? The question can be answered, yet again, only with an insistence on the variability of practice. The typology of covers is broad, from Natalie Imbruglia's 1997 hit *Torn* at one extreme (so close in every detail to an earlier version by Norwegian singer Trine Rein as to occasion journalistic outrage),[25] to at the other extreme The Verve's *Bittersweet Symphony* (also 1997), which, although closely based on an old instrumental version of The Rolling Stones' song *The Last Time* as arranged by their manager, Andrew Oldham, has changed and added enough to be legally a new entity (albeit still the object of a court case for plagiarism). The distance is that between something akin to a 'performance' in the WECT sense and something actually on the boundary of a category more like that of 'tune family'.

Frank Sinatra's celebrated *My Way* (1969), itself a cover of an earlier French song with new English words, has been imitated, adapted and parodied many times. Sinatra, in his version, makes the most of the emotionalism and the personal, even confessional, mode of address, typical of the ballad genre. Digging into the verbal meanings, his jazz-derived phrasing giving the singing the effect of authenticity, he unquestionably ends up establishing the song in the popular mind as **his** composition. Elvis Presley's 1977 cover follows the outlines of Sinatra's version closely; it is inconceivable that he did not have this version in his mind. However, the setting is stylistically shifted (from large orchestra to rock band, from jazz-style rhythms to rock backbeats, etc.). And Presley's singing, rhythmically less varied than Sinatra's, is much more dramatic in timbre and pitching: the echoey chest

25. It is interesting, of course, that what in a different musical sphere might have been accepted as an adequate reproduction of an original is here denied credibility precisely because it is heard as adding nothing new. By contrast, 'copy bands', whose sole *raison d'être* is to reproduce iconic performances with ritualistic exactitude, are regarded as perfectly acceptable.

voice and extravagant glissandi (for which he was well known) produce an effect that marks the 'way'of the song's title as emphatically Elvis Presley's. The cover here, then, acts as a tribute, alluding to a performance that we are assumed to know, but speaks from a different point in the music culture. Sid Vicious's 1979 version with the Sex Pistols might also be described as a tribute, albeit a negative one. The opening verse is turned into a parody of the tradition which Sinatra is taken to represent (interestingly, Vicious's voice-production, diction and 'sobbing' phrasing suggest that he associates this tradition with classical music); the personal soul-baring is made to sound pretentious and self-indulgent. After this, a drastic punk restyling launches itself violently at the conventions of 'classic' popular music, offering the 'way' of punk with absolutely no apologies. Harmonies and melody are stripped down to the basics, so that the focus is on the aggressively speech-like vocalism (shout, sneer, snarl, with exaggeratedly demotic diction and deliberately bad intonation) and the ruthlessly regular rhythmic drive. The conjunction of disgust and self-disgust is typical of punk. We might regard this recording as an example of an ideologically motivated cover: there is a conscious effort to make a statement which is in opposition to, and indeed 'mutilates', an existing aesthetic.[26]

Still, though, this could not work without a target. And, while we can say that covers are located on a spectrum, moving from exact copies at one end, through tributes, reinterpretations and distinct stylistic shifts, to ideological attacks at the other end, in all cases there is a dependence on an **originating moment**: an existing version, a starting point or defining interpretation, against which the cover will be measured, to which it will relate. This origin is not a 'first cause' but more a transiently privileged moment of departure within networks of family resemblances, bearing comparison with similar moments within the networks of repetition, Signifyin(g) and remixing. It would be misleading to view such moments as equivalent to 'works', although we might, perhaps, consider them symptoms of 'work-ness' (or the work-concept might be thought of as a historically specific extrapolation from the more general system that I am describing in terms of family resemblance networks). While the sheer variability of

26. Frank Sinatra, *My Way*, Reprise RS 20817; Elvis Presley, *My Way*, RCA PB1165; The Sex Pistols, *My Way*, 'The Great Rock 'n' Roll Swindle', Virgin CDVD 2510.

process that has been sketched above renders any generalisation, still more any prophecy, dangerous, it may be that this sort of picture – networks of interconnected moments, coalescing into temporary hierarchies marked by the installation of 'root' points and specific input references – offers the best available model of a possible emergent politics of popular compositional practice.

Musical Works, Musical Labours

To pursue the progressive potential of this model very far would require much more than action on the level of compositional practices alone, for they are embedded in business structures that are completely predicated on the legally protected individuality of musical works, the financial hierarchies benefiting from this arrangement, and the quasi-romantic auras painted around these works and their 'creators' that are used to help sell them. It can hardly be accidental that the rise of the 'work' parallels and intermeshes with that of the 'commodity', nor that the history of that sort of 'individuality' necessary to the former coincides with that of capitalism, whose success was powered, as the work of Weber and Tawney gives us good reason to believe, by exactly the same species of property-conscious individualism. Fetishism of the work is not too far away from that fetishism of the commodity to which Marx drew attention, both in its characteristic psychology and in its social basis in the effacement of collective labour. Goehr attributes the success of work thinking to 'conceptual imperialism',[27] but it becomes easier to understand the political power that concepts can undoubtedly possess if we grasp the material forces in which they are rooted and which they help to sustain. The fact that digital technology and the world success of African-American musical practices, with their potential to subvert work thinking, have arrived at the same moment that the market has tightened its grip on musical production through ruthless maximum exploitation of ownership rights is one of the great ironies of the late twentieth century, but is readily explicable once we situate the rôle of transnational capital correctly in the analytical picture; this force will turn any 'raw material' into grist to its mill.

One way to address critically the conceptual level of this imperialism is to crack open the terms of its discourse. Just as 'recording' can

27. Goehr (1992), p. 245.

refer to a process, a moment in a network, as well as an object, so, too, 'work' can have an active and processual, as well as a reifying, sense; a musical work can be a **labour**.[28] Turning to Raymond Williams's indispensable *Keywords*, we find etymological corroboration of the way that 'the basic sense of the word, to indicate activity and effort or achievement' was shifted in favour of 'a predominant specialisation to regular paid employment' as a result of the development of capitalist productive relations.[29] It is easy to see how this might connect with the idea of the product of such relations being a 'work' (and the place of manufacture, a 'works').[30] The *Oxford English Dictionary* confirms that the earlier usage can be traced back well into the first millennium AD; it often seems to be connected with a sense of passing time (as in 'the work of a moment') and to have an ethical dimension (as in 'good works'). Examples of the second usage – work as product – can also be found before the year 1000, but seem to become much more common from the fifteenth century (which is about the date when the specialised application to 'art-works' begins, too). Williams shows as well how, in one usage, 'working' became associated with a particular social class, and how this history was intertwined with the etymological history of 'labouring' and 'labour': scope there, one would think, for some discursive labour by radical musicians and musicologists. James Brown's many recordings may well constitute a body of works, but when he is described as 'the hardest working man in show business', the significance of this phrase for his African-American audience, one suspects, is not limited to an awareness that Brown has been an exemplary black capitalist.

28. Is it possible that the word 'opus' contains an analogous dialogics? From around the sixteenth century, of course, this term can denote a musical work, although what exactly Listenius's *'opus perfectum et absolutum'* (*c.* 1527) means may be disputable, as Goehr points out (ibid., p. 116); but *opus Dei* in the Benedictine usage referred to the *activity* of prayer.
29. Raymond Williams, *Keywords: A Vocabulary of Culture and Society*, rev. edn, London, Fontana, 1988, p. 335.
30. Think of the Manchester-based company Factory Records, not to mention the commonplace image of 'assembly-line' musical production, applied not only to the Tin Pan Alley, Motown and Brill Building 'song-factories' but also to Haydn's symphonies, nineteenth-century Italian operas and English oratorios. The custom-built masterpiece resists the extreme extensions of this image, but also partly accedes, through the institutionalisation of compositional pedagogy (massed ranks of composers' apprentices); here we are more likely to be asked to think in terms of a discourse of craftsmanship, the 'composer's workshop'.

There is a lineage for such discursive critique among radical ethno-musicologists, where the late John Blacking and Charles Keil among others have emphasised a distinction between 'music as process' and 'music as product', often with (perhaps somewhat rosy-spectacled) appeals to evidence of non-commodity music-making in precapitalist societies or among marginalised groups within capitalist society. Lydia Goehr ends her book by asking how far the work-concept may have constrained and disadvantaged musicians, and concludes, eloquently, that

> Music as an end could never, on aesthetic grounds alone, fully justify the social or political means involved in its composition, performance and reception. The question, therefore, still asks for a more satisfactory answer, one that will force us to think about music, less as excused and separated, and more as inextricably connected to the ordinary and impure condition of our human affairs.[31]

While truly radical change in this direction might depend, I have argued, on a broader re-evaluation of 'individualism' and 'ownership' than seems presently to be in view, this seems no reason to question the value of attempts at change within the purely musical sphere – attempts to 'un-work' the practice, so to speak.[32]

Among the many implications that such moves would have, two are of particular interest here. First, the effects might be felt not only in the vernacular sphere, as one would expect, but also on the classical canon (which in any case now resides there to a considerable extent). If, for example, Richard Williams is right to suggest that Bill Laswell's reconstructions, by rewriting Miles Davis and Bob Marley in the light of later musical developments, reveal what they were 'really' (that is, latently) about, we might say that this is what good performance (and good composing too) in the WECT tradition has always done also:

---

31. Goehr (1992), pp. 285–86.
32. This would be somewhat analogous to contemporary movements to defend remaining environmental 'commons' – including the ecological and cultural knowledge of 'tribal' peoples. The project would be politically fraught, no doubt. Keil has called for a campaign to abolish music copyright altogether. I would be with Keil in spirit, but, as Steve Feld has suggested in his dialogue with Keil on this issue, it is far from certain that penniless musicians, especially those in 'third world' countries, for whom copyright represents one of the few routes out of poverty, would agree. See Charles Keil and Steve Feld, *Music Grooves: Essays and Dialogues*, Chicago, University of Chicago Press, 1994, pp. 313–24.

they take what is given and create the past through the ear of the present; this is the historical projection of intertextuality. Just as today's popular music practice is, as we have seen, somewhat less different from practice in that WECT tradition than is sometimes excitedly claimed, so, too, Western art-music practice (as distinct from the associated theory) may have been less faithful to *Werktreue* principles than is often supposed. One task now, therefore, may be to rescue historical performing practice from the *Diktat* of the composers and their philosophical, musicological and pedagogical allies.

A second interesting point brings us back to the question of authoriality. The move from 'work' to '(inter)text' can result, ironically, in a deepening of that very aestheticist isolation which troubles Goehr about the work-concept. In some postmodernist versions of this move, as the 'author' disappears, textuality as such appears to take centre-stage, writing 'humanity' out of the script. Swimming, distinction-free, in a sea of intertextual relativism, we (whoever 'we' now are) may lose all basis for resistance to an anonymous 'view from everywhere'. But all moments are not commensurate, and the ethics of musical practice that we badly need requires an identifiable agency – the Bakhtinian author – where responsibility can be seen to reside. The misogynistic strand in 'gangsta' rap can be defended on the grounds that it belongs to a much older Signifyin(g) thematics within African-American culture; similarly, the solipsistic political quietism typical of much recent dance-club culture can be explained in terms of self-referencing circularities in the music. In both cases, a dense, internally spiralling intertextual practice makes such hand-washing easy. But the singular moment, each performance-event, is ethically unique. Responsibility cannot be ducked, any more than it can (for intertextual relationships of a rather different type) in any case where a late-twentieth-century performance of *The Magic Flute* does not raise the issue of sexism, or where a *Ring* does not somehow, explicitly or implicitly, build in an encounter with the fascistic potential of Wagner's original. To imagine that the defence of such singularity implies a return to a culture of 'works' would be unimaginative. Rather, these moments, of a huge variety of types, operating within intricate cultural networks of resemblance and difference, are what I would like to term unique **instances**; they are, in short, examples of what may be called (and what we can try to feel our way towards) 'work-in(g)-practice'.

4

Work and Recordings: The Impact of Commercialisation and Digitalisation

Catherine Moore

A dormant literature, music requires the awakening of interpretative performance. Until recently, recordings were fixed, and also permanent, documentation of a performance. For instance, the radio broadcast of Bruckner's *Fifth Symphony* conducted by Wilhelm Furtwängler on 25 October 1942 is preserved on record as a finite and specific interpretation of a recognisable musical work.[1] In fact, it can be argued that every performance is a unique 'work' whose character should be permanent.

When a musical work becomes a recording, however, the technology used in making the recording can blur the definition of 'permanent'. In March 1967 Otto Klemperer went into London's Kingsway Hall with his New Philharmonia Orchestra and a recording team from EMI Records to record Bruckner's *Fifth Symphony*.[2] Not only is Klemperer's interpretation of the symphony very different from Furtwängler's, but the construction of the recording differs as well, because this is a studio recording. In a studio recording parts of a piece are played several times, and then the sections (in the form of numbered takes) deemed best by the producer and artist are edited together into a master tape. But it is important to understand that the resulting performance could conceivably be remade using other takes.

This resulting performance can also be remade by a record label's marketing or A & R (artists and repertoire) department. In the case of new recordings, the A & R department typically has the first say

---

1. Music & Arts CD 538, Anton Bruckner, *Symphony No. 5*, Wilhelm Furtwängler, Berlin Philharmonic Orchestra. Catalogue numbers may differ from country to country; when a recording is reissued, on the same or a different label, it is usually assigned a new catalogue number.
2. EMI Classics CDM 63612, in the 'Studio' series.

about a project; the marketing staff are involved only after the record is completed. In the case of recompilations, however, the rôles are often reversed: the marketing staff may well invent the theme, and then the A & R staff are asked to provide material that suits the theme. This scenario is different from that of a producer re-editing a complete symphony, because artistic concerns are secondary. The marketing staff are searching not for the finest takes but for a saleable recompilation of material from archival master tapes. As a result, movements (or even shorter segments) are removed from a complete musical composition and placed in a new context, usually in association with a theme whose appeal is non-musical. Examples of this practice in classical music are 'Eternal Russia', 'The Women in My Life' and the top-selling 'Karajan Adagio'.[3]

As for recordings of popular music, both technology and business are frankly acknowledged to be a necessary part of the creative process.[4] Most in the business embrace this, but as the business is reshaped in the 1990s, some critics are damning. American-born British writer Donald Clarke is blunt: 'The twin problems, fuelling each other, have been overuse of technology and the sound of money shouting'.[5]

Fred Goodman, exploring the consequences of heeding the call of 'money shouting', does not shrink from aptly identifying the rock music industry as driven by commercial, not artistic, ends.[6] If his peers find him too cynical, they need to take a clearer look at what continues to drive the industry: ever greater consolidation into vertically integrated companies that crave products with cross-promotable synergy. Today, stock market prices (something Goodman does not explore) are almost as important as chart position.

3. Deutsche Grammophon 437 946, 437 743 and 445 282, respectively. Extracted movements on 'Karajan Adagio' include the Air from Bach's *Third Orchestral Suite*, the Adagio molto from Vivaldi's *Sinfonia in B minor* [RV 169], 'Aase's Death' from Grieg's *Peer Gynt* music, the Adagietto from Mahler's *Fifth Symphony* and the Andante from Brahms' *Third Symphony* (as listed in *Schwann Opus* [catalogue], Vol. 8, Fall 1997, p. 1054).
4. The term 'pop' (or 'popular') is used here to represent various genres of popular music: pop, rock, rap, country, dance, etc.
5. Donald Clarke, *The Rise and Fall of Popular Music: A Narrative History from the Renaissance to Rock 'n' Roll*, New York, St Martin's Press, 1995, p. 493.
6. Fred Goodman, *The Mansion on the Hill: Dylan, Young, Geffen, Springsteen, and the Head-on Collision of Rock and Commerce*, New York, Times Books, 1997.

people used to make records
as in a record of an event
the event of people
playing music in a room
now everything is cross-marketing
it's about sunglasses and shoes
or guns or drugs
you choose

(from *Fuel* by Ani DiFranco)[7]

Recordings Transform Consumers into Listeners

Despite the pressures that technology and commerce exert on a musical work, it is important to emphasise that without recordings many works would now be lost to all but a small group of scholar-specialists. Live performance is experienced by listeners first simultaneously and later in personal recollection. Recorded music captures interpretative performance and creates a collective or public recollection. Individually, recordings render a work immutable, but collectively they reveal the very same work to be changeable and able to accommodate varied interpretations.

Whereas written music immortalises the composer's artistic creation, recorded music immortalises the interpreter's performance as well. However, what we might commonly refer to as 'Toscanini's Beethoven 5th',[8] or 'René Jacobs' *Poppea*',[9] are, in some respects, not works but re-creations of works. Performers, even those who contribute music to the score (as in the case of Jacobs' *Poppea*), are re-creators, not creators. Markedly different performances of the same work provide listeners with something they cannot get from reading a musical score and can only rarely experience in concert. Further, recordings will prove to be the preserver of a literature of 'works'

---

7. 'Little Plastic Castle', Righteous Babe Records RBR012, 1998. I am grateful to Charles Stanford for suggesting these lyrics and to Jason Korenkiewicz for background information about Ani DiFranco.
8. The Fall 1997 *Schwann Opus* classical catalogue lists no fewer than eight recordings of Beethoven's *Fifth Symphony* conducted by Arturo Toscanini (p. 183). Not counting complete symphony cycles, some 120 recordings of this symphony are listed (pp. 7 and 183).
9. Harmonia Mundi HMC 901330/32, Claudio Monteverdi, *L'incoronazione di Poppea*, conducted by René Jacobs.

whose day in the concert hall may well be done, or which never got the chance to be heard in the first place.

Regardless of how the consumer purchases recorded music – at a retail store, via download or by mail-order – once that music is in the home, he or she becomes a listener. Today, listeners have access to a wealth of musical works that is almost without boundary. It costs less to stay at home with recordings, and even the wealthiest person fifty years ago could not hear the range of music that an ordinary person can hear on record today. Moreover, listeners who have the opportunity to hear a work repeatedly find that their curiosity about that work is increased rather than simply satisfied, and they may find that their perceptions of a work, a composer or an interpreter will change. The composer's canon can expand at home, as it has ceased to do in public performance, and the range of interpretation possible at home can never be made available in live performance. A listener listens differently every time, and a good performance promotes active listening.

Listeners' Judgement Helps Determine a Work's Future

Active listening ensures that a musical work lives in its repeated hearing by an individual listener. Recordings are interesting to people for three reasons: as information, instruction and musical experience. The first is motivated by curiosity: 'I've never heard this piece and would like to'. The second is usually tied to interpretation: interpretative variations can change your view of a piece and give historical perspective. The third is perhaps the most important: for the general listener, the experience of music on record is of a kind he or she cannot get elsewhere. This experience is becoming more and more desirable, because much concert programming is not unusual repertoire. A recording is also an experience that is just as valid as a live performance. It is ideal for any who want emotional or intellectual stimulation, and we are much more likely to find that stimulation on record, not live.

A recording takes the abstract idea of a musical work and makes it into a tangible consumer product. The listener experiences the product, and if he or she experiences it as music, it becomes, by certain criteria, a work. If we allow that a listener's judgement can define a work, then recordings provide the essential vehicle through which judgement – and art – can survive.

Digitalisation – Art Becomes Information

Digitalisation undermines the idea of the permanently recorded performance because it facilitates remaking. Once music becomes digital information, it can be manipulated at will. What was a 'work' is now malleable information. It is as if you chopped Michelangelo's 'Day of Judgement' fresco into four hundred million identically shaped jigsaw puzzle pieces, or poured the dots of a pointillist painting into an hourglass like sand.

The first step in the digitalisation of music was the binary encoding of a master tape, which stored the audio signal from the studio or concert hall as a series of on/off, zero/one codes and allowed rapid access to any point with computerised accuracy. Unlike other significant recording and playback developments – acoustic 78s, electric 78s, monaural LPs and stereo LPs – digital recording did not improve recording quality or sound reproduction.[10] The relative fidelities of analogue and digital sound are succinctly described in a chart accompanying an article by John Markoff about analogue computer chips: 'Digital chips [are] ideal for processing large amounts of data, [but] they are not suited for communicating with the real world, which is full of the gray areas that lie between 1 and 0'.[11] When that real world is music, 'a digital chip can only **approximate** the details of the curve of a sound wave. [...] The digital version of the music is transferred to a CD, which lacks the sonorous subtleties of an analog recording but can be copied more precisely'.[12]

The first digital pop record from a major label was 'Bop Till You Drop' (Warner Bros 3358, 1979) by Ry Cooder, who sought to be at the cutting edge of recording technology. The album was moderately successful: on the US album chart for 15 weeks, peaking at No. 62. The first commercially successful digital pop record was Herb Alpert's 'Rise' (A & M Records 3714, 1979). Alpert was not particularly concerned about technological advances, but 'Rise' sold more than one million copies and established digital recordings in the

---

10. Although the idea of digital LPs was certainly sold to consumers as a new and improved product, digital sound is not better than analogue sound. And since an LP is an analogue playback medium, there was in fact nothing 'digital' about these specially marked (and premium-priced) LPs.
11. John Markoff, 'In Milan, a Subtle Artisan Finds a Medium in New Analog Chips', *The New York Times*, 27 July 1998, pp. D1 and D4, at p. D4.
12. Loc cit. The emphasis is mine.

marketplace. The album peaked at No. 6 on the chart, and was on the chart for 39 weeks; the single of its title track hit No. 1, and remained on the singles chart for 25 weeks.[13]

Like movies, pop records are products of the studio, and digital recording did indeed improve production techniques and allowed for a much greater number of independent tracks to be fed into the recording console in the studio and editing suite. Multitracking is an especially important part of producing pop records, because many recordings are extensively remixed to suit specific radio formats or cross over into the dance scene.[14] In a remix, an instrumental introduction may be radically shortened or completely removed; the vocals moved forward or blended back virtually into the beat; or the beats per minute may be increased or decreased. If we consider a pop single or album to be a musical work, it is a work often constructed in a manner that can be readily remade. Digitalisation facilitates both its construction and its remaking.

This is not to say that classical recordings are, by contrast, faithful documents of complete performances that take place in the recording studio. Classical producers and engineers are not passive handmaidens who merely ensure that microphones and tape machines are operative and then wait for the musicians to finish playing. In recent years, classical labels have asked producers to add electronic effects with synthesizers and sampled bass and percussion to medieval music;[15] and to blend two human voices into a hybrid meant to replicate the singing of an eighteenth-century castrato in the soundtrack of the film *Farinelli*.[16] But we need not turn to such extreme fabrications to find classical recordings that are conscious creations of the studio, even though they do not add anything that the composer did not intend. Producer John Culshaw's cycle of Richard Wagner's *Der Ring des Nibelungen* is an artistic creation as a recording, and it is with no disrespect to the music's composer or conductor (Georg Solti) that this colossal enterprise (fourteen and a half hours on 19 LPs [now 14 CDs]

13. I am grateful to David Steffen for the information about both recordings.
14. Richard Middleton and Serge Lacasse address various aspects and implications of remixing in their contributions to the present volume.
15. 'Vision: The Music of Hildegard von Bingen', CDC 72435 55246 21. This CD was created by Angel Records as a 'contemporary' follow-up to the multi-million-selling 'Chant', a US reissue of Gregorian chant recorded by Spanish monks in the 1960s (released in other territories as the 2-CD set 'Canto Gregoriano').
16. 'Farinelli: Il Castrato, Bande originale du film', Auvidis/Travelling K1005.

and recorded over eight years, 1958–65) is known simply as 'the Culshaw *Ring*'.[17]

Together with his Decca recording engineer, Gordon Parry, Culshaw went through Wagner's score and production book and looked at the composer's stage directions. They had also seen the four operas in performance, and realised that many of the stage directions could be suggested audibly by special effects in the recording studio. The producer exercised his artistic judgement, not accepting that the music alone could speak for itself. Recording is itself an art form, and if that art form can be used to help people understand the work better, then technology serves music.

Culshaw also understood that his *Ring*, the first on record, needed to sell. He knew that he needed to create a market for something never before heard complete on record by making it as interesting as he could. Not only did this inventive producer create a market for Decca's *Ring*: he also created a market for the *Ring* on other labels. The commercial significance of the cycle is as important as its groundbreaking technological influence.

The second step in the digitalisation of music was the Compact Disc, a consumer software device from which digital information is read by a CD player's laser beam scanning an optical disc. Launched in 1983 (1984 in the United States), the CD has proven to be a saleable and convenient playback medium, appealing to consumers in developed music markets around the world. In 1997 CDs made up 70.2 per cent of total net unit shipments in the US market. The second largest share is cassettes, 18.2 per cent.[18] One of the reasons for the success of Compact Disc is worldwide compatibility: a CD bought anywhere in the world will play in one's home player. Although the information on the disc is digital, it must be re-converted to an analogue signal (by the CD player) in order to become audible music. Digital information has neither sound nor substance.

More recent digital developments do away with a disc or tape altogether: digital information is simply transmitted electronically to a radio or computer. With downloading, or digital distribution, there is no physical product; this absence of physical product radically

---

17. The story of the undertaking, which began in the age of mono, is perhaps best told by Culshaw himself: John Culshaw, *Ring Resounding*, New York, Viking, 1967. Decca/London 455 555 (14-CD set).
18. Recording Industry Association of America (RIAA), *1997 Annual Report*, p. 31.

changes the economic model of the recording industry – an industry notable, and unusual, for its character as a volume-driven, not profit-driven, business. Record companies, via their distributors, regularly discount their newest and most popular items, seeking to gain market share from competitors at the expense of high-profit revenue.

Composers, too, explore new capabilities of digital music-making in which a computer offers them a way to compose music that is not subject to varied interpretations by performers. 'For Milton Babbitt the promise of technology was to give the composer complete control of his composition even through the contingencies of its perfor-mance.'[19] Others write pieces that require interaction between com-puters and live musicians and, therefore, consider the quality of a computer's 'musicianship'. Robert Rowe, a composer and expert in music technology, has developed a 'real-time interactive music pro-gram, Cypher',[20] whose two main components, a listener and a player, allow a computer to be a responsive participant in live perfor-mance. Rowe believes that interactive 'systems are not concerned with replacing human players but with enriching the performance sit-uations in which humans work'.[21] Nevertheless, he also believes that 'we must concentrate on improving the musicianship of our emerging [computer] partners.'[22]

The Medium is Measured

Like LPs, whose 25–30 minutes per side replaced the four-minute sides of 78s, the Compact Disc lengthened uninterrupted playback time. For example, home LP listeners had been able to hear Steve Reich's *Music for 18 Musicians*, a continuous 57-minute piece, only with a fade-out and fade-in unsatisfactorily linking the two sides of the record. But CD (ECM 1129) restored the piece to its intended whole. The normal capacity of an audio CD is 75–80 minutes.

For the music industry, recordings are tangible, finite consumer products. They are not musical works but inventions whose function is to be the primary medium for carrying musical works to the

19. Simon Frith, *Performing Rites: On the Value of Popular Music*, Cambridge, Mass., Harvard University Press, 1998, p. 245.
20. Robert Rowe, *Interactive Music Systems: Machine Listening and Composing*, Cambridge, Mass., MIT Press, 1993, p. 39.
21. Ibid., p. 262.
22. Loc. cit.

listener. Home listening is now the norm, so when someone says, 'I heard Beethoven's *Seventh Symphony* last night,' we assume that it was heard at home, not in concert. Home listening is motivated not only by economic necessity (a concert ticket is usually more expensive than a CD) and a modern search for privacy but equally by the availability of a vast array of music on CD. If we consider Marshall McLuhan's equation of medium and message, we now comprehend musical messages as Compact Discs. Simon Frith writes about recording technology and the 'musical object' and declares: 'There's no doubt here that the fetishization of the recording has meant the demystification of the work'.[23]

Certain classical pieces readily fit the three dominant formats in the history of sound recording: arias, encore pieces by Fritz Kreisler, and Domenico Scarlatti keyboard sonatas matched 78s; Haydn and Mozart symphonies fit LPs; most Bruckner and Mahler symphonies fit on one CD. Longer pieces that don't fit the medium are cut to fit (a symphonic movement on several 78s) or excerpted (a portion of a movement becomes a discrete piece; repeats are removed; arias are edited). Although shorter pieces cannot be analogously stretched, they can be joined to others to form a larger entity. One CD example is 'A Venetian Coronation 1595', a programme of period music that might (just) have been played on that specific historical occasion.[24] A similar example from the LP era is 'The Triumphs of Oriana: Music to Entertain Elizabeth I', where the producer selected music that might have been played at an Ascension Day tournament for Queen Elizabeth.[25] Such inventions, large or small, ought not to have the same status as the normally defined musical work, but their coherence, and recorded permanence, ought to merit a certain 'work-status' *sui generis*.

It would seem safe to assume that the musical works that best 'fit' the consumer medium of choice should have some priority or inviolability, but this is not necessarily the case. There are relatively few pieces that fill a CD on their own, so combinations of pieces, or smaller components of pieces such as movements, choruses or even musical themes are the rule, not the exception.

The motivation to fill the available space has also affected certain

23. Frith (1998), p. 244.
24. Virgin Classics 59006, 1990.
25. Argo ZRG 643, 1970.

performing conventions. In the Renaissance and Baroque periods, an entire book of madrigals or printed set of concertos or sonatas would not often have been played straight through at one sitting. When all the pieces are brought together on a single CD, however, modern performers anticipate that the listener will hear them all together. As a result, efforts are made to turn the sequence into an appealing musical programme. Methods used to vary the sound include singing motets alternately with one voice to a part and with a larger choir; playing some vocal pieces on instruments; using a wide variety of accompanying instruments; and playing some Baroque sonatas without continuo. The desire to hold the listener's attention through the whole 'invented work' is paramount. Some of these adjustments to performing conventions would also be feasible in concert, but most would probably not.

In the case of popular music from the era of 78s, songwriters provided plenty of material, from show tunes to patriotic songs; and dance records brought the big bands into private middle-class homes. The introduction in the late 1940s of the LP did not immediately change pop composition, nor did CD: songs are still singles, and singles are short. Unified theme albums, as described below, have inspired pop composers to a greater or lesser extent since the 1960s. Identifying a classical equivalent to the popular music 'themed album' is not straightforward, because the pop album often becomes a live, touring show, whereas the classical one rarely does. The pop tour exists in large part to promote the album, and record companies recognise that touring is a necessary promotional expense. Although classical artists frequently tour, it is exceptional for a tour to share a title and a programme with an album. Most classical record programmes, in fact, are not suitable concert programmes. When such a linkage does occur, the intention is clearly to use a pop industry technique to sell more records. Although many pop albums are increasingly difficult to replicate live, a situation that has led to criticism by fans of live shows for using prerecorded music and lip-synching, the pop tour remains a valuable means to achieve multi-platinum-album sales.

Newer configurations such as audio DVD,[26] launched in the late

---

26. DVD is an abbreviation of Digital Versatile Disc, originally Digital Video Disc, almost always referred to only by its initials. Capacity is predicted to be from seven to thirty times that of a CD.

1990s, contain many hours of music on one CD-sized optical disc. The extra capacity of DVD could be used not just to extend playing time but also to provide multichannel home audio and an exponential increase in sampling rate and signal-to-noise ratio, both of which are believed to enhance the quality of digital audio. It is generally assumed that DVD will succeed primarily as a convenient and affordable video and multimedia carrier.

It is interesting to note that the newest medium for music delivery, computer downloading, necessitates a return to splitting pieces up into segments that can be transmitted economically. Although an affordable means to download longer pieces of music will no doubt emerge, the short-term effect is one of fragmentation.

Commercialisation

In practice, commercialisation can change the definition of a musical work if the 'work' is not deemed saleable. Depending on the type of music, popularity or commercial success has varying time-spans and sales criteria. For instance, a film soundtrack of rap music may sell hugely for six weeks, then disappear completely, but a jazz recording with a link to a television show may stay at the top of the jazz chart for several months before tapering off to steady, though modest, sales. A rap CD needs to sell 500,000 units in the United States before it is deemed a success, but a jazz record that reaches 50,000 units worldwide is also a success.

In terms of the recorded musical work, the single has been the standard unit-measure of pop music more consistently than the album. As an artistic goal, the creation of a well-constructed and unified album was pursued most consistently in the period 1965–1983, and it can be argued that the release of Nirvana's 'Nevermind' in 1992 signalled the start of another album-centred period. This current period, however, is less artistic than commercial. In order for an album to reach gold and platinum sales plateaux, it needs to contain four or five hit singles.[27] Producing an album with several hit singles does not

---

27. Gold and platinum sales are certified by the industry-governing organisations in various countries; sales are measured as units shipped to retail. Certification levels are different for singles and albums and are roughly proportional to population: for example, a platinum album is one million units in the US; 300,000 in Britain; 300,000 in France; 100,000 in Italy.

necessarily mean that the album is conceived as a unified artistic whole.

Hit singles are important because they become hits through radio play and thus introduce the album to a wide public. The marketing rationale for this emphasis on singles is that the public will hear the single, then buy the album. However, a significant number of artists have made albums that contain only one hit song, and consumers are reluctant to pay for a whole album unless they hear more than one single. As a result, the successful album must contain several singles that will get on the radio.

Composers, artists and record companies all seek to produce commercially successful products. They believe that they create music for a general audience that is attracted to heavily promoted product and, especially in the case of classical music, is unfamiliar with the existing recorded repertoire. As a result, they redefine the recorded repertoire.

For recordings of classical music, this redefinition has several implications. One, the recompilation of old material into concept CDs, has already been described. Some concepts, such as 'Karajan Adagio', are derived from the music itself. Others are meant to appeal to certain lifestyles: 'Mozart in the Morning' (Philips); 'Out Classics' (BMG). Still others are cross-promotions with non-music items such as a book series ('Penguin Classics'/Decca and 'Classical Music for Dummies'/EMI) or lingerie (several classical compilations made for the retailer Victoria's Secret). Intended to grab the attention of non-classical (even non-music) customers, recompilations are usually not put together as cohesive musical programmes. Sometimes, the programme is incohesive because its marketing-driven concept is extra-musical. Sometimes, the problem is that the material made available for the recompilation is not of consistent sonic or artistic quality.[28]

This is not to say that musically rewarding recompilations are impossible or unknown. Serious producers who do this become companions to the composers, and the resulting CD is no longer just the composer's work. One key to the invention of rewarding CD programmes is the producer's ability to recognise music that is comparable and place it in a context that will enhance the music. There is a

---

28. Reasons for the non-availability of desirable material can include damage to an original master tape, the refusal of permission by artists and uneconomically high royalty rates.

parallel to concert programming here: if an unfamiliar piece of repertoire (often, but not always, from the early or modern period) is sandwiched between, say, Beethoven and Brahms, it will almost certainly make an unfavourable impression on the listener. However, if the same piece is heard in a musical context of related repertoire – Pierre Boulez's programmes with the Ensemble Intercontemporain are models of the kind – its impression upon the listener is often more meaningful and intelligible. Moreover, a becoming context is fairer to the composer. If the programme is on record and can be replayed, the listener gains enormously. 'The Triumphs of Oriana' and 'A Venetian Coronation 1595' described earlier are cases in point. Some programmes, such as 'Songs to Shakespeare' (Arne to Tippett) and 'Souvenirs de Venise' (Rossini to Fauré), successfully span several historical periods.[29]

Another implication of efforts to redefine the recorded classical repertoire may seem new, but is not. Many new recordings of classical pieces are sold on the reputation of the artist, not the repertoire or even the composer. Often, the artist's name and likeness dominate the cover art and promotional campaigns. What is new in recent years is that, increasingly, classical artists are selected for their marketability, not their accomplishment. The marketing assumption by the record labels is that the eye of the consumer is quicker to attract than the ear. The packaging of artists for their looks is a long-standing practice in popular music; the extent to which classical music will succeed by doing the same is as yet unknown.

Nevertheless, the artist-centred approach to marketing classical music is the result of assumptions about what makes a recording saleable. It is a record-company marketing department's job to understand what consumers want and then execute a strategy to reach those consumers. Most classical recompilations, and some classical new recordings, are motivated by the belief that there is a large untapped market of record buyers who do not know anything about classical music. Reaching that market is believed to be simply a matter of repositioning the product through chic or faddish concepts and catchy, even risqué, commercial artwork, and by selling the artist as a pop personality.

Another assumption is that once bitten, neophyte classical record buyers will return again and again to explore the rich, virtually

29. Hyperion CDA66480 and CDA66112, respectively.

boundless, world of classical music. Most record labels subscribe to this assumption, even though there is still no evidence that buying 'Beethoven's Greatest Hits' leads to Mahler or Bach, or even to the *Missa Solemnis* and late Beethoven quartets. Conceived as 'one-offs', recompilations seek to reposition classical music and reach new pop consumers. Theoretically, they would sell more recordings to a wider customer base, thereby expanding the size of the classical market.

The small size of the classical market is particularly evident in the United States, where sales of classical records have been less than 4 per cent of total record sales for a number of years. In 1995 2.9 per cent of unit sales in the US were classical; 3.4 per cent in 1996; 2.8 per cent in 1997.[30] As for Europe, although classical market share has been significantly higher than in the US (typically 10 per cent or higher), recent contraction is evident in the 1997 figures: Britain 7 per cent; Italy 7 per cent; Germany 9.9 per cent; France 7.5 per cent.[31] Further, sales of so-called classical 'crossover' records (such as 'Three Tenors' and 'Carreras Sings Mario Lanza') are now usually included in the classical sales figures, resulting in skewed sales figures for 'serious' classical recordings.

Although record labels are concerned about the saleability of their products, and performers want maximum sales in order to advance their careers, classical composers may or may not be concerned about the saleability of what they write. Frank Martin and Michael Tippett are unquestionable examples of the composer *qua* composer. Aaron Copland followed his uncommercial second symphony, arguably his best work, with the deliberately commercial third symphony, much film music, *Billy the Kid*, *Rodeo*, and *Appalachian Spring*. Maurice Ravel could be both saleable (*Boléro*) and not (*L'Enfant et les sortilèges*). George Gershwin was a very good pop composer who was, and increasingly is, sold as a classical composer.

Business Inserts Consumer Economics

The economics of the seller/buyer relationship affect the artistic bond implicit in the creator/listener relationship by adding financial reward

---

30. RIAA (1997), p. 29. Figures refer to units, not value.
31. International Federation of the Phonographic Industry [IFPI], [Report 1998], p. 90. These IFPI percentage figures refer to value, not units. Worldwide, classical market share has declined from 6.1 per cent in 1991 to 4.5 per cent in 1997, with an estimated retail value for both of those years of US$1.7 billion (ibid., p. 91).

as a measure of success. However, heeding commercial signals is not always a negative thing: in a public symposium after his 22 July recital, part of a 14-recital complete Bach cycle at Alice Tully Hall in New York City during the 1998 Lincoln Center Festival, English organist Christopher Herrick described the way the commercial success of one CD of Bach organ music (trio sonatas) led to follow-ups (toccatas) and ultimately convinced the head of Hyperion Records to approve the recording of a complete cycle. Forty years ago, even the completion of John Culshaw's *Ring* depended upon the sales verdict for the first opera, *Rheingold*.

Consumer demand clearly had a positive artistic effect in these cases, but evaluating consumer taste is not always easy, and consumer research is often tendentious. Further, some business analysts even urge organisations to look beyond consumer demands: '... if the goal is to get to the future first, rather than merely preserving market share in existing businesses, a company must be much more than customer led. Customers are notoriously lacking in foresight'.[32]

Despite such warning, and the fact that consumer research is not an exact science, it is rare for a pop record company to record a style of music that has no consumer track record at all. Companies with the most sensitive and wide-reaching feelers – otherwise known as A & R departments – strive to detect what teenagers, in particular, are listening to, then quickly sign, record and release records in that hot trend. Other companies, almost without exception, will follow that trend. The key is quickness: as soon as the trend starts to fade, new material in a new style should be in the pipeline, ready to satisfy the most active music consumer age-group: 10–19.[33] Classical labels also follow trends such as period instrument performance, Russian repertoire from 1890 to 1940, and what can be labelled 'choral mysticism',

32. Gary Hamel and C.K. Prahalad, *Competing for the Future*, Boston, Harvard Business School Press, 1994, p. 99. The same sentiment, as expressed in the 1950s by Akio Morita, the cofounder of Sony Corporation, is often cited as central to Sony's corporate culture: 'Our plan is to lead the public with new products rather than ask them what kind of products they want. The public does not know what is possible, but we do.' Thomas W. Malnight and Michael Y. Yoshino, *Sony Corporation: Globalization*, Boston, Harvard Business School Case Study, 1991, p. 2.
33. Share of US recorded-music unit sales in 1996. The next-largest age group in 1996 was 25–34. These same two groups held the top share, and were within one percentage point of each other, from 1991 to 1995. Veronis, Suhler & Associates, *Communications Industry Forecast*, 1997, p. 222.

encompassing music from Gregorian chant to Arvo Pärt. The last category, in particular, is a deliberate attempt to reach the 25–50 age-group, which accounted for more than 44 per cent of the US market in 1996.[34]

Earlier in this chapter (p. 89), I characterised the music industry as one driven to 'ever-greater consolidation into vertically integrated companies that crave products with cross-promotable synergy'. Most record labels today are owned by media conglomerates that seek to own a media 'property' with the potential to be sold, more than once, to the same consumer. The same company can reap the profits from a movie, its soundtrack, T-shirt, soft toy and other spin-off products, all from the same property. Music is but one outlet, and, more often than not, the music must fit the rest of the products, rather than standing on its own. The assumption in cross-marketing is that consumers see the products as discrete items, linked but not identical. But consumers do have limits of tolerance in this regard, and may come to a point where a reissued, repackaged, re-edited recording is no longer considered to be a new musical work. Repackagers of music need to be especially sensitive to consumer perceptions of 'new', particularly when most recompilations are priced at top level, even though they reuse previously released recordings. All consumer industries increase their markets by introducing new products, and marketing staff need to consider the extent to which the following external factors are perceived by music consumers as new: packaging, plastic or cardboard CD box, endorsement, altered track order, recombination with other music, price category and the addition of video.

The economic impact of music downloading by consumers is currently the subject of much concern and speculation in the recording industry.[35] For music producers, the digital distribution revolution may force disclosure of real costs for the first time, as the industry seeks to devise a fair and profitable range of distribution, service and downloading fees. But just because a record label has a very expensive

34. Loc. cit. This is a conservative estimate calculated by combining two age-groups: 25–34 (23.9 per cent) and 35–44 (20.2 per cent). The highest age-group identified in this report is 45+ (15.1 per cent).
35. It is important to distinguish here between the recording industry and the larger music industry, which is increasingly woven into the even larger entertainment industry. The music industry will not disappear, but the recording industry, as a producer of product, may.

contract with an artist, should the cost of that contract be passed on to consumers? By the same logic, consumer prices should go down if a record is a huge success and recoups its costs.

Pricing, and predicting revenue from, a digitally distributed 'product' – now perhaps more aptly called a 'service' – takes on a new, qualitative dimension that was not a factor in physical (analogue) distribution.

> Information should not be subject to economies of scale: its value is qualitative, not quantitative – three pages of a book or three hours of TV are not worth thrice as much as one. But our physical distribution of information had so far been largely based on economies of scale, because of the analog form of this information.[36]

In the above quotation, Philippe Boutié is not writing specifically about downloading music or distributing physical CDs, but his point about relative value is certainly apt. At present, services such as Music Boulevard (a division of N2K Inc.) charge a fee of US$0.99 for downloading a single, regardless of its length. This is typical of what various services are offering. At the time of writing, album-length units of music are not priced separately from their value as a multiple of singles.[37] Unsurprisingly, record companies are not keen to have whole albums available for download until they can be assured that the revenue they will receive from downloading will equal what they now receive by distributing a manufactured product. What really worries them, however, is that their accustomed monopoly as the definitive creator of musical works on record will no longer be safe. It is not hard to imagine that once downloading becomes technologically viable, affordable and sufficiently widespread, record labels will become superfluous.

In the future, the music you download at home into your computer may simply be charged by the minute, using a meter to measure your

36. Philippe Boutié, 'Will This Kill That?', *Communications World*, April 1996, pp. 34–38, at p. 38.
37. On 17 August 1998, there were 38 'e-mod' (i.e., downloadable) singles from 20 artists featured on the Internet web site of Music Boulevard: 19 pop/rock singles; 13 jazz; 6 classical. The largest number of singles from one artist was the five from Candy Dulfer in the jazz category, four of which were remixes of the same song, *Gititon*. File sizes were given in megabytes: the largest was *Stupid Message* by The Specials (10.6MB), in the pop/rock category; the smallest, *Ostinato (#146 from Mikrokosmos)* played by Max Levinson (2.8MB), in the classical category.

consumption, just like telephone calls or electricity. But such metering takes no account of whether an opera should cost more per minute than a symphony because production costs are higher, or whether the pop album whose star commands a higher-than-average royalty rate, and whose albums are expensive to produce, should cost more than the album by a new singer-songwriter who accompanies herself on acoustic guitar.[38]

Those in the recording business who are sceptical about the future of music downloading emphasise that their typical customer is still the collector, and that this consumer, by definition, likes to collect physical objects and line them up on a shelf. Commercially, however, digital distribution is attractive because it eliminates much in physical distribution that is costly and cumbersome: warehouses, packaging and shipping (both to a retail outlet and back as excess inventory). Simply put, digital distribution removes inventory altogether. It is attractive also because that lack of physical inventory actually allows sellers to expand the range of 'digital' inventory they offer. This virtually limitless selection is advertised to consumers by retailing pioneers such as Amazon for books and Music Boulevard for music. For now, this is essentially a mail-order business shipping physical products. The striking difference is that the possibility of delivering 'digital' books seems remote, whereas 'digital' music is the norm and downloading is already taking place.

In a future without concrete recordings, a database of identifiable musical works will need to exist so that consumers can order, download and pay for them. To maximise efficiency and completeness, the ideal database would be created and administered by the major record companies, the companies who own the master tapes. However, having spent huge amounts of money to acquire 'content' (a term which also applies to catalogues of films or television programmes) to gain advantage over their competitors, companies are unlikely to want to act as collaborators in the distribution of that content without adequate legal and financial safeguards. A wide-ranging communal database would suit consumers' needs, but content owners may prefer to establish individual, competing databases.

How works will be identified in the future, especially works that

---

38. Such price differentials have been used before on LP and CD: developing artists are often lower-priced, and some major distributors' highest price category is reserved for superstars.

are recordings but are never released as physical products, is unclear. Questions about selection of material for the database – whether material would stay in the database 'forever', whether every one of the tens of thousands of CDs released every year in the present day would or should be in the database, and whether every master tape now in a label's vault will be available – will probably be decided by market forces. But once market forces take command, categories of music such as classical and jazz will surely be marginalised again, just as they are today, because promotional priority will always be given to what is the most popular and easily saleable.

Technology Inserts a Reinterpreter

By inserting a reinterpreter, technology has the power to unbalance the fruitful and fundamental composer/interpreter relationship. The person controlling the technology can be the recording engineer, the producer, the tape editor or the consumer at home. Even the original composer and interpreter are potential reinterpreters, and in any of these hands, technical reinterpretation can alter or obscure musical interpretation.

Although music lives through the interpretation of performers, the consequences of reinterpretation need to be addressed. To what extent did the original composer wish or plan that a reinterpretation should be in fact a recreation? For pre-electronic compositions, it seems clear that limits on subsequent performers are implicitly narrow: a Beethoven sonata can be played on any type of piano; a Bach partita on modern or Baroque violin; a Stravinsky ballet suite by any orchestra with the requisite number of players and instruments. By contrast, compositions that use electronic or computer elements may implicitly invite interpreters to alter the composition more radically.[39]

If the original composition is meant to be mutable in performance, the onus shifts to the performer to create a cohesive whole: a musical work. When the performer is the person operating the technology in live performance, a cohesive whole emerges. However, if performers have the opportunity to alter an earlier performance that now exists only as a recording, they are unlikely to want such alterations. Even

39. For these purposes, improvisatory and/or aleatoric factors are not taken into consideration.

though most musicians change what they believe about a piece over the years of their career, they always have a cohesive view. For instance, they would not dream of tacking part of a 1975 conception on to a 1984 conception. Encouraging such reconstruction is to acknowledge that technology is no longer in the service of the performer or composer.

Pop engineers and producers are acutely aware of the effect that recorded sounds have on listeners' reactions to a piece, and they create their sounds accordingly. But their classical counterparts often fail to understand how recording technology becomes part of the listener's perception of a musical work, and of the calibre of its performance. For instance, you may think that a composer's string writing is very harsh, but the harshness may be the result of the recorded sound. Some artists even appear to instruct the recording engineer to obtain a particular sound. To cite one example, the Italian Baroque string ensemble Il Giardino Armonico are well known, and frequently praised by record reviewers, for their 'aggressive' sound. I have heard many of their recordings, so when I heard them in concert I was most surprised to hear a warm, smooth sound. It appears that the group has deliberately chosen a 'signature sound' that sets them apart from the many other groups who record the same repertoire.

Prior to the development of digital recording technology in the late 1970s master recordings existed on analogue tape. In order to release any analogue recording on CD, its analogue master must be copied in digital format so that the metal stamper that presses the CDs can be manufactured. As a result, we now have digital tapes of a very large portion of the predigital recorded repertoire. Writing in *The New York Times*, Paul Griffiths imagines how the resulting digital material could be used:

> There are, for example, enough recorded samples of Maria Callas's voice in existence to supply multitudinous instances of how she sang every note of the scale (and a good many in the cracks) in all kinds of musical contexts. ... The editor would simply select from the whole repertory of recorded Callas notes, and adjust the volume, color and attack of the chosen example to suit the phrase. We might then have Callas's Brünnhilde or even Callas's version of music she would never conceivably have touched: Callas's Berio, Callas's Dufay, Callas's Dylan.[40]

40. Paul Griffiths, 'Callas Sings Bob Dylan? Could Be', *The New York Times*, 11 January 1998, Arts and Leisure section, p. 39.

Whether you now take your music home in the form of a disc, a cassette or digital information, various technological means are under development to enable you to change a recording at home. The first of these is already available in programmable CD players: the listener can choose the order in which tracks are played back, including a random sequence determined by the CD player at the touch of a single 'Random Play' button. On the pop side, any carefully crafted album can be scrambled at will, but some classical labels utilise this feature and include alternative tracks, so that different versions of a piece can be reconstructed at home. Two examples are Handel's *Messiah* on Harmonia Mundi and Puccini's *Madama Butterfly* on Vox.

In the former (performed by conductor Nicholas McGegan and the Philharmonia Baroque Orchestra on Harmonia Mundi HMU 907050/52), alternative versions of certain pieces are added to the end of each of the oratorio's three parts; each part occupies a separate CD. Programming instructions in the booklet show the listener how 'to recreate any of nine distinct documented performances of Messiah **from Handel's time.**'[41] In the latter (performed by conductor Charles Rosenkrans and the Hungarian State Opera House Orchestra, Vox Classics VOX4 7525), the world première recording of the original 1904 La Scala version of the opera is complete and in sequence on CD 1, CD 2 and the first eight tracks of CD3. The rest of CD3 and all of CD4 contain revisions made by Puccini for performances in Brescia and Paris. 'If you have a multiple-disc, programmable CD changer, you may follow the chart [listing Acts and tracks] to program the complete La Scala, Brescia, and Paris versions of the opera.'[42]

Other innovations that encourage consumer manipulation of a recording include interactive CD-ROMs and Internet web sites that allow remixing of pop albums. One example is Todd Rundgren's CD-I (Compact Disc Interactive) version of 'No World Order', which allows consumers 'to manipulate and reassemble various components of the musical recordings themselves'.[43] Because this is too much trouble for the general public, and is very likely too crude to interest those consumers with some knowledge of audio technology, such remixing

41. *Schwann Opus*, (Fall 1997), p. 437. The emphasis is original.
42. From the CD's accompanying booklet, p. xxvii.
43. Paul Théberge, *Any Sound You Can Imagine: Making Music/Consuming Technology*, Hanover, NH, Wesleyan University Press, 1997, p. 253.

capability will probably remain a multimedia novelty feature that may appeal to audio-engineer home amateurs. Most artists and producers are unlikely to encourage home remixing. Whether consumers or fans will come to demand it remains to be seen. It would remove most of the boundaries we now use to define a musical work, though it seems a lot of trouble to go through just to make something you can call your own.

Without boundaries, works have no identity. If we wish to preserve identity, we face a wide range of forces, from the individual home consumer to international economics, that threaten to blur the boundaries. Conflict arises from the fact that boundaries are commercial or technological, but standards are artistic. Whether a musical work exists on vellum, as a recording, or in a composer's imagination, standards of artistic worth are meaningful only if non-negotiable.

5

The Practice of Early-Nineteenth-Century Pianism

Jim Samson

'Formerly one could expect from a performing virtuoso that he eluci-
dated, interpreted and clarified a masterwork; nowadays one wants to
admire the skill of an individual …. Formerly it was the piece that
mattered; now it is the person that counts'.[1] August Kahlert's observations epitomise a shift from works to practices within the pianism
of the early nineteenth century. He was documenting the final stages
of a post-Classical virtuosity whose heyday was the 1820s and 1830s,
and within a relatively short time-span the trend he describes had
been reversed. Already by the mid-century, a genre- and performance-
orientated culture had been been largely 'returned' to a work-orientated culture. In this essay I will characterise that journey (from genre
and performance to work) in terms of changing configurations within
the practice of pianism.

My understanding of the term 'practice' is somewhat indebted to
Alasdair MacIntyre, although I am by no means supportive of his
clean separation between the interests of a practice (with its own setting, history, tradition, values and ideals) and those of its enabling and
supporting institutions (structured in terms of power and status).[2] It
is enough to say that recovering a practice means more than documenting the institutions of music-making. Unlike an institution, a
practice has an ethos; it exercises virtues as well as skills. Characteristically, it offers choices to its participants within certain parameters.
Its relevance to my work is that it builds the performer – the act of
performance – centrally into the historical study of a repertory. Inter-

---

1. August Kahlert, 'Das Concertwesen der Gegenwart', *Neue Zeitschrift für Musik*,
   Vol. 16 (1841), pp. 105–6.
2. Alasdair MacIntyre, *After Virtue*, London, Duckworth, 1981. I am grateful to
   Richard Evans for introducing me to MacIntyre's work.

estingly, the term crops up rather often in the chapters dealing with popular music in this volume, and it may be no bad thing to approach art music repertories from a perspective more commonly employed in popular music studies. David Horn's characterisation of a 'popular music event', for instance, comes close to invoking a practice in MacIntyre's sense, though without a constitutive ethos or authenticity. And I might add that Horn's characterisation could be applied almost as it stands to an early-nineteenth-century benefit given by a pianist-composer.

It will already be clear that my investigation of a specific performative practice has implications for the periodisation of music history, and in particular for Lydia Goehr's thesis that the work-concept acquired a regulative function around 1800.[3] On one hand, my history of a practice militates against any single global caesura around that time, and, indeed, against any uni-linear reading of history; one would need to invoke Fernand Braudel to make any sense of this dislocated chronology. On the other hand, my history invites us to consider whether the practice has its own caesura; if so, we might be looking to the years around 1850, by which time a recital culture was in formation, institutionalising a work-concept peculiar to pianistic practice. That, too, is probably overschematic, but there are other reasons to privilege the mid-century as a marker of what has been called the invention of tradition.[4] Without elaborating the point here, I refer to further changes in the structures of concert life,[5] to publishing enterprises (especially the Breitkopf & Härtel collected editions), to pedagogy (the dissemination of a structural, as opposed to an aesthetic or generic, sense of form),[6] and even to perceptions of popular culture. I am tempted to wonder, then, whether there may not be an unbroken continuity between the invention of tradition that followed

3. Lydia Goehr, *The Imaginary Museum of Musical Works: An Essay in the Philosophy of Music*, Oxford, Oxford University Press, 1992.
4. *The Invention of Tradition*, ed. Eric Hobsbawm and Terence Ranger, Cambridge, Cambridge University Press, 1983.
5. I have discussed this in 'Music and Society', in *The Late Romantic Era: From the Mid-19th Century to World War I (Man & Music*, Vol. 7), ed. Jim Samson, London, Macmillan, 1991, pp. 1–49.
6. Especially in Germany in the 1840s. For a discussion of the rôle of Eduard Krüger and Adolf Bernhard Marx in this see Jeffrey Kallberg, 'Small "Forms": In Defense of the Prelude', in *The Cambridge Companion to Chopin*, ed. Jim Samson, Cambridge, Cambridge University Press, 1992, pp. 124–43.

in the wake of 1848 and the efforts of a recent generation of scholars to categorise that invented tradition, notably within German scholarship.[7]

The larger context for these reflections is a research project on virtuosity, on which I have been engaged for some time. This project focuses on the *Transcendental Studies* of Liszt, and my observations here on the practice of virtuoso pianism – the practice that helped shape the work of Liszt (as also Chopin) – will use as its reference point the *Etude en douze exercices*, the earliest version of the 'Transcendentals', which was composed when Liszt was a fifteen-year-old pianist just emerging from a period of study with Czerny. My central premise is that an early-nineteenth-century pianistic culture was in a special sense a performance culture, in that it was centred on, and invested in, the act of performance rather more than the object of performance, which was usually, but not always, the musical work. My concern, then, is with a 'pre-recital' pianism, and only at the end of the essay will I venture some thoughts on the crystallisation of a work-concept within the practice.

A polarity between the work-as-text and the work-as-performance became increasingly marked during the nineteenth century, notably in the reception histories of early-nineteenth-century repertories: consider the reception of Beethoven, as against that of Rossini or Paganini. In one case, there was a developing conviction that the notational form embodied a kind of intentional knowledge, an 'idea' which originated with the composer and was made available to the listener; in the other cases, where the text is typically more fluid and often in search of 'completion' by the performer, the listener would be encouraged to focus on the medium as much as the message: to appreciate a sensuous or brilliant surface persuasively and directly communicated by the performer rather than to search out a form of knowledge embedded (concealed) in sound structures by the composer. At the risk of reading history backwards, I venture that already during the eighteenth century this division between notational and acoustic forms was plotted and enabled. That century greatly strengthened the work-concept, establishing the relative autonomy of the work by loosening the threads binding it to genre and social function. It also 'created' the virtuoso, an international figure in whom the activity of performance gained (or regained) its own measure of

7. See Reinhard Strohm's remarks on this in Chapter 6, pp. 134–40.

autonomy.[8] And it is fair to say that until recently this activity has not been subject to the kind of scholarly scrutiny afforded to musical works.

Part of my concern is to correct that imbalance. This means investigating the rôle of the performer (recovering the practice). But it also means exploring the performance-orientated musical materials characteristic of that practice (recovering the repertory). My approach, then, is primarily historical. However, my larger project on virtuosity will in addition involve analytical enquiry, and I will offer a brief prefatory word on analysis here. Whatever precise form it may take, analysis interprets the musical work as a real presence in our present-day culture, a presence imbued with meanings that were made concrete only in relatively late stages of its reception. In other words, it is concerned with an active present (Liszt for today) rather than a recovered past. It speaks of our world in at least three ways. First, it adopts the esoteric languages promoted by an ethos of professionalism. Second, it invests in the status of the work as a text. This ontological issue is genuinely problematic, since the work is not actually a text, any more than music is a language. Performance is a constituent of it, and it is reasonable to explore ways in which analysis, especially when addressing a repertory involving the concept of virtuosity, might find a way of absorbing that performance dimension. Third, it appropriates its object. In other words, we construct the Liszt *Etudes* (relativistically) in the image of our own world. It is partly in acknowledgement of this relativism that analysis has tended to invoke context in recent years, and it has usually done so in one of three ways. Either it has confronted context (through homologies of compositional and contextual structures: the 'good fit' approach). Or it has been absorbed by context (courting the dangers of over-interpretation that Umberto Eco warns us against).[9] Or again: it has itself absorbed context, notably through some applications of semiotic theory.[10]

My own 'line' is to preserve a more traditional sense of disciplinary integrity for analysis, recognising that it asks useful questions of the work – and of a kind that nicely complements my historical questions.

8. See Sylvette Milliot, 'Le Virtuose international: une création du 18ᵉ siècle', *Dix-huitième siècle*, Vol. 25 (1993), pp. 55–64.

9. Umberto Eco, *Interpretation and Overinterpretation,* ed. Stefan Collini, Cambridge, Cambridge University Press, 1992.

10. Robert Samuels, *Mahler's Sixth Symphony: A Study in Semiotics*, Cambridge, Cambridge University Press, 1995.

Analysis forms, in other words, one prong of a two-pronged enquiry. Thus in the larger project (but not in this essay) there will be some attempt to analyse individual exercises in the *Etude en douze exercices*, mapping out repetition structures, motivic interrelationships and harmonic grounds; and there will also be some consideration of the work as a cycle. The latter will involve an analysis of tonal associations across the twelve exercises, of conspicuous continuities between ends and beginnings, notably through top-voice identities, and of a descending *fauxbourdon* motive that appears explicitly at strategic points in several of the exercises and is arguably present more latently in some others. All of these may be regarded as 'associational structures'. While they may indeed strengthen the cohesion of the cycle for many listeners, they can be regarded only as hierachical, and therefore unifying, within an unhelpfully general meaning of the term. I will also examine grouping structures, based on the strategic placement of the four *cantabile* exercises, although I acknowledge that such structures (I identify four groups, one consisting of a single exercise) are concerned with boundaries rather than territories: with form rather than process. The premise of such analytical work, whether carried out on individual exercises or on the cycle as a whole, is that the resulting focus on form and structure, on a sense of work-character and individuation, can usefully complement the quest for musical materials that is my primary concern at this initial stage. And that brings me to history.

Recovering the Practice

Here, my approach might be located in relation to three others. I am not attempting a social history, which characteristically locates the causes of a repertory but risks depleting a sense of its immanent value. Nor a stylistic history, where context remains largely untheorised. Nor yet a full-blown sociology of musical language, which sets out – with daunting ambition – to identify the social trace left on musical materials themselves. (Very crudely, we might take Knepler, Einstein and Adorno to exemplify these three approaches.) If we were to seek a reference point, it would be Dahlhaus's reflections on hermeneutics in history.[11] These reflections offer two things of particular value:

11. Carl Dahlhaus, 'Hermeneutics in History', in *Foundations of Music History*, trans. J. B. Robinson, Cambridge, Cambridge University Press, 1983, pp. 71–84.

first, criteria for identifying unjustifiable readings (we should take care to ask appropriate questions of the past); second, the useful implication that the repertory may be revealed by, and may at the same time reveal, the practice (we understand what motivates the answers partly from the answers themselves). In this sense, we would be encouraged to draw together elements of the social and stylistic histories of music, not least through their convergence on the instrument and the performer. This, then, represents the second prong of my two-pronged enquiry. If I had to label this approach, I would call it a 'critical hermeneutics'; and it is on this that I will focus during the remainder of this essay.

The larger framework would be a structural history of the practice, of a highly reductive kind. Such a structural history immediately invites criticism for its rationalising tendencies, yet I would wish to argue that any practice exhibits centralising (and temporally stabilising) impulses that counter its sequential qualities. Like a structure or a system, a practice will change fundamentally only when there have been functional changes to the nature of its components or to their interaction. Such changes will usually be cumulative rather than abrupt, but at some stage they coalesce into a new, relatively stable, configuration. Briefly, I take the piano recital, a surprisingly stable and resilient institution, as the reference point for my history, and I go on to propose a simple, three-fold structure: pre-recital, recital and post-recital. For the age of the recital itself, I locate the practice within a network of social and cultural agencies: grounded by the institution; focused on an object, albeit an 'ideal aesthetic object' (the musical work); and cemented by an ethos, its adequate interpretation; by interpretation I understand here a dialectic of self-expression and convention. We might refine the history by identifying a period of induction extending from the establishment of the solo recital to the consolidation of modern programming, and even, at risk of forcing the argument, a later *kairos*, or point of perfection, in the early twentieth century. This takes us almost up to the reification of interpretative forms associated with the recording industry, which prefigures, I gently suggest, today's post-recital age.

Now, the pre-recital culture of the early nineteenth century functioned within a very different configuration, one not yet centred on the musical work and on its interpretative forms. It was grounded by different institutions, principally the benefit and the salon; supported by different agents, notably the piano manufacturer and the music publisher; focused on an event (the performance) rather than an object and concept (the work and its interpretation); and held together by a different ethos, which I would describe as a balance between mercantile values and the aesthetic values of a developing instrument. Liszt put this succinctly, describing his own efforts to '[steer] a course between the Ideal and the Real, without allowing myself to be overly seduced by the former, nor ever to be crushed by the latter'.[12] Interpretation played a subsidiary rôle within the pre-recital practice – a component of its product rather than the product itself. A performance, after all, may exemplify or promote many things other than a musical work: a technique; an instrument; a genre; an institution; a direct communicative act. It was in the age of the recital that these functions, including the last, became subordinated to the claims of the musical work.

I think it important, incidentally, to differentiate my structural history of a practice from grand narratives of music history based on style systems and notional traditions. Of such grand narratives I remain suspicious. In particular, they are unkind to practices, largely because practices are more concerned with acts (including performance acts) than with works. Little historical justice is done to the overlapping and interactive musical practices of the late eighteenth and early nineteenth centuries, for instance, by reducing them to two competing style paradigms: 'Classical' and 'Romantic'. My repertory – a dominant strand of culture that produced Chopin and Liszt – is virtually lost in this reading. Far from describing a progress towards Romantic individualism and subjectivity, this repertory actually tolerated a much greater degree of stylistic uniformity than anything we find in so-called Viennese Classical music. As the practice was increasingly institutionalised and popularised under a commercial imperative (through benefits, salons, conservatories, tours and 'seasons'), there was a corresponding reification of genres, forms, materials and performance styles. Nor should this surprise us greatly, given the tendency of any mercantile culture (including today's 'popular music') not just to embrace standardisation, but also, to borrow Adorno's formulation, to standardise its apparent individuality. It is in fact this latter paradox that goes some way towards defining the condition of

---

12. In a letter to Lambert Massart. See Franz Liszt, *An Artist's Journey*, trans. and annotated by Charles Suttoni, Chicago and London, University of Chicago Press, 1989, p. 88.

a post-Classical virtuosity, a condition whose essential separateness has been more widely registered in German scholarship than in Britain and America.[13]

Post-Classical virtuosity was, then, an art of conformity, where individuality was often translatable as novelty and interpreted, at least by the more high-minded critics, as a kind of excess (which raises questions of taste that will not be considered in this essay). I am not, of course, suggesting that pianist-composers did not possess or seek unique qualities: only that those qualities were associated with a characteristic deployment of recognised skills rather than the biography of the artist or the demands of the work. 'Brilliance' and 'expression' were first and foremost categories of performance, and it is worth stressing that they were capable of reaching their public without the help of musical works at all: I mean, of course, through improvisation. It has often been noted that this art, now more or less lost to us, played a vital, if perhaps ambivalent, rôle in the pianism of the late eighteenth and early nineteenth centuries: ambivalent because of its potential both to stretch and to freeze compositional conventions. (We should be cautious of the written record here, incidentally: I have in mind the models of improvisation presented in method books, and, in general, the ways in which composer-pianists themselves represented the nature of their inspiration, where Mozart rather than Beethoven formed the exemplary model. Ours is not the only age in which the rhetoric and the reality may be at odds.)

I am unable to explore the practice of improvisation adequately here, beyond suggesting that it may open a window on the shared musical materials of the post-Classical virtuoso repertory. It seems likely that by the 1830s simple, formulaic schemes were the order of the day in improvisation, standard frames designed to offset and promote ever more brilliant or ever more sentimental treatments: a natural outcome of the popularisation of the practice, and one whose effect was to congeal, rather than to dissolve, established generic and affective categories by promoting, in effect, a shared material content in the practice. On the other hand, improvisation continued to play a crucial, and probably a strengthening, rôle in shaping the detailed substance (as opposed to the large-scale design) of early-nineteenth-

---

13. See, for example, Izabella Amster, *Das Virtuosen-Konzert in der ersten Hälfte des 19. Jahrhunderts*, Wolfenbüttel, Kallmeyer, 1931, and Konrad Küster, *Das Konzert: Form und Forum der Virtuosität*, Kassel, Bärenreiter, 1993.

century piano compositions. Above all, it facilitated and developed what we may call 'instrumental thought', where the instrument itself – its potentialities and its limitations – took on a highly proactive rôle in the generation of material. In other words, the spontaneity of improvisation directly encouraged the idiomatic, sharpening the focus on instrumental devices and helping, in effect, to create a fetishism of technique. From a very different perspective, this, too, promoted a shared material content in the practice. And this brings me to the next stage of my critical hermeneutics.

Recovering the Repertory

Rather than identifying musical structures, my project will seek to identify the musical materials of post-Classical pianism. Ultimately, this will have to mean confronting the social nature of those materials and exploring the mechanisms involved in their realisation and perception. (In other words, there may be a resonance for social history, for performance studies, and maybe even for music psychology.) A useful comparison might be made with a mass-cultural form such as rock music, another performance- and genre-orientated musical culture. I suggest that, for both repertories, pattern perception is achieved not so much by relating materials to larger units that define them as patterns (although that does, of course, occur) as by matching them with analogous materials across a wider repertory. The identification of a material content in this way is, of course, an historical project, privileging the contemporary moment of a repertory as well as the preceding moment, the world that helped to shape it. Yet its aim is historical sympathy rather than historical authenticity. Hermeneutic approaches involve us in a dialogue with the repertory in its contemporary setting. Their primary concern is to recover the repertory, to situate it, although they remain alive to the chimerical nature of this quest – not least because it is a dialogue, whose course is dependent on our own situatedness.

My initial approach, then, will be to propose three 'ideal types' of musical material derived inductively from the wider repertory. All three types are defined by convention and are partly embodied in musical figures, each of which can signify a dimension of the larger practice, codifying the practice, as it were, through a material content that freely crosses the boundaries of individual works. My ideal types are genre markers, 'affective' or musical-rhetorical figures and idiomatic figures. (I should say that for my larger project on virtuosity, it is the last that primarily concerns me.) I will also propose a fourth ideal type, formal motives, although I recognise this as a less secure classification for present purposes. In general, this approach is designed as one way of making concrete the point of intersection between the practice and its repertory, thus enabling useful generalisations about a history centred on practices rather than composers, works and institutions. If nothing else, it serves as a corrective to the customary focus on work-character in nineteenth-century music. And, again, I am struck by a parallel in the essays on popular music within this volume (Horn, Middleton). In popular music research the term 'signifying' apparently describes a set of strategies playing on pre-existing materials. That is actually a rather good description of the composer-performer's activity within my practice, where, incidentally, improvisation and composition are closely linked.

It remains, then, to say a word about these ideal types. Genre markers signify not only a genre, but, depending on the genre in question, a wide range of functional and aesthetic associations: extra-musical reference, pedagogy, vocal influence, improvisation, virtuosity, and even musical form, as form was understood in the early nineteenth century. It has been noted (by Adorno and Dahlhaus, among others) that the potency of genre declined with the rise of aesthetic autonomy and of the musical work.[14] It might be added that the rise of the work brought with it a tendency to problematise musical meaning: an inevitable consequence of individuation, and something we might well associate with a Romantic ideology. Self-contained works, in other words, resisted the closure and clarity of meaning conventionally offered by a genre title. In contrast, there was relative stability of reference in a post-Classical, i.e. pre-Romantic, pianistic culture, together with a clearer sense of ontological hierarchy. Here, the musical work had a contingent quality: it exemplified a genre, which in turn exemplified an aspect of the practice. The boundaries of works were consequently blurred, dissolving constantly and naturally into the world around them. At the same time (but beyond the scope of

14. Theodor Adorno, *Aesthetic Theory*, ed. Gretel Adorno and Rolf Tiedemann, trans. Christian Lenhardt, London, Routledge & Kegan Paul, 1983, pp. 285–89; and Carl Dahlhaus, 'New Music and the Problem of Musical Genre', in Dahlhaus, *Schoenberg and the New Music*, trans. Derrick Puffett and Alfred Clayton, Cambridge, Cambridge University Press, 1987, pp. 32–44.

this essay) genres were increasingly treated as 'topics' within the practice, and the ordering of these topics by way of plot archetypes had some potential to replace, or at least to complement, the structuring devices of a Classical repertory.[15]

Referring specifically to Liszt's *Etude en douze exercices*, we would note that within the early nineteenth-century practice there would have been a rather greater awareness of the generic contrasts between individual exercises in a collection than our own structuralist age has encouraged. (Much the same was true of variation sets, where, for example, individual variations might have a distinctive generic character, and, incidentally, would often have been individually applauded in performance.) On occasion, the genres feeding into études and exercises were even incorporated in the title, although it is dangerous to infer too much from titles in what was, in that respect, at least, a permissive age. Such references were not in any case essential to generic recognition. The genre markers in the Liszt exercises are transparent enough. They refer, for instance, to a prelude, signifying a practice of improvised preluding, which was a familiar part of public pianism (no.1); to a pastorale, relatable to one of the most popular genre pieces at the turn of the eighteenth and nineteenth centuries (no.3); to a hunting piece: 'hard pastoral', if you like (no.4); to a *marche brillante* in the manner of Beethoven or Weber (no.8); to a romance, characterised by a delicate balance between core elements, vocally inspired and even, at times, literally singable, and by decorative extensions and interpolations that are idiomatically pianistic, even if they partly stylise vocal practice (no.9); to a toccata, with a brilliant *perpetuum mobile* in double notes: a monument to 'equal-finger' virtuosity (no.10).

Of their nature, such genre markers promote intertextual readings, where the work exemplifies the genre as distinct from making its own statement. They focus, in other words, on shared materials, albeit at a level of some generality. In a rather more integral way, musical-rhetorical figures work towards a similar end, drawing our attention to the shared expressive substance of a repertory, its store of common expressive devices. These were the still vital residue of a fully-fledged theory of 'affects' derived from rhetoric, through which composers of the seventeenth and eighteenth centuries set out to represent both the

15. See Marta Grabosz, *Morphologie des oeuvres pour piano de Liszt*, Paris, Editions Kime, ²/1996 (orig. edn. 1986).

world of nature and the inner world, the 'passions of the soul'. While their codification by theorists might not have related precisely to compositional praxes, they constituted in principle a form of 'ideal imitation', or *mimesis*, and were thus transparently related in function not only to genres but also to tonal types (key characteristics). In the early nineteenth century *figurae* were still active in genre pieces, although they were increasingly threatened by the replacement of the affective with the characteristic. More fundamentally, they were threatened by the emergence of formal archetypes promoting *telos* and argument (although even in sonata-form movements they maintained a presence). The decline of *mimesis* (and therefore of *figurae*) in the nineteenth century signified a loss of faith in the capacity of signs to relate to things in a straightforward and simple manner. Yet, for all that, it would be wrong to imagine that tonal types and *figurae* ceased altogether to play an active rôle in the nineteenth century. If anything, a post-Classical pianistic practice tended to freeze them, along with genres, into a kind of fixity, albeit one often involving their translation into the idiomatic terms of the piano.

The identification of such *figurae* is, however, fraught with difficulties. For one thing, they are often so generalised in character that they are barely distinguishable from the syntactic constituents of the music: scale figures, schematic progressions, and the like. That, in turn, begs the question of their authenticity, given that they were never templates for composition but, rather, theoretical abstractions: part of a much larger attempt by music theorists to codify elements of a 'living language'. All the same, that 'shared expressive substance' was real enough, even where classificatory devices may be found wanting. And its residue is still present in nineteenth-century music, for all the investment in subjectivity, the apparent rejection of commonalities. Right at the end of the Romantic century, Mahler could engage in a play of meanings that still depended heavily on the connotative values assigned to genre markers, 'affects' and rhetorical figures.

There may be value, then, in testing out the *figurae*, since they point to qualities that can be differentiated from the constitutive motives or figurations of a piece. These qualities are reducible, in many cases, to rather basic relationships of a kind whose expressive function (as sensuous surface) is rather easily subordinated by present-day listeners to their analytical function (as formal components), especially when the association with a text is lacking. Immediate repetition is a case in point, when it involves either voice-transfer or sequential transposition. To modern ears, this is a process rather than a figure; as such, it might be considered not just ubiquitous in the early-nineteenth-century repertory, but actually integral to the construction of the music rather than part of its *decoratio*. The same could be said for a 'figure' such as *variatio*, whose rhetorical rôle (as a form of emphasis) is difficult to separate from its formal function. The case is somewhat different with figures identifable by shape, interval or texture. These can range from such simple gestures as rising or falling shapes to axial figurations, specific intervallic types and double-note textures. All of these can be found in the Liszt exercises, and it is worth identifying them as figures: holding them up for inspection as semi-autonomous features rather than surrendering them to larger contextual functions. We may, for instance, consider the expressive charge contained within a simple gesture of melodic ascent. Or the potency of the chromatic progression labelled *passus duriusculus*, as recently discussed by Peter Williams, especially when isolated as an expressive event relative to surrounding diatonic harmony.[16]

And so to my third category, idiomatic figures: the most important for the larger purpose of my project on virtuosity. These figures are, by definition, welded to the instrument, and in that sense are expressive of a performance-orientated rather than work-orientated culture. They represent the performer as technician and virtuoso, and they stand, in a way, for 'instrumental thought', for the instrument itself. Of their nature, they are unavailable to structural analysis, of whatever persuasion. For all such analysis (by no means only Schenkerian) is reductive in quality: concerned with formal, motivic or harmonic relations at a level beyond the surface play of figures. It may be worth dwelling on this for a moment by at least mentioning two very different attempts to explore the idiomatic. The first, by David Gagné, is strictly analytical.[17] This analyst begins with structure and, from a Schenkerian perspective, reveals how the composing-out of a structure is influenced by particularities of medium. The second, by Tomi Mäkelä, starts, in contrast, from materials, and thus draws us away

16. Peter Williams, *The Chromatic Fourth during Four Centuries of Music*, Oxford, Oxford University Press, 1998.
17. David Gagné, *Performance Medium as a Compositional Determinant: A Study of Selected Works in Three Genres by Mozart*, PhD dissertation, City University of New York, 1988.

from the particularities of the individual work.[18] Mäkelä groups figures into what he calls types and forms, listing the occurrences of each and then arriving at summary percentages. The contrast in methodology here arguably points to a larger compositional distinction between composers who work from, and composers who adapt to, particular instrumental media. Or, at least, to a distinction between what I have termed instrumental thought and a constructivism that starts from concepts rather than sounds, where thematicism is a dominant principle and 'mere' figuration is demoted. The 'mere', incidentally, can usefully remind us that there may be implications for value in the tendency for a thematic discourse to signify the work as text, while figures signify the work as performance.

The story of piano virtuosity is partly the story of such figures. They are the most transparent embodiment of instrumental thought available to us, and, as such, they document a medium-sensitive approach to composition that penetrates through from the general conception of a work to the specific details of its execution. It should be stressed that there is considerable historical continuity in the development of such idiomatic figures. They took their character from a lengthy process of individuation in instrumental media (although, in many cases, that process involved a 'translation' of devices from other media to the keyboard), and their subsequent development was increasingly linked to a fetishism of technique that was given expression in such genres as variations (or divisions), where figurative patterns acquired considerable brilliance and sophistication, and in toccatas, where monomotivic writing of considerable density and concentration was cultivated.

Without elaborating the point here, I will simply indicate how the briefest inspection of the opening pair of Liszt exercises allows us to attempt some initial partitioning. Thus at the beginning of no.1 the right hand divides into chord-based, scale-based and changing-note figures, all of which recur in various forms later in the piece; indeed, a rather basic contrast between arpeggio and scale is fundamental to the piece and supports its prelude-like character. Subsequent bars then introduce (broken) octave figures and *Rollfiguren*, the latter a device shared with violin virtuosity, together with characteristic

18. Tomi Mäkelä, *Virtuosität und Werkcharakter: Zur Virtuosität in den Klavierkonzerten der Hochromantik*, Munich and Salzburg, Emil Katzbichler, 1989.

'mixtures'. This performative play of figures, stressing the tactile, the technical, the immediate, in turn sets the compass reading for the second exercise, although additional figures are introduced here (including rapid repeated notes). And it would be possible to map out the entire cycle in such terms, adopting an additive or combinative approach to its musical materials. Already, a repetition structure emerges from this map, and it should be added that this structure, the play of figures, will often run counter to the repetition structure dictated by metrical and phrase-structural relationships: by 'analysis', if you like.

It will be worth adding a word on my fourth ideal type, formal motives, although I do so tentatively. Formal motives are first and foremost analytical data, defined as such by a reading of structure. As an 'ideal type', the formal motive might be said to embody the work as a discourse and therefore to signal the performer as an interpreter of the work. In short, it invites us to reflect less on material content than on formal design. Yet, in many cases, it is recognisable prior to the possibility of analysis, i.e. on first hearing, as a class of material, and one often tending to a nonidiomatic character. Thus there are classes of motive common to the rondo, just as there are others common to the 'first subject' of a sonata or the principal theme of a nocturne. At the same time, there can be a rhetorical dimension to the relation of material to function. Just as a popular generic theme (say, a waltz or a barcarolle) may become the unexpected basis of a sonata-form movement (as in the Chopin *Ballades*, for instance), so, too, a musical idea whose 'cut' is that of a formal motive may in the end fail to function as such. In other words, we may identify what we take to be a formal motive from its qualities as an ideal type of musical material. The expository formal motive at bar 5 of the first of the Liszt exercises is a case in point, defined by its harmonic placement (the first structural downbeat on the tonic), phrase structure and internal repetition scheme. Here, motivic definition emerges briefly from figuration, and the fact that the formal implication is not realised in no sense annuls our initial identification.

Beyond the Practice

At this stage, it may be worth returning to the question of analysis, if only to pinpoint the contrast between analytical approaches and the sort of hermeneutics I am attempting here. When analysis was instituted as a discipline, at the turn of the nineteenth and twentieth centuries, it formalised a century-old tendency for the profiles of individual works to emerge sharply from music as a whole, and specifically from larger generic groupings. The work, clearly defined against a generic background, would be legitimised by its structure, which in turn could be revealed by analysis. Analysis, then, highlights the antinomy that exists between those genre markers (and other musical-rhetorical figures that stress the music's relationship to larger groupings) and those elements of a schematic structure that solidify it, through a reductive, integrative process, into the original and durable 'ideal aesthetic object' that we call the musical work.

At the same time, analysis brings into focus another antinomy, one already plotted in my introduction. We might describe it as an opposition between text and performance, each of which is in a sense contained by the musical work. Reducing the work to a text strips it of a sense of authorship or ownership, a sense that someone worked to produce it. It dehumanises and neutralises the work. A text, then, is an object constructed of notational symbols. Although it was produced at a particular historical moment as an outcome of someone's activity, it lives on ahistorically as a durable presence in our culture today. A performance, on the other hand, is itself an activity: it is time-specific, singular and expressive, asserting the work, but at the same time instantiating it in a unique and particular way. It realises one of the many possible worlds prescribed by the text, and it does so, of course, within certain contextual constraints, including the skills and personality of the performer. On the one hand, there are analytical functions, which reveal the properties – the constructedness – of a text. And since, in all cases, these functions involve a reduction from explicit 'surface' to implicit 'structure', they remain non-idiomatic; one might almost say performer-proof, except that a performer may choose to underline or suppress them. On the other hand, there are idiomatic figures. These are essentially surface properties, determined by the potentialities and limitations of an instrument. And since they are properties of an instrument as well as a text, they freely cross the boundaries of individual works, blurring their distinctiveness, and highlighting their participation in a shared performance culture.

It has been common for our age in particular to view the work as a musical whole, intentionally shaped: its configuration fixed once and for all in its notation. Yet, as has been much noted in recent years, the ascendancy of the work as a cultural concept belongs to a specific historical period. There was a shift from genre to work, or perhaps rather a separation of genre and work roughly congruent with the separation of 'popular' and 'significant' (formulaic and original) repertories during the nineteenth century. At the same time, there was a separation of text and performance. Like genre and work, these were far from cleanly divided prior to the nineteenth century (witness figured-bass realisation, ornamentation and other forms of extemporisation). But as the notated text congealed into a fixed form, supposedly representing its author's intentions, so the performer became increasingly an interpreter: subordinated to the work but at the same time marked off as special by the uniqueness of his/her interpretation. From being a fused pair in the eighteenth century, performance and text had been well and truly split apart by the early twentieth. Stravinsky and Busoni might be taken to represent polarised responses to this divided culture, where the one fetishised the text and the other the performance. For Stravinsky, interpretation 'got in the way' of the composer's intentions as represented by the text. For Busoni, those intentions were imperfectly reflected in the text but could be accessed by the inspired performer through the text. In effect, Busoni reordered a Platonic degenerative sequence, such that the performance, though subsequent to the text, might be closer to the 'ideal form' of the work.[19]

Much of the thrust of this chapter has been to 'recover' (in the spirit of a critical hermeneutics) the practice of early-nineteenth-century pianism and to find ways of discussing its repertory beyond reducing it to stylistic generalities on the one hand and separating it into discrete works on the other. Putting it negatively, that means filtering out practices and values that are deeply ingrained in our way of thinking today. Putting it positively, it means making a genre- and performance-orientated culture concrete through useful generalisations about its musical materials. There has been space to attempt little more than the basic mapping out of an approach to these tasks, so I will end by sketching very briefly the implications for subsequent research. It goes without saying that Liszt, like Chopin, was a highly individual composer. Yet that individuality was hammered out from the performance-orientated materials of what I have already described as an art of conformity, and in response to a work-concept

19. This view of Busoni's conception comes close to that identified by John Williamson in Chapter 9, p. 200.

already well established in other practices. Partly, this meant a reinvestment in the individuality of earlier masters, in ways that are by no means confined to the piano medium. That is what most existing analytical writing tends to highlight, in my experience: it is the perspective of the present-day subject. But it was also a matter of promoting an image of the instrument itself that was already part of the ethos of post-Classical pianism. Here, we approach, I suggest, the perspective of the historical subject. As well as the most potent symbol of a mercantile culture, the piano was increasingly viewed as a universal and all-inclusive medium of musical experience: capable of saying all in its own terms and embodying in itself (in its very name) the symbolic power of contrast. These two representations of the piano might be described glibly as the real and the ideal, although if I were to develop this point, I would want to argue that the one was a precondition of the other.

It would be easy enough to demonstrate that my ideal types of musical materials were transformed by the ascendancy of this second image of the piano in alliance with a work-concept. Briefly, the effect was to problematise generic meanings, to dissolve musical-rhetorical figures into something approaching an indivisible expressive continuum welded to the medium; and, most important of all, to transform idiomatic figures from a performance-orientated surplus to a work-orientated essence in what amounted to a conquest of virtuosity by the musical work. But I suspect it may be even more useful to invoke the perspective of the historical subject: to demonstrate, in other words, that, even when transcended, the figures were remembered, and that this memory, distinguishing Chopin and Liszt in an essential way from other canonic repertory of the mid-nineteenth century, might stand for what I would like to describe as the hidden trace of the performer in the work.

6

Looking Back at Ourselves: The Problem with the Musical Work-Concept

Reinhard Strohm

The Impatience with the Work-Concept

In the title of this symposium, in some of its papers and in other recent writings on the musical work-concept, I sense an impatience with the work-concept that may do more harm than good to musical scholarship.

The work-concept has, of course, deeply influenced our musical culture; it is as 'real' as any aesthetic idea can be, and many generations of musicians have believed in it. When, however, the title of our symposium presents 'reality' and 'invention' as equal options for its definition, the verbal opposition implies that 'invention' means here 'a fake', 'a fabrication'. As a historical statement, this would seem frivolous; I can only conclude that it is a rhetorical statement making a tongue-in-cheek reference to the demystificatory rhetoric which paints European cultural traditions of the nineteenth and early twentieth centuries as deeply devoted to fakes, 'myths' and 'imaginary museums'.

In fact, when musical scholars spoke seriously of 'The Myth of the Netherlands School', the 'Myth of Nationalism' or 'The Myth of the Musical Work', they expressed a commitment to demystification and thus to truth and morality. Here, the term 'myth' is to be read not in the dignified sense of 'a hallowed tale' but in the common-parlance sense of 'something fabricated'. What is the point of accusing a historical conceptual notion of being fabricated? Perhaps these are the offshoots of a Puritan rationalism that denies value or legitimacy to things that are not real, and perhaps there is an intention of warning young people off concepts, canons or distinctions that intellectuals have thought up to deceive them. A general mistrust of concepts characterises the tradition of philosophical realism so common in Western popular religion and Anglo-American political philosophy. This tradition outlaws concept as a carrier of truth and draws the consequences by elevating universal concepts that for normative reasons cannot be denied, such as God, Beauty, Nation, Work, to the rank of material existence. In the modern world, where scientific standards have changed more drastically than philosophical ones, the philosophical realist has turned positivist and falls into his own trap, now needing to argue that God, Beauty, Nation, Work, etc. are unreal and therefore untrue. When it is sometimes claimed that no musical works exist but only individual texts or performances, this same sort of disappointed realism may be involved.

In the moderate nominalist tradition, on the other hand, the reality of words and concepts is accepted but only as a shaded reality: while being able to consider as potentially true what does not materially exist, this tradition also recognises the contingency of the connections between words and things. This was the point of the chapter title 'The Invention of the Masterwork' in my book on fifteenth-century music. What I am trying to describe there is a conceptual construct which, when first invented, may have served vested interests or even fostered deception, but which nevertheless became a cultural reality because people acted on it.[1]

Thus the rhetorical charge of 'fabrication' can perhaps be laid aside. Even so, there would remain the diagnosis, to which, among others, Lydia Goehr has contributed,[2] that the musical work-concept (as a 'regulative' concept), with its associated notions of a canon of works and great classical masters in composition, is a strategy for rationalising music whose alleged claim to exclusive dominance must now be

---

1. Reinhard Strohm, *The Rise of European Music 1380–1500*, Cambridge, Cambridge University Press, 1993, pp. 412–88 ('France and the Low Countries: The Invention of the Masterwork', covering the period *c*. 1450–*c*.1485). A more recent contribution on the 'invention' of the musical work-concept and related concepts is Reinhard Strohm, 'The Humanist Idea of a Common Revival of the Arts, and its Implications for Music History', in *Interdisciplinary Studies in Musicology. Report from the Third Interdisciplinary Conference, Poznan, 1996* , ed. Maciej Jabłoński and Jan Stęszewski, Poznan, Society for the Advancement of the Arts and Sciences, 1997, pp. 7–25.
2. Lydia Goehr, *The Imaginary Museum of Musical Works: An Essay in the Philosophy of Music*, Oxford, Clarendon Press, 1992.

challenged.[3] Charges of exaggerated dominance do indeed concern truth and – at least, in the sense that they imply a 'guilty party' – a specific historical period, cultural tradition or ethnic/social group that has set it all up. The peculiarity of this discourse deserves archaeological investigation. By analysing moments in the recent history of the debate about the musical work-concept, I shall attempt to identify historiographical and philosophical premises of the discourse and to relate them to a consideration of what I see as an ongoing crisis of modernity. As I hope to show, the historical diagnosis of the work-concept as a past we should reject is, to some extent, a self-diagnosis.

The concept of the musical work has been 'on the run' for a considerable time now. The literary avant-garde, as far as its own orbit was concerned, utterly demolished the reputation of the autonomous artwork in the 1950s and 1960s.[4] To describe it today, for example, as a glorious tradition now unfortunately coming to an end would appear derisory, and to believe in its future might have to be considered as naïve. Since the 1960s, many musicians have taken this process as accomplished fact. Still today, however, the musical work-concept provides a major target for attack by musicians and musicologists. The case against the work-concept in music is made on the grounds of its allegedly unabated dominance or inherited status. It is made in the name of scholarship as well as of the suffering consumer, sometimes supported by reference to world traditions, and often presented as a brand new proposition.

Michael Talbot's 'blurb' for the Symposium (see Introduction, p. 2) is a case in point. Here, the conflict is situated between popular

3. See, in particular, Goehr's discussion of the *Werktreue* concept as practised during the twentieth century (*The Imaginary Museum of Musical Works*, pp. 244–57, where the author claims that the Romantic aesthetic of the work-concept has continued to be the dominant view and identifies the belief in its constitutive concepts as 'conceptual imperialism' (p. 245).

4. Carl Dahlhaus and others saw its decline approaching in the 1960s; see Dahlhaus, 'Plädoyer für eine romantische Kategorie. Der Begriff des Kunstwerks in der neuesten Musik', *Neue Zeitschrift für Musik*, Vol. 130, 1969, and also id., 'Über den Zerfall des musikalischen Werkbegriffs', *Beiträge 1970/71 der Österreichischen Gesellschaft für Musik*, Kassel, Bärenreiter, 1971 (repr. in id., *Schönberg und andere*, Mainz, Schott, 1978, pp. 279–90), where several of the arguments of the present article are laid out. See also the preface (probably written in 1957) to Roman Ingarden, *Untersuchungen zur Ontologie der Kunst*, Tübingen, Niemeyer, 1962, trans. as *Ontology of the Work of Art*, Athens (Ohio), Ohio University Press, 1989.

assumptions of the past and enlightened alternatives of the future, which makes the task of eradicating a reified work-concept appear quite easy. Assurances that it 'crystallised in relatively modern times' and is rare in a world context seem to suggest that there is no really heavy price to pay for abandoning it. On the other hand, the power of the work-concept over people's beliefs appears inflated ('axiomatic until quite recently'), and its use is derided as a popular reification.

Or, to quote two passages from Richard Middleton:

> There is a suspicion that this type of musical production is peculiar, at least in its origins, to that system, with all its associated social, aesthetic and discursive apparatuses, which Leo Treitler has termed the WECT: the West European Classical Tradition. (Acronyms can serve the reificatory function, useful on occasions, of displaying the object for the fascinated scrutiny characteristic of the museum visitor.) As the authority of this system apparently implodes in the late twentieth century – at the same time, ironically, as it completes its dissemination to the last corner of the globe – it seems natural to question the sustainability of the work-concept.

> From a historical point of view, the fact that this difference between vernacular music and the WECT could emerge so strongly is not too surprising. Just at the time, around 1800, when 'popular music' as we understand it was emerging as a distinct category so, too, were developing all the ideological and institutional accoutrements of the work-concept: the autonomy aesthetic, the 'serious' listener, the canon, music academies, 'great man' music history, and so on. Popular music, defined with a new intensity as 'different' – in fact, as 'low' and 'trivial' – could to a large extent continue to operate differently precisely because of this placing in the hierarchy. Pop was saved from complete assimilation to work-thinking by its vulgarity.[5]

The historical ascendancy of the work-concept, situated around 1800, is viewed as an ingredient or even an agent of cultural hierarchisation; reification is blamed on a concept and its users, whom the text itself reifies and derides, making Treitler's jocular acronym a vehicle for denunciation; the 'system' and its 'apparatuses' – as under Stalin – are placed on the side of the work-concept and its 'accoutrements', including 'great man' history; assimilation to work-thinking is presented as something from which cultural traditions should be 'saved'.

5. Richard Middleton, Chapter 3, pp. 59 and 60–61.

From the broad sweep of challenges to the musical work-concept made in these and many other contributions, three central charges might be distilled: the charge of mere contingency, or haphazard origins in a relatively recent and circumscribed cultural milieu; the charge of reification and petrification of living culture; and, probably most poignantly, the charge of excessive power over people's culture today.

It has been shown, however, that all these arguments already characterised the polemics of the modernist avant-garde and would usefully be considered in the context of the whole criticism of idealist and Romantic aesthetics.[6] This debate, then, belongs to a previous generation. Why are we kicking what is already doomed? Why are prophecies of the imminent demise of the work-concept getting louder as the demise recedes behind us? An answer is suggested, perhaps, by Peter Bürger, who distinguishes between 'the discourse of the end of the idealist aesthetic' and the real achievement of that end.[7] This might point to some kind of dialectical relationship between the continuation of the discourse and the continuation of its subject.

Terms and concepts reflect our own past, and the transition from establishing them to complaining about their influence can be very short indeed. To give some examples of how a dialectic can operate: the 'WECT' may be the only world tradition that has established the regulative notion of the musical work, but it is also the only one to worry about it; the reification of musical culture that we enact when looking at its manifestations through the looking-glass of works or composers ('composer-centredness', as described by Michael Talbot in this volume), is in itself not so much a fact about us as a reified way of looking at ourselves. Indeed, the critical concept of 'reification' has arisen not from without but from within the Western cultural tradition (Karl Marx) and has been used in the arts to defend an abstract or universal aesthetic including the work-concept against commercialisation and 'fetishism'(György Lukács). We have inherited not only the offending cultural practice but also the embarrassment about it. A parallel example can be seen in the charges levelled against

---

6. See Peter Bürger, 'Die Negation der Autonomie der Kunst durch die Avant-garde', in id., *Theorie der Avantgarde*, Frankfurt am Main, Suhrkamp, 1974, pp. 63–75. A survey of the avant-garde's challenges to the musical work-concept can be found in Goehr (1992), pp. 257–84.

7. Bürger (1974), p. 88.

musicology of having promoted 'canonisation' or 'composer-centred-ness': musicology has not only created or developed this critical terminology but has also conducted real battles against 'shrinking repertoires' and the musical hero-worship that the music industry forever tries to impose.[8]

The contingency – and therefore the limited applicability – of the work-concept is supposed to be addressed by the historiographical discourse concerning a 'watershed' in music history around 1800, to be considered below; also, more recently by the rapid consolidation of a period paradigm for the two centuries running from the eighteenth-century Enlightenment to Post-modernism, this new paradigm frequently being referred to as a 'sea change'.[9] But the impatience with which we are talking ourselves away from this past seems to imply anxieties about unsettled relationships with it: far from being able to live with the idea that Romantic and modern Western culture has run its course, we resent its persistence and attempt to domesticate it into a circumscribed historical paradigm.

The greatest worry may be about power, not only of the old work-concept over alternative practices, but also concretely over our lives. Hence the opera buff or concert-goer who grows impatient with a ritual that chains her to an armchair for five hours, concentrating on one man's invention; hence the impatience of the exasperated museum visitor with having to digest one reified object after another. This cultural fetishism (consumerism) is but the tail-end of our own aesthetic tradition. The attitudes of non-Westerners to art and ritual have not yet been learned by us. Similarly, the rhetoric of 'myths', demystification and of the 'sea change', and the historiography of paradigms and watersheds, may keep an idealist aesthetic in power and exert demagogic power precisely because these are handy reductions of the old progressivist, idealist and realist philosophies. What generates these reductions is not yet clear, but I suggest a close connection

8. On attempts to berate the Western tradition for such critical terms as 'canon' or 'museum character', whose very existence documents a long-standing unease with the respective cultural practices, see Reinhard Strohm, 'Collapsing the Dialectic: The Enlightenment Tradition in Music and its Critics', in *Congress Report IMS, London, 1997* (forthcoming), Round Table 'Historiography'. The term *Werktreue*, be it noted, was coined by early modernists as a weapon for the defence of musical practice against the exaggerations of the *Ausdrucksästhetik*.

9. This aspect, too, is discussed in my paper quoted in the preceding footnote.

with anxieties over the collapse of Western values and Western status in the world.

I am not worried about the demise of the work-concept; but I worry about the things it was meant to describe. And equally: about the things that the concept has been found unable to describe. Not by coincidence is much of this symposium addressed to the 'alternatives': to phenomena that are not works or work-related, and to the question of overlap. Can we hope to describe non-work phenomena in measured relation to a central term when that term is weighed down by consumerism and impatience? The musical work may not yet be a thing of the past, but the musical work-concept has long become a tool to redefine our past in our bid to cope with the difficulties of the present.

Metahistorical Significance?

In the historiographical section of this essay it will be necessary to relate present-day constructions of the history of the work-concept to those of the generation writing in the 1960s and 1970s. One such construction is the hypothesis that dates the emergence of the modern work-concept around 1800 (or in the late eighteenth century: I have yet to see a critical enquiry into the data underlying the datings). This hypothesis, which would seem to imply the historical contingency of the concept, ties it in with other perceived, and allegedly relevant, historical changes around 1800, and assigns to earlier appearances of the work-concept a lesser or more casual status. My argument is that the hypothesis is inseparable from the special pleading of our predecessors in favour of a metahistorical significance of the musical work-concept. It would seem extremely difficult to defend a contingent origin and a metahistorical significance of the same thing at the same time.

Michael Talbot sums up the historiographical tradition, running from at least the 1950s until today, that tends to cumulate all or most relevant changes in musical life in the West in a few decades around 1800.[10] This period is seen as 'a watershed' in the evolution of music; other important historical changes in Western culture affecting music are said to concur with this verdict. The greatest assuredness about this hypothesis is found in the most recent writings, for instance in

10. Michael Talbot, Chapter 8, pp. 168–71.

Goehr: 'Given certain changes in the late eighteenth century, persons
… were able for the first time to comprehend and treat the activity of
producing music as one primarily involving the composition and performance of works. The work-concept at this point found its regulative rôle'.[11] The credibility of the assertions 'for the first time' and 'at
this point' would depend, it seems to me, on a demonstration that
these things had never happened before, which is manifestly impossible; although this does not necessarily devalue the assertion itself. A
historical statement can be incredible and yet efficient, as in, for
example: 'They lived happily ever after'. This formula implies 'end of
story: it is not my task to delve into future events'. Similarly here,
although with inverted time-direction, Goehr implies that to investigate the previous 40,000 or so years of music history for equivalent
phenomena would be unfeasible for her. I recently heard a famous
eighteenth-century specialist claim that it was precisely in that century
that people 'for the first time got together and sat down just in order
to listen to music'.[12] And in similar vein Michael Talbot notes 'the formation, for the first time, of a universal musical "canon"'.[13]

The possibility that the musical work acquired distinctive features
in the decades around 1800 was also a concern for Carl Dahlhaus,
who commented on it in his publications of the 1960s, 1970s and
1980s; parallels can be found in the writings of Zofia Lissa, Hans
Heinrich Eggebrecht, Walter Wiora and other writers.[14] The whole

11. Goehr (1992), p. 113.
12. William Weber, in his keynote address to the conference *Concert Life in Eigh-
     teenth-century Britain* (on the 250th anniversary of the Holywell Music Room,
     Oxford), held in Oxford on 3–5 July 1998 (I quote from memory).
13. Talbot, p. 169.
14. Zofia Lissa, 'Über das Wesen des Musikwerkes', in id., *Aufsätze zur Musikäs-
     thetik*, Berlin, Henschel, 1969, pp. 7–35; Hans-Heinrich Eggebrecht, 'Opus-
     musik', in id., *Musikalisches Denken. Aufsätze zur Theorie und Ästhetik der
     Musik*, Wilhelmshaven, Heinrichshofen, 1977; Rainer Cadenbach, *Das
     musikalische Kunstwerk. Grundbegriffe einer undogmatischen Musiktheorie*,
     Regensburg, Bosse, 1978; Walter Wiora, *Die vier Weltalter der Musik. Ein uni-
     versalhistorischer Entwurf*, Stuttgart, Kohlhammer, 1961; trans. M. D. Herter
     Norton as *The Four Ages of Music*, London, Dent, 1966; id., *Das musikalische
     Kunstwerk*, Tutzing, Schneider, 1983; id., 'Das musikalische Kunstwerk der
     Neuzeit und das musische Kunstwerk der Antike', in *Festschrift Carl Dahlhaus
     zum 60. Geburtstag*, ed. Hermann Danuser and others, Laaber, Laaber Verlag,
     1988, pp. 3–10.

debate has been summarised by Wilhelm Seidel.[15] This group of writings has profoundly influenced the current discourse and its continuation in Goehr's book and more recent contributions: the connections between the older group and this new one are closer than is usually acknowledged. However, certain ideas that our generation has borrowed from those writers may need revision.

First, as concerns the emergence of the work-concept around 1800, no coherent account has been given of its relationship with previous eras or, indeed, of alternative concepts that might have survived parallel with it. Dahlhaus and Wiora, for example, rated the significance of the changes occurring towards 1800 as greater than that of the transformations they recognised in the musical aesthetic of the Renaissance, but they were unable to trace a developmental path between these two eras (except for the emancipation of instrumental music, on which see below). In an isolated attempt to identify an early countermodel to the modern work-concept, Dahlhaus interpreted the perceived stature of at least certain compositions by Handel or Palestrina as that of *exempla classica* : not works but specimens of classical workmanship.[16] This would have built a bridge towards the classical and humanist tradition that surely should have been taken into account. It must be conceded, however, that famous composers wrote works for consumption and on commission from at least the fifteenth century onwards, so the production of *exempla classica* was probably not uppermost in their minds. Generally speaking, the rôle of the work-concept before the mid-eighteenth century has remained nebulous. Goehr, following Seidel, takes up the challenge of the humanist influence by commenting on Listenius's *opus perfectum et absolutum*, but goes only so far as to insist that the identity of that concept with the modern one cannot be proven; it may in fact be quite similar (see also below).

The second main weakness of the hypothesis centring on 1800 is its ambivalence of historiographical purpose. Some of Dahlhaus's and Seidel's characterisations of the post-1800 work-concept were conceptual, for example, the idealist invocation of a composer's

---

15. Wilhelm Seidel, *Werk und Werkbegriff in der Musikgeschichte*, Darmstadt, Wissenschaftliche Buchgesellschaft, 1987.
16. Dahlhaus, 'Exemplum classicum und klassisches Werk', in *Epochenschwelle und Epochenbewusstsein*, ed. Reinhart Herzog and Reinhart Koselleck, Munich, Fink, 1987, pp. 591–94.

intention; others were material or notational, such as that of finiteness of the text; yet others social, such as that of autonomy from external functions. Many of these definitions were negative: the absence of social function, of text-relatedness, of performative freedoms, of patronage, and so forth, was considered just as significant as the presence of structural unity, of compositional intention, etc. Wiora distinguished more clearly between features concerning the *Gehalt* (essence, substance) of the musical work and its *Daseinsform* (form or mode of existence, for example in society).[17] This labour of defining the musical work-concept looked over its shoulder at the perceived parameters of the social history of music while trying at the same time to satisfy idealist notions of type and structure. In other words, the aim of these scholars was to establish a self-sufficient, philosophically viable concept while making this very concept fit historical contingencies observed around 1800. Writings from that period, such as those of Kant, Herder, Körner and Nägeli, were scrutinised for conceptualisations of contemporary music, with predictably ambiguous results.

Now, it is not entirely clear to me whether Dahlhaus and his colleagues were pursuing a philosophical work-concept that could exist outside time or a historical, practical one to which Beethoven's contemporaries merely gave philosophical meaning. But that, I suggest, was the point of the argument: German, modernist historiographical notions of classicism, the Enlightenment and the fate of European music made it easy for these scholars to identify the formation of a cultural practice, at a crucial time in European history, with a wide conceptual model of lasting significance. This model was the ultimate confirmation that the European musical tradition was *sui generis* in the world context. In its characteristic blend of idealism and historical structuralism, this discourse is one of the twentieth century defining itself in music; the work-concept that emerged here was our own, not the one prevalent around 1800.

But are not the documented views of Beethoven's contemporaries independent evidence? To some extent, the evidence may be tautological. Although in itself a historical fact of great interest, continuity between the views of Beethoven's time and those of the later twentieth century should not be taken uncritically as a confirmation of historical fact; it may simply mean that the language has not moved on.

17. Walter Wiora, *Das musikalische Kunstwerk*, Tutzing, Schneider, 1983.

Tautological or circular reasoning infects the present discourse also through the tendency to make historical observations reinforce each other: for example, the idea that the work-concept originated around 1800 because other important changes also happened in music then (emancipation of instrumental and absolute music, concert life, free-lance composers, etc.), and that these changes, in turn, happened because they were related to that of the work-concept.

A third weakness of the hypothesis is the factual frailty of several of its historiographical arguments. Take first the 'emancipation of instrumental music': most of our writers agree that the work-concept could not be fully formed until it applied to instrumental music. In fact, the emancipation of instrumental music from about the fifteenth century onwards is traditionally described as a steady development towards work-character that it did not attain before the classical symphony. If so, why should vocal music not have attained it earlier? Why did it have to wait for the symphony? The presence of text is seen as a concession to extra-musical and functional influences that might obscure the purity of the work-concept.[18] Apart from the danger of circular reasoning, mentioned above, the background of this hypothesis seems to be undiluted idealism: a principle that does not operate everywhere is not operating at all, and it is better to set the stakes for a definition too high than too low. One wonders, then, how vocal music after 1800 managed to fulfil the conceptual criteria (did it learn from the symphony to disregard text?), and also why text is viewed as the sole bearer of extra-musical influence, whereas instrumental medium and performance conditions, for instance, are discounted. Texted music of the Baroque era, for instance, could be much more 'autonomous' as an artistic endeavour than some instrumental music of the nineteenth century. The contrived theory that the emancipation of instrumental music helped the establishment of the work-concept also in the realm of vocal music depends on an assumption that the function of text and social relevance in vocal works changed radically around 1800, for which there is no evidence at all. On the contrary: the history of oratorio, opera, song and church music just after 1800 confirms the continuing relevance of external meaning and function in vocal music. Really, the argument about instrumental music is

18. See, for example, Carl Dahlhaus, 'Epochen und Epochenbewußtsein in der Musikgeschichte', in *Epochenschwelle und Epochenbewusstsein*, pp. 81–96, at pp. 90–91.

correct only when turned on its head: although instrumental music, in the shape of musical works, became more 'emancipated' over the generations, this meant only that it caught up with vocal music in this respect.

What I see as the greatest flaw of these arguments is the idea that function or relevance for social practices should, generally, have been a hindrance to music's possession of work-character. Many writers, including Dahlhaus, seem to have confused artistic dignity or relevance, i.e. work-character, with the absence of functionality. This is disproved by most Western music composed after 1800, which has been functional in many ways but nevertheless dignified. On the other hand, the belief 'that music should not hang on the coat-tails of another practice in order to be accorded the dignity and meaningfulness of art' was, in my opinion, not 'new-found' around 1800, to quote from Michael Talbot's present essay,[19] but had already been demonstrated by the Renaissance conception of *musica* and its status among the arts and practices. There had been a very long cohabitation of work-like significance and functional determination in music. The last time when there was no other purpose to music than a ceremonial or otherwise functional one was not the eighteenth century, but the Neolithic age; it would be absurd to claim that the ancient Greeks and Romans did not at least intermittently enjoy the art of music for its own sake, and examples of pure sensualism or commercialism in the appreciation of music are numerous in both the Middle Ages and the Renaissance.

This also affects the argument over structural or sonorous autonomy in early music. Dahlhaus and others assumed automatically that medieval or Renaissance compositions always borrowed 'work-like' unity, as well as artistic dignity, from texts. But it is difficult, for example, to find many textual explanations for the appearance of clausula recomposition, the isorhythmic motet or Mass structures, or even for the Baroque canzona and sonata structures. The parameters of intertextuality, artistic emulation, compositional individualism, the pursuit of patronage, and so on apply here, and they all lead away from the functionality suggested by the (sometimes) liturgical texts. The unitary structure of a cyclic tenor Mass is counterposed to the functionality of its performance in an almost ostentatious gesture of structural independence; precisely because the timescale and function of the

19. Talbot, p. 172.

Mass service is taken for granted, the listener will perceive the divergent organisation of the music – not the texts – as structurally meaningful. Also, the unity and the intertextual features of Renaissance polyphony (including the emulation of similar works by other composers) are primarily sonorous and thus aesthetic, not representational or functional. The music of Renaissance motets and madrigals often confers unity on texts that in themselves are neither complete nor especially autonomous. Harmony, mode and tonality in early music are generally factors giving structure and coherence, not just performative modes. In terms of rhetoric, they correspond to *dispositio* or *elocutio*, not *pronuntiatio*.

An Age of the Work-Concept?

While the German and other European modernist scholars never gave up the search for various material and conceptual distinctions between earlier musical works and those created after the late eighteenth century, but kept some distance from a heavy-handed watershed theory, Lydia Goehr and other Anglophone writers have now opted wholeheartedly for a more paradigmatic approach, placing certain criteria in a much more privileged position than others. This allows them to separate the work-concept of the nineteenth century quite strictly from those of preceding centuries, but only at the cost of employing extra philosophical reasoning that had not served any such historical narrative before. These elements had to be reconciled in a new fashion.

Lydia Goehr seems to be influenced by Zofia Lissa's criticism of Roman Ingarden's ontology of the musical work;[20] she concludes a long analytical chapter on the work-concept with a call away from philosophical analysis and towards history: a 'change in emphasis' from ontology to musical practice.[21] I am unclear, in any case, about the very possibility of an ontology of a historical phenomenon; but even if there are ontologies that do justice to the historical intricacies of their subject (the modern philosophers discussed in Goehr's

---

20. Ingarden (1989), paragraphs 1–8; Lissa, 'Einige kritische Bemerkungen zu Ingardens Theorie des musikalischen Werkes', in id., *Neue Aufsätze zur Musikästhetik*, Wilhelmshaven, Heinrichshofen, 1975; English trans. in *Roman Ingarden and Contemporary Polish Aesthetics*, ed. Piotr Graff and Slaw Krzemien-Ojak, Warsaw, Polish Scientific Publishers, 1975, pp. 129–44; see also Lissa (1969).
21. See especially Goehr (1992), pp. 86 and 89.

opening chapters do not qualify), the philosopher's contingent experience and cultural-historical awareness of the subject may be parochial. A lack of professional experience may also entail a lack of critical distance from current discourses. Professional acquaintance with music before 1800, which fewer and fewer people now have, must inform a philosophical interpretation of nineteenth-century music. Otherwise, the danger of, for instance, erroneous assertions of uniqueness or novelty is just too great.

Goehr's categorial approach was to be fed from historical evidence of the *Daseinsformen*, the contingent modes of existence or even the 'substance' of historical music. Sometimes, however, it still mixes philosophical rigour and historical judgement in a confusing manner. For example, the large defining rôle given in the first chapters to the varying degrees of notational 'adequacy' and performative freedom in Western music may be due to a misunderstanding of a technical sort shared with other philosophers. I should not like to suggest, as Goehr seems to imply, that the possibility of playing Bach or Tartini with non-notated trills or divergent ('improvised') notes militates against the work-concept, or that the practice of beginning the performance of a Beethoven sonata by playing its first note demonstrates *Werktreue* concepts in operation.[22] The boundaries of convention, individual control and significance in musical production have been redrawn in various ways since at least the Middle Ages: a perspective hoping to glean philosophical evidence from these fluctuations may well be too narrow. On a world scale, of course, the normative relevance of having to play the first note, or of having to add certain understood embellishments to a written score etc., may indeed allow for distinctions between cultural traditions or repertories. Within the Western musical tradition since at least Guido of Arezzo, however, the developing boundaries between notation and performance are unlikely to permit hard distinctions between 'work' and 'non-work', or the presence or absence of the respective concepts. It is a fact that much Western 'non-work' music shares the notational and other modes of existence of 'work' music. For example, leaving out the first note of the *Summer Canon*, or of a children's song or dance-tune, is just as silly as doing it with Beethoven's sonata Op. 31 no. 1, but this fact alone does not suffice to turn those pieces into works.

Goehr's central claim is built around the watershed theory

22. Ibid., p. 285.

mentioned above. In fact she appears to have made this historio-graphical decision in an *a priori* manner, shifting the burden of proof that something obeys the regulative work-concept on to music composed before 1800. The corollaries – musical practices and concepts before this time – are investigated on the prior assumption that the central claim applies, not in order to find out whether it does.[23] Much of Goehr's historical argument thus involves the fending off of rival claims on the work-concept arising from earlier practices (and a little from modern and post-modern times, where the argument is, however, carried off convincingly). The generalised justification for 'drawing a line' against the past is presented as the philosophical aim to avoid infinite regression. This would also be a preference of the historian; but of course such a general principle does not justify, as is almost claimed, a specific cut-off date for the emergent work-concept. Goehr's discussion of Listenius and his formula of the musical *opus perfectum et absolutum*, which follows Seidel's account but departs from his conclusions,[24] raises the stakes against Listenius's status as a witness to the work-concept both in principle and casually. The first, by demanding positive evidence that the regulative work-concept is what Listenius's formulation means; the second, by holding it against this author that he does not specify 'repeatability'. In truth, Listenius does specify that the *opus* is complete in written form – which in Western music since Guido of Arezzo automatically implies repeatability. But Seidel's discussion of Listenius, and therefore Goehr's understanding of him, is incomplete. Eggebrecht, Wiora, Cahn, Niemöller and the present writer have all elaborated on the humanist and classical background of the idea of *musica poetica*.[25] These other

23. This is acknowledged on p. 119, for instance.
24. Seidel (1987), pp. 3–5.
25. See Eggebrecht (1977); Peter Cahn, 'Zur Vorgeschichte des "Opus perfectum et absolutum" in der Musikauffassung um 1500', in *Zeichen und Struktur in der Musik der Renaissance. Symposium, Jahrestagung der Gesellschaft für Musikforschung Münster (Westfalen) 1987*, ed. Klaus Hortschansky, Kassel etc., Bärenreiter, 1989, pp. 11–26; Klaus Wolfgang Niemöller, 'Zum Paradigmenwechsel in der Musik der Renaissance. Vom *numerus sonorus* zur *musica poetica*', *Abhandlungen der Akademie der Wissenschaften in Göttingen, Phil.-Hist. Klasse*, 3. Folge, Göttingen, 1995, pp. 187–215; Strohm (1993, 1997); id., 'Music, Humanism, and the Idea of a Rebirth of the Arts', in *Music as Concept and Practice in the Late Middle Ages*, ed. Reinhard Strohm (*New Oxford History of Music*, revised edn., Vol. 3), Oxford University Press, forthcoming; Wiora, 'Das musikalische Kunstwerk der Neuzeit und das musische Kunstwerk der Antike'.

writers have recognised, for instance, the influence of Quintilian and
Horace on Johannes Tinctoris, who in the 1470s uses the term and
concept of the musical *opus* as a regulative yardstick by which a piece
of music can be evaluated just like a famous and enduring literary
work.[26] The claim that Renaissance humanists introduced the concept
of the musical work as a regulative concept by transferring its general
idea from the classical tradition of the other arts is in many ways
underpinned by musical production and its modes of existence in the
era of the Franco-Netherlandish composers from Dufay to Josquin, as
well as by other contemporary opinions (see also below on the rôle of
the composer). An interesting focus on the coexistence of the concept
with the performative tradition is provided by the lines that a French
humanist wrote about Ockeghem *c.* 1470: 'He sang marvellous songs,

26. Strohm, 'Music, Humanism, and the Idea of a Rebirth of the Arts'. The passage
     in Tinctoris's *Liber de arte contrapuncti* (1477) reads as follows:

     'Hac vero tempestate, ut praeteream innumeros concentores venustissime pro-
     nuntiantes, ... infiniti florent compositores, ut Johannes Okeghem, Johannes
     Regis, Anthonius Busnois, Firminus Caron, Guillermus Faugues, qui novissimis
     temporibus vita functos Johannem Dunstaple, Egidium Binchois, Guillermum
     Dufay se praeceptores habuisse in hac arte divina gloriantur. Quorum omnium
     omnia fere opera tantam suavitudinem redolent ut, mea quidem sententia, non
     modo hominibus heroibusque verum etiam Diis immortalibus dignissima
     censenda sint. Ea quoque profecto numquam audio, numquam considero quin
     laetior ac doctior evadam, unde quemadmodum Virgilius in illo opere divino
     Eneidos Homero, ita iis, Hercule, in meis opusculis utor archetypis. Praesertim
     autem in hoc in quo, concordantias ordinando, approbabilem eorum compo-
     nendi stilum plane imitatus sum'.
     (J. Tinctoris, *Opera theoretica*, ed. Albert Seay, Rome, 1975, Vol. 2, pp. 12–13.)

     'In this age, however, even leaving aside the innumerable singers who perform
     so beautifully, ... an endless number of composers flourish, for example,
     Johannes Okeghem, Johannes Regis, Anthonius Busnois, Firminus Caron and
     Guillermus Faugues, who can be proud to have had as their teachers in this
     divine art the recently deceased Johannes Dunstaple, Egidius Binchois and
     Guillermus Dufay. Almost all the works of all these [composers] exude such
     great sweetness that they should, in my opinion, be considered worthy not only
     of humans and heroes but of the immortal gods themselves. And indeed, I never
     hear them, never study them, without coming away the happier and wiser;
     therefore, just as Virgil used Homer as model in his divine work, the *Aeneid*, so,
     too, do I use them, by Hercules, as models for my writings. This is particularly
     true of the present work, where my arrangement of the harmonies is a straight-
     forward imitation of their praiseworthy style of composition' (author's transla-
     tion).

and left new written [pieces] behind, which all the people now hold in honour'.[27]

The tradition of this work-concept persists and develops throughout the sixteenth to eighteenth centuries, in ways quite comparable with the evolution of the 'modern system of the arts' (Kristeller), which likewise was already in place by the fifteenth century.[28] What distinguishes the fifteenth-century state of the regulative work-concept in music from the one Goehr is assigning to 1800 is obviously a quantitative matter: the concept gradually became more influential and universal (for example, outside its original cultural domain), and also in some ways more 'regulative', for example, by becoming more familiar to patrons and listeners. The watershed theory implies, problematically, that two different states of a continuity are placed on the same developmental axis; instead of softening this historiographical construction by admitting long-term developments of many kinds, Goehr exacerbates the problem by equating the passage from the eighteenth to the nineteenth century with a hard-and-fast distinction between different functions of a philosophical idea.

Thus, *pace* Goehr, it remains to be shown how a philosophically tenable distinction can possibly be made to accord with historical and, indeed, historiographical developments. Kant's distinction between 'constitutive' and 'regulative' ideas and their uses, which lies at the basis of Goehr's theory and which she defends against the wider application of the 'normative' or 'regulative' function of genres or even individual things proposed by Warren and Wellek,[29] is definitely not a historical concept, let alone a historiographical one.[30] Kant would reject outright the hypothesis of a historical development from a constitutive to a regulative idea: he says that 'transcendental ideas

27. See Reinhard Strohm, '"Hic miros cecinit cantus, nova scripta reliquit"', in *Johannes Ockeghem. Actes du XLe Colloque International d'Etudes Humanistes*, ed. Philippe Vendrix, Paris, Klincksieck, 1988, pp. 139–65.
28. Paul Oskar Kristeller, 'The Modern System of the Arts: A Study in the History of Aesthetics', *Journal in the History of Ideas*, Vol. 12, 1951, pp. 496–527; see also id., *Renaissance Thought II: Papers on Humanism and the Arts*, New York, Harper and Row, 1965, pp. 163–227.
29. René Wellek and Austin Warren, *Theory of Literature*, Harmondsworth, Penguin, 3/1963, p. 102.
30. See Immanuel Kant, *Kritik der reinen Vernunft*, Part 2: *Transzendentale Dialektik, Anhang* (III. 8), in id., *Werke*, Darmstadt, Wissenschaftliche Buchgesellschaft, 1983, Vol. 4, pp. 563–82.

are never of constitutive use';[31] i.e., if an idea was at one time 'regulative', it was so at all times, since apart from regulative and constitutive uses no third category is given. Moreover, he speaks only of the 'regulative use of ideas of pure reason' (this the title of his chapter), not of 'regulative ideas' as such.

Goehr circumvents the difficulty with a historical argument, distinguishing between the regulative use of the work-concept as seen from 'within the practice' and as seen from without. 'Practice' here is a historical notion (not the opposite of theory) which is largely concerned with subsidiary constitutive concepts, such as the tradition of concert performances or musical notation – traditions which might be fluctuating – whereas the 'regulative concepts function stably because they are treated as if they were givens and not 'merely' as concepts that have artificially emerged and crystallised within a practice'.[32] Seen from without, however, the regulative concept can 'emerge' in a contingent and variously conditioned process.[33] And this is what it did towards 1800.

That the work-concept occupies a philosophically distinct status before and after 1800 arouses suspicion because it piles a powerful metahistorical argument on top of much evidence deduced from mere cultural history, as if the latter **were not enough**. There is an analogy here with Dahlhaus and Wiora, who approved of the idea that German idealist culture of Goethe's and Beethoven's time had raised its artistic practice to a level that was *sui generis*. That the work-concept supposedly occupied a regulative status simultaneously, and in combination, with other concepts that were only constitutive, exposes this construction to the challenge of defining musical practice and the priorities of musicians. What degree of consensus was actually needed? Could some practitioners have held the work-concept to be 'merely' contingent and constitutive, but different concepts to be regulative, say, the 'beautiful' or the 'musical', not to speak of 'composer-centredness'? These alternative candidates are by now part of the discourse, and I would hate to see Goehr having to adjudicate between them. Equally problematic is her implication that the (messy) process of emergence should have come to an end after 1800, when, somehow, everything had fallen into place, and the regulative concept

31. Ibid., p. 565.
32. Goehr (1992), p. 104.
33. Ibid., pp. 107–8.

was 'first able' to function explicitly – and that this cleaner state of affairs should have continued up to the late twentieth century.

It is essentialism to subordinate a historical tradition to a single and central definition that at the same time acts as its chronological, classificatory criterion. We are facing a theory of 'The Age of the Regulative Work-Concept'. This resembles the old idealist narratives which proposed that this was the age of Romanticism, and **therefore** what earlier ages had to offer along this line was not Romanticism but something else. Something else it surely was, but not because Romanticism was still to come. Ages do not differ in that one 'properly' answers a description formulated by us, the other not; whether ages answer descriptions depends on our selecting convincing ones for them in the first place.

Thus the Dahlhausian hovering between an idealist view of a musical concept or category 'above the times' and a statement about historical contingencies is exacerbated. Goehr's history of the work-concept implies the confusion of philosophical aesthetics with historiography. It lets keywords (such as *Werktreue*, a term that is not even at home in the nineteenth century) serve as categorial expressions of an age. In that sense, it is idealistic and also 'imperialistic': it imposes from outside categories that concern us more than them. There is a coincidence or tautology linking this remarkable late-twentieth-century effort to rationalise musical history with the alleged nineteenth-century effort to centralise and dominate all sorts of musical practice: the charge of 'conceptual imperialism' made against the idealist tradition must be laid also at Goehr's door. Further evidence of this can easily be found in her exaggerated and oversimplified descriptions of musical practices in both the eighteenth and nineteenth centuries (in chapters 7 and 8, respectively). Goehr's nineteenth century has not created 'popular' music nor indulged in folk song and exoticism; it has not appreciated performers (when they were good) above works, nor tried to create new 'non-work' genres such as the *Etude* or the *Albumblatt*, nor cultivated amateur music-making on a massive scale. I forgo addressing details of the eighteenth-century chapter, which gives an altogether unbelievable picture of musical reality, is full of generalisations and is largely concerned with secular ensemble music to the exclusion of other types. It has the assertion 'without the work-concept' emblazoned in its title and expresses a capital verdict of 'NOT YET' throughout.

Alternative Narratives

Michael Talbot's chapter 'The Work-Concept and Composer-Centredness' immediately bears out the problems inherent in Goehr's book by articulating concern over the distinction between 'works' and 'non-works', and over the different ways in which a work-concept might affect their respective creation. This suggests to me that the specialised music historian has difficulties in recognising a narrative which is mainly a tale about the development of a concept from one philosophical category ('constitutive') into another ('regulative'). In fact, when the distinction is applied to a particular work, it might not show. Talbot notes: 'Whatever the new-found regulative rôle is, it makes no discernible difference to the product considered in its own right'.[34] By way of constructive criticism, Talbot then shifts the ground from a consideration of works to that of their creators; what had been acknowledged by many previous writers as a typical *Daseinsform* of a musical work – to be created by a known author – is now a category of its own helping to construct musical history. It even overrides, in certain circumstances, the force of the work-concept to designate a musical culture, for example, when works and non-works by the same composer are treated in the same way by his contemporaries.

This last point implies the possibility that Talbot's 'composer-centredness' was relevant at a time when Goehr's work-concept was not, and indeed earlier. 'Composer-centredness' is in many ways apparent in historical circumstances where our knowledge of the status of works is limited. To give just two examples: the contemporary debates around Monteverdi's *seconda prattica* emphatically concern composition and the rôle of the composer, as, for instance, when the achievements of earlier masters are adduced (de Rore, de Wert, Marenzio), or when, in the preface to Monteverdi's fifth book of madrigals, the 'regulative' idea for the act of composing is revealed to be 'truth', culminating in the programmatic dictum that 'the modern composer creates' (*fabrica*) 'on the principles of *verità*'.[35] This, be it noted, in the genre of the madrigal, whose overt functionality prevents, for some scholars, their full appreciation as musical works. Other examples are the historiographies and chronologies of certain genres such as

34. Talbot, in this volume, p.170.
35. Claudio Monteverdi, *Lettere, dediche e prefazioni*, ed. Domenico de' Paoli, Rome, De Santis, 1973, p. 392.

Venetian seventeenth-century opera or Roman oratorio (Ivanovich, Spagna), where the composers of the music are acknowledged as co-authors and in any case famous men, being recommended to the general listening public. Today, the individual status of the opera's musical setting as a work and performance is subject to debate. I once attempted to characterise the status of late Baroque opera music as event-like rather than work-constituted;[36] this idea has since been taken up by others but I see more of a dialectic now between the 'written-ness' and work-character of this genre and the transient aspect of the performance event. To be sure, contemporary documents other than librettos – scores, archival entries, narrative accounts – very often speak of opera as a work created by a certain composer.

'Composer-centredness' is to a much higher degree a phenomenon of musical practice and circulation – modes of existence – than is 'workhood' (a term used by Goehr), which would be part of an 'essence' for Wiora. Talbot's criterion seems to merge more easily with social history, but this leads to a diffusion or ambiguity of historical categories. The question 'what sort of composer-centredness?' looms even larger now than in Goehr's case with the work-concept. Talbot points out, for instance, that the use of the plural form for the collected compositions of a single author, oeuvres or Werke, after c.1800 tended to upgrade even obvious non-works, arguing that it was the composer-centredness which in these cases constituted the cultural sea change. The fact that all the musical products of a certain individual were given blanket attention seems new and decisive to him. This example does not quite harmonise with the information that already in 1477 Tinctoris summarily admired the 'works' (opera) of Ockeghem and Dufay (see above). On the other hand, the observation reminds me of discussions in the 1970s concerning the preparation of the thematic catalogue and the collected edition of Wagner's works, when it seemed odd but inevitable that his musical entries into friends' diaries (Albumblätter, or just 'musical signatures') should receive opus numbers and be listed and critically edited alongside the music dramas.[37] This kind of composer-centredness was definitely a

36. See Strohm, Italienische Opernarien des frühen Settecento (1720–1730), 2 vols, Cologne, Volk, 1976 (= Analecta musicologica, 16).
37. To avoid misunderstandings, I am referring here not to the separable Albumblätter but to functional items such as WWV 101, 105, 106, 112 and 113, and to various arrangements and fragments: see John Deathridge, Martin Geck and Egon Voss, Wagner-Werkverzeichnis (WWV), Mainz, Schott, 1986.

late-twentieth-century phenomenon, although ostensibly centred on a nineteenth-century composer who was a centre unto himself. It is patent that Wagner would not have included all these occasional, private documents in a collected edition of his 'works'.

None of my examples, which seem to match Talbot's observations in different ways, supports the hypothesis of a watershed around 1800. Nor, to a surprising extent, do many of his own observations. Although he invokes the collected editions of the 1790s, there were earlier ones, for example, that of Hasse (completed but destroyed by war in 1761). Conversely, the attention to the lifetime production of Mozart and Haydn, insofar as this entailed the scrutiny of all the works or products together, was a trend beginning not in the 1790s but in the 1850s. The contemporary critical reception of Beethoven does not yet compare *Fidelio* with other Beethoven works published or composed simultaneously – this happened in the wake of the 'great composer' biographies and editions of the mid-century – but placed the opera along other contemporary operas and thus contributions to the progress of the genre. Mozart reception was tightly genre-bound in many ways until the late nineteenth century. Thus the advances of composer-centredness even in this small segment of reception history are remarkably spread out. Going further afield: Talbot's observation that classical record anthologies only recently became more composer-centred than performer-centred seems a pertinent glimpse at the post-1960s market; that critics and listeners should distinguish between the quality of a composition and its performance in a given situation, is clearly postulated by Johann Krieger and endorsed by Mattheson in 1725, although Talbot bewilderingly uses the quotation again to support the 1800 theory.[38]

Much is contained in Talbot's chapter on the substantial shifts of the status of composers in the medieval and Renaissance periods.[39] Single-author manuscript collections are said to be very rare before 1500, when the single-author prints (first of Josquin, Mouton, Isaac, Obrecht and Agricola) started to appear. What happened earlier in this direction, for instance, in the case of Machaut, is said to have to do with special, additional factors (the factor of emerging composer-

38. Talbot, p. 176n.11.
39. On the important developments occurring in the fifteenth century, see Strohm (1993) and Rob C. Wegman, 'From Maker to Composer: Improvisation and Musical Authorship in the Low Countries, 1450–1500', in *Journal of the American Musicological Society*, Vol. 49, 1996, pp. 409–79.

centredness, perhaps?). Rather than adduce further examples of composer collections before 1500, I wish to stress that Petrucci's idea of
printing single-author musical editions had a sweeping success in the
sixteenth century and brought composer-centredness into the homes
of patrons, connoisseurs and amateurs alike. Lasso's *Magnum opus
musicum* was a composer-centred collection of all his available motets
made by his sons, for the patrons and general public. It was not a
motet collection aimed merely at users of the genre, but it attempted
to show the highest of the master's characteristic achievements, which
were to be found in the most regulatively work-like genre, the motet.
Throughout the sixteenth and seventeenth centuries, the enormous
circulation of written or printed music of all genres by dead but
famous composers is nothing if not composer-centredness out there
in the marketplace. Finally, it is to the great credit of Talbot to have
reminded us of the initial 'spark' in matters of the work-concept and
all the related traditions: 'the decision of the Universal Church ... to
have a universally employed musical setting for its liturgy' and the
developments flowing from that.[40] The paragraph could almost have
been written by Wiora: compare his *The Four Ages of Music*.[41]

It seems, indeed, that the advances of both composer-centredness
and a regulative work-concept are spread out over many centuries of
Western history, in the same sense in which the bourgeoisie 'always
rises'; this situation just cannot be historiographically controlled with
one-line developmental models and philosophical categorisations. At
the very least, the temporal distances over which astonishingly similar phenomena can be observed suggest drastic changes of pace. I
would add: reversals of direction, multiplicity not only of developmental lines but also of developmental pace and type, and, finally, a
decisive amount of retrospective bending of all the evidence for the
sake of creating for ourselves a digestible past. This brings me to my
last section, which has so far attained the form only of single theses.

Theses

1 The historical narratives that diagnose a major watershed or categorial breakthrough in the development of the work-concept and
   related phenomena around 1800 evade the burden of proof that

40. Talbot, p. 182.
41. Wiora (1961), pp. 130–32.

ought to be placed on them: to show that previous phenomena were essentially – philosophically – different.

2 Chronological tendencies towards a pragmatic and normative higher status of the work-concept and composer-centredness in Western music can be observed over the whole of its history. The problem of 'infinite regression' cannot be solved by throwing a spanner in the works. Rather, the various stages of the development should be evaluated *sine ira et studio*.

3 Philosophical concepts, and in particular the notion of a 'regulative use of transcendental ideas' (Kant), are not suited to make up the criteria of a historical chronology. The identification itself of the musical work-concept with one of these regulative [uses of] ideas is spurious. It remains a historical phenomenon like others, subject to the possibility of divergent, parallel, intermittent and contradictory manifestations.

4 The decision to use philosophical categories to mark out specific processes in German musical history is inherited from European idealist and modernist scholars, who were motivated by their personal (tautological) identification with this past that they considered, in a world perspective, to be *sui generis* (Wiora).

5 The more recent, negatively valued use of the same idealist categories may be a product of the present anxiety over the collapse of the values of modernity and the fear of an isolation of the European cultural tradition in the world. It may function as a conservative attempt to define ourselves as 'children of 1800'.

6 Negative evaluations of the 'imperialist' work-concept dovetail with many other reificatory characterisations of the last 200 years to form a 'divided retrospection' with Oedipal connotations: an abominable father's age, the enlightened/modern age (after 1800), is contrasted with a happy grandfather's age, which had retained contact with the pastoral traditions of the rest of the world, until alienation through enlightenment and the work-concept took place.

7 It should now be acknowledged how much the universal awareness and the embrace of alternative traditions in the world of today is a result of the European tradition itself. Humanism, Enlightenment and its aftermath as well as other tendencies have brought Europeans in line with the world, have in fact conceptualised 'the world' as a cultural idea.

8 It is time to delimit (in the sense of 'cancel its limitations, erase its

borders') European cultural historiography altogether, including its musical history, by accepting and reinforcing the overriding tendency of our tradition, over the whole of its course, towards the universal and extraneous.

7

'The Work': An Evaluative Charge

Philip Tagg

Writing entries for the *Encyclopedia of Popular Music of the World* (*EPMOW*, forthcoming) is not an easy task. One recurrent problem is that concepts applied to the description of musical structure in the classical repertoire cannot always be used in the same way when denoting ostensible equivalents in the field of popular music.[1] Terminological convention also varies in the classification of harmonic practices as well as in the meaning of basic terms like 'beat' and 'chorus'. However, it is perhaps conventional musicology's notion of 'the work' that is the most awkward to use in the description of popular music. The problem can be illustrated by the following attempt to provide a definition of 'turnaround' for *EPMOW*.

> 1. (original meaning): a short progression of chords played at the end of one section in a song or instrumental number and whose purpose is to facilitate recapitulation of the complete harmonic sequence of that section or of another section within the same number; 2. (transferred meaning) any short sequence of chords, more than two and usually less than six, recurring consecutively inside the same piece of music.

The obvious difficulty here is one of terminology relating to what might or might not be called 'the work'. Note the clumsy expression 'song or instrumental number' and the way in which 'number' and 'piece of music' are used as synonyms. The question is how to refer to something that, within a given musical culture or subculture, is generally perceived as a musical continuum of determinate duration and of sufficient internal structural cohesion to be understood as sonically identifiable in itself from whatever precedes or follows it, as well as from other similarly integral sets of sequences of musical sound. The

---

1. For example: riff versus ostinato, tune versus melody.

concept is really quite simple, even self-evident. The problem is that I felt unable to use the word 'work' to denote this concept when defining 'turnaround', and that this notion is avoided also by most popular music scholars. Why?

The simple answer is that the notion of a musical work sounds pretentious, or at least incongruous, when used in popular music contexts. The aim of this essay is, therefore, to lay bare some of the mechanisms underpinning the practical problem of terminology just mentioned so that eventual alternatives can be based on firmer musical, historical, social and linguistic foundations than has often been the case with other terms employed in popular music scholarship.[2] The main part of this text seeks, in other words, to unravel some of the semantic and historical values attached to the word 'work', starting with its definitions and equivalents in various European languages.

Meanings and Values of 'The Work'

The English word 'work' has a multitude of meanings. Of particular relevance to our understanding of 'the musical work' are the following four:[3]

(i)   the application of mental or physical effort to a purpose;
(ii)   a thing done or made by work; the result of an action; an achievement;
(iii) a person's employment or occupation etc., esp. as a means of earning income;
(iv)   literary or musical composition.

2. For example, 'iconicity' is used incorrectly by John Shepherd and Peter Wicke in their book *Music and Cultural Theory* (Cambridge, Polity Press, 1997), while 'intertextuality' was generally used in an imprecise 'blanket' sense during a recent symposium organised by the Institute of Popular Music (University of Liverpool, 11–13 September 1998). Even such basic terms as 'beat' and 'rhythm' are also often used without clear definition or distinction (see Garry Tamlyn, *The Big Beat: Origins and Development of Snare Backbeat and Other Accompanimental Rhythms in Rock 'n' Roll'*, PhD dissertation, University of Liverpool, 1998).
3. The following reference works have been consulted for definitions, translations and synonyms: *Cassell's Compact Dutch Dictionary*, London, 1965; *Cassell's German Dictionary*, London, 1978; *Cassell's Italian Dictionary*, London, 1978; *Cassell's Latin–English, English–Latin Dictionary*, London, 1968; *Collins Spanish Dictionary*, London, 1982; *The Concise Oxford Dictionary of Current Eng-*

It is important to note that these meanings are ordered according to the chronology of their first recorded usage in the English language. The *Oxford English Dictionary* traces the original meaning of the word – 'application of mental or physical effort' – back to the Old English and Anglo-Saxon word *weorc* and considers the second meaning of the word – the result or effects of work, also in the sense of 'deed', including its ethical aspect (e.g., 'By your works shall ye be judged') – to have been in common use not much later. However, the majority of sources quoted by the *Oxford English Dictionary* in relation to the fourth meaning of the term – 'literary or musical composition' – date from the fourteenth century or later.[4]

Whoever consults *Roget's Thesaurus* for synonyms for 'work' in relation to the topic of this symposium is dispatched to such semantic fields as:

> 1. *exertion*: effort, struggle, strain, stress, trouble; labour, industry, work, hard work, donkey work, manual labour, grind, drudgery, slavery, compulsion, toil, chore, job, task. 2. *production*: creation, origination, invention, undertaking, authorship, performance, output, throughput, execution, accomplishment, achievement. 3. *composition*: combination, construction, production; ballet, musical piece, work of art, picture, portrait, sculpture, literary work. 4. *form*: shape, formation, structure, structuration, expression, formulation; organisation, pattern, constitution, fabric, texture. 5. *(musical work)*: piece, composition, opus, work; number, tune, track. 6. *skill*: masterpiece, chef d'oeuvre, pièce de résistance, masterwork, magnum opus, stroke of genius, coup-de-maître, feat, tour de force, work of art, objet d'art.

Labor Sive Opus?

The first striking distinction in these definitions of, and synonyms for,

lish, Oxford, Clarendon Press, 1995; *Dicionário Inglês–Português* and *Dicionário Português–Inglês*, Porto Editora, n.d.; *Langenscheidt's Standard Dictionary of the French and English Languages*, London, Hodder & Stoughton, 1968; *Greek–English Lexicon*, ed. Henry G. Liddell and Robert Scott, Oxford, Clarendon Press, 1871; *The Oxford Paperback Greek Dictionary*, Oxford, Oxford University Press, 1997; *The Oxford Paperback Russian Dictionary*, Oxford, Oxford University Press, 1996; *Le petit Robert*, Paris, Société du Nouveau Littré, 1970; *Roget's Thesaurus*, ed. Betty Kirkpatrick, Harlow, Longmans, 1987; *Swedish Dictionary*, London, Routledge, 1993 (Stockholm, Prisma, 1993).

4. See also Richard Middleton's Chapter 3, p. 85.

the English word 'work' is that between, on the one hand, work in its original sense (or work as experienced by the majority of people who have ever worked) and, on the other hand, work as the tangible outcome of work in its primary sense. In other words, English uses the same word ('work') to cover two concepts which in the majority of other European languages are denoted by separate words. For example, *douleia* and *ergo(n)* in Greek, *labor* and *opus* in Latin, *Arbeit* and *Werk* in German and the *arbete* and *verk* of Scandinavian languages, not to mention the *travail, trabajo, trabalho* and *oeuvre, obra, obra* of French, Spanish and Portuguese respectively, all underline the same dichotomy of, first, work as tiresome toil, tribulation, etc., and, second, work as the end-product of effort expended, more often than not by someone other than the person using that product.[5] It is obvious that the notion of a literary or musical work relates not to the former (*douleia, labor, lavoro, Arbeit, travail*, etc.) but to the latter: to *ergo(n), opus, opera, Werk, oeuvre*, etc. In other words, we are clearly referring to a product viewed (or heard) primarily from the perspective of the beholder, i.e. with the *ergo technés*, the *Kunstwerk*, the *oeuvre d'art* (the 'work of art') – not, in the case of music, with the *douleia tou mousikou* or the *Arbeit der Musiker* or the *travail du musicien*. In short, the notion of 'musical work' refers not to the labour invested by composer or musician to generate the product or to derive income from it but to the product of that labour from an 'end-user perspective'. Equally clear distinctions are made in these languages between, say, *un grand travail* and *une grande oeuvre* (or the equivalent pair of words in German, Spanish, etc.), each of which literally means 'a big work' but would translate more correctly as 'a lot of work' and 'a great work' respectively. It is interesting to note here that English, in order to compensate for having only the single noun 'work', distinguishes the two concepts by qualifying that same noun either quantitatively ('a lot') or evaluatively ('great').[6]

---

5. It is worth noting in this context (i) that *travail, trabajo* and *trabalho* derive from *tripaliare*, popular Latin for 'to whip with the *tripalium*', a birch rod sporting sharp thorns used by Roman masters on their slaves during forced labour; (ii) that the word has entered the popular Latin languages of former Roman colonies – although Italian distinguishes between *travaglio*, carrying the sense of pain, torment, distress or labour in particular, and *lavoro* (from *labor, laboris*), for work in general; (iii) that *douleia* originally meant slavery (cf. *doulos* = slave).
6. It should be noted that English accords 'work' a much larger, and 'labour' a much narrower, range of meanings than do other languages. For example, Russ-

As self-evident as these observations may appear, they still constitute, as the difference between 'a lot of work' and 'a great work' suggests, much more than a mere philological nicety; for although, from
a European perspective, the English language may be idiosyncratic in
the manner just described, other languages – French, German, Greek,
Portuguese, Russian, Spanish, Swedish, and, to a lesser extent, Italian[7]
– all include some element of evaluation in their distinction between
the equivalents of *travail* and *oeuvre* in relation to the production of
art. The next part of this essay discusses such elements of evaluation
in relation to music.

Opus, Work and Aesthetic Value

'Beauty', it is said, 'is in the eye of the beholder'; and since with the
musical work we are dealing with a product whose use-value resides
in its capacity to please, disturb, excite, entertain or otherwise com-
municate a series of affective or gestural states and processes,[8] the
notion of a 'musical work' can assume an evaluative dimension,
depending on whether the work pleases, disturbs, excites, entertains,
or otherwise provides the required aesthetic use-value. Now,
although beauty may be in the eye or ear of the beholder (in the singular), beauty and other notions of aesthetic value are not only an
individual matter: they are just as much a collective issue, simply
because similar opinions and values are held by many beholders (in
the plural), this community of taste being more often than not related
to other cultural as well as to social and economic aspects of commu-

ian distinguishes four separate concepts relating to 'work': (1) *rabota*, meaning
work in general; (2) *trúd*, meaning labour, toil, etc.; (3) *proïzvedennïe*, meaning
a work of art, a production or product; (4) *iskússtvo*, in the sense of workmanship, craft or art.

7. Because of the particular meaning of *opera* as 'opera', the distinction in Italian
between *lavoro* and *opera* is to some extent less clear than that between *travail*
and *oeuvre* in French or *Arbeit* and *Werk* in German, the Italian for 'masterwork'
being *capolavoro* rather than the direct linguistic equivalent of *chef d'oeuvre* or
Meisterwerk.

8. This characterisation of aesthetic use-value is not unlike that provided by
Horace: Aut prodesse volunt, aut delectare poetae / aut simul et iucunda et
idonea dicere vitae' (Poets want either to benefit or to entertain or to say things
that are at the same time pleasing and relevant to life): *Ars poetica*, lines 333–34,
quoted by Gioseffo Zarlino in *Le istitutioni harmoniche*, III (Venice, 1558);
reproduced in Oliver Strunk, *Source Readings in Music History*, London, Faber
& Faber, 1952, p. 229.

nity. The observation may seem trite, but it is easy to overlook its importance, the existence of such a community being a *conditio sine qua non* for the social survival of any set of musical practices.[9]

Now, the existence of different communities of aesthetic value within society does not in itself produce a moral, ethical or terminological dilemma: on the contrary, the function-related aesthetics of, for example, different music clubs (*vú hà*) in Ewe culture play an important part in codifying the rôles and characters of different groups within the larger community (young or old, fast or slow, male or female, etc.).[10] Differences of aesthetic community can in this way be structured horizontally rather than vertically, and can be considered of equal status or as mutually complementary within a larger social structure in a manner homologous with the polyrhythmic structure of much Ewe music, which demands the simultaneous occurrence of clearly articulated, contrasted figures in different metres entering at different points in time as prerequisites for the construction of an integral sonic whole. No: our terminological problems start with social stratification, because if groups or classes within society are organised hierarchically, people belonging to (or aspiring to belong to) a ruling class will tend to assume that the aesthetic values

9. For example, the commercial viability of any format radio relies totally on the assumption that community of musical taste is a reasonably reliable indicator of other collective characteristics, e.g. lifestyle, social status or economic status. Such assumptions have also theoretical and empirical underpinning in social science, as the following quotation illustrates. 'Concerned by the Nazi and Stalinist use of radio and movies for state propaganda in the 1930s, a number of scholars turned to look at the impact of the mass media on society. [Ernst] Krenek, [Herbert] Blumer, [Theodor] Adorno and [Harold] Lasswell were soon joined at Columbia University by [Robert] Merton and [Paul] Lazarsfeld who founded the Office of Radio Research which became the Bureau of Applied Social Research. They, with their students, did a whole set of studies on the media industries, their program content, and effects on their audiences. ... Ironically, what began in the 1930s as a concern with totalitarian political propaganda became, by the 1950s, the intellectual fountainhead of "motivation research" – the prime tool of Madison Avenue advertisers' (Serge Denisoff and Richard A. Peterson, *The Sounds of Social Change*, Chicago, Rand McNally, 1972, pp. 4–5). Format radio mushroomed in the USA in the 1950s, its income deriving from advertising and the target audience from community of musical taste.

10. See the explanations provided by the Ghanaian musicologist Klevor Abo (a pupil of J. H. Kwabena Nketia) in Philip Tagg, '"Universal" Music and the Case of Death', *Critical Quarterly*, Vol. 35 (1993), pp. 57–58.

of that class are commensurate with class superiority in other cultural, as well as in economic, terms. One common way of justifying such a viewpoint is to try and link the intrinsically transitory habits, mores and values of the privileged class to phenomena that appear to transcend the historically specific and culturally relative nature of the social system over which this class presides.

For example, in such societies as those of Ancient Egypt, Mesopotamia and China the ruling classes sought in various ways to establish links between their music, including its structuration, modes of reception, etc., and supposedly immutable or universal truths, including the position of stars, mathematical ratios and the cycle of seasons, thereby creating the impression that the aesthetic values of their class and, consequently, the social system over which they ruled, were as immutable or universal as the phenomena with which they were held to be linked.[11] Of course, all the social systems just alluded to, together with the aesthetic values of their ruling classes, have died out; they have been replaced by competing social systems and sets of values. The rise of capitalism and the bourgeois revolution in Europe, understood here as a lengthy historical process and not as an individual event, brought about one such substitution, in that one set of irrational tenets about music (those of the medieval church) were replaced with a new, but equally confused, set of aesthetic values.[12] Indeed, the overridingly metaphysical character of Romantic music aesthetics, especially that of German-speaking intellectuals of the

11. See: Robert Anderson, 'Egypt (I)', in *The New Grove Dictionary of Music and Musicians*, ed. Stanley Sadie, London, Macmillan, 1980, Vol. 6, pp. 70–75; Paul Crossley-Holland, 'Non-Western Music', in *The Pelican History of Music*, ed. Alec Robertson and Denis Stevens, Harmondsworth, Penguin Books, 1960–68, Vol. 1, pp. 13–135; Hans Hickmann, *Ägypten*, Leipzig, 1961; Jan Ling, *Kompendium i musikhistoria*, unpublished teaching materials, University of Göteborg, 1974; id., *Europas musikhistoria – 1730*, Uppsala, Esselte, 1983; Wilhelm Stauder, 'Mesopotamia', in *The New Grove*, Vol. 12, pp. 196–201.

12. See: Dénes Zoltai, *Ethos und Affekt. Geschichte der philosophischen Musikästhetik von den Anfängen bis zu Hegel*, Berlin, Akademie-Verlag and Budapest, Akadémiai Kiadó, 1970; Georg Knepler, *Musikgeschichte des 19. Jahrhunderts*, Berlin, Henschelverlag, 1961; Jan Ling, 'Musik som klassisk konst. En 1700-talsidé som blev klassisk', in *Frihetens former – en vänbok till Sven-Eric Liedman*, Lund, Arkiv, 1989; *Music and Aesthetics in the Eighteenth and Early Nineteenth Centuries*, ed. Peter le Huray and James Day, Cambridge, Cambridge University Press, 1988; Carl Dahlhaus, *Nineteenth-Century Music*, trans. J. B. Robinson, Berkeley, University of Californa Press, 1989.

time, is well documented, to the extent that what was to become known as 'classical music' was frequently held to transcend the supposedly petty concerns of everyday existence.[13]

As part of this process, the official image of a composer became less that of a skilled worker or tradesman, e.g. Bach or early Haydn, providing a service for courts and church, and more that of the genius who, it was often assumed, relied on the magic of artistic urges to produce 'works' (oeuvres, Werke), not in order to make a living but for the edification and entertainment of certain social couches.[14] These 'works' could then be managed by agents charging entrance fees to concerts or recitals and commodified by publishers in the form of sheet music sold to persons prosperous or famous enough to own a decent piano or to put on musical soirées in their parlour. In fact, although the European notion of a musical work (and of its concomitant evaluative charge) dates back at least as far as Tinctoris,[15] the practice of cataloguing a composer's works by opus number first became commonplace in the merchant city of Venice towards the middle of the seventeenth century. Indeed, it is in the following terms that the New Grove entry for Opus cautions those scholars who might

13. See, for example, Ludwig Tieck, 'Phantasien über die Kunst für Freunde der Kunst' (1799), and Wilhelm Heinrich Wackenroder, 'Die Wunder der Tonkunst' (1799), both cited in Per Druud-Nielsen, Musik og betydningsinhold, unpublished teaching materials in music aesthetics, University of Århus, 1983; Dahlhaus (1989), pp. 16, 56, 94–95, 171. The quintessence of nineteenth-century transcendentalism in relation to music exudes from the pen of De Lamennais, who wrote: '[Music] ... lifts man above earthly things and imports him to a perpetual upward motion ... Music's goal is infinite beauty. Consequently it tends to represent the ideal model, the eternal essence of things, rather than things as they are. For, as Rousseau so correctly observed, "Outside the individual being existing on his own, there is nothing beautiful apart from that which is not"' (Hughes Félicité Robert de Lamennais, Esquisse d'une philosophie (1840), part II, book 8, chapters 1–2, and Book 9, chapter 1, as quoted in le Huray and Day (1988), pp. 351–55. The Rousseau quotation is left untranslated by these editors – understandably so, for its meaning is rather obscure: 'Hors le seul être existant par lui même, il n'y a rien de beau que ce qui n'est pas'.

14. For an historical account of this process from Bach and early Haydn to late Haydn and Beethoven, see Dahlhaus (1989), pp. 171–75.

15. In 1477 Tinctoris mentions Ockeghem, Dunstaple, Binchois, Dufay and several other composers (see the present essay by Reinhard Strohm, p. 143n.26: 'Quorum omnium omnia fere opera tantam suavitudinem ...'). Significantly, it was during a flourishing period for early mercantile capitalism in Northern France (Chartres) that Tinctoris worked before moving to the court of Naples.

assume opus numbers from that period to be chronological in relation to composition or performance date:[16]

> Numbers were not applied until publication, and then often by the publisher, not the composer ... Where the same work appears with two publishers, it may have different numbers assigned to it ... Until 1800 opus numbers were more common in instrumental than in vocal music and they have rarely been applied to stage compositions at any period largely because numbering was related to publications, not to pieces.

This information corroborates earlier observations about 'work' as a term denoting not the composer's actual labour but the product of that labour from an end-user viewpoint; it also underlines the notion of 'work' as commodity, here in the shape of sheet music, whose use-value for the publisher resides in its potential for capital accumulation. But there is more: we learn also that opus numbers were assigned to instrumental music much more than to vocal music or to stage compositions. Now, it is most likely that the reasons for this practice were purely logistical, i.e. that one composer could produce any number of sonatas or *concerti grossi*, each requiring its own number for purposes of unique identification in a catalogue, but rarely more than one song and certainly no more than one stage work bearing the same name. However, in pursuing the historical values embedded in the concept of a musical work, it is worth recalling a passage from Hegel's *Aesthetics*:

> What the layman (*Laie*) likes in music is the comprehensible expression of emotions and ideas, something substantial, its contents, for which reason he prefers accompanimental music (*Begleitmusik*); the connoisseur (*Kenner*), on the other hand, who has access to the inner musical relation of tones and instruments, likes instrumental music for its artistic use of harmonies and of melodic intricacy as well as for its changing forms; he can be quite fulfilled by the music on its own.[17]

16. David Fuller, 'Opus', in *The New Grove*, Vol. 13, p. 656. The first composer to whose instrumental works opus numbers were systematically assigned by the publisher was apparently the Brescian violinist Biagio Marini (1587–1663).
17. Friedrich Hegel's *Ästhetik* (Berlin, Aufbau-Verlag, 1955), quoted in Zoltai (1970), p. 260: 'Der *Laie* liebt in der Musik vornehmlich den verständlichen Ausdruck von Empfindungen und Vorstellungen, das Stoffartige, den Inhalt, und wendet sich daher vorzugsweise der begleitenden Musik zu; der *Kenner* dagegen, dem die inneren musikalischen Verhältnisse der Töne und Instrumente zugänglich sind, liebt die Instrumentalmusik in ihrem kunstgemässen Gebrauch

It would be foolish to propose any direct causal link between the practice of numbering instrumental works and Hegel's valorisation of
instrumental music, and equally misguided to try to date the first
widespread evaluative use of the term 'work' to the early nineteenth
century. Clearly, Hegel's ideas about music are unlikely to derive from
the commercial logistics of music publishing and much more likely to
be influenced by ideas of the German *Aufklärung*. To paraphrase
Charles Ford rather drastically,[18] this intellectual and artistic movement, with its *Empfindsamkeit*, its *Sturm und Drang*, etc., differed
considerably from the Enlightenment in France or England, not least
because the socio-economic base of the German bourgeoisie in the
eighteenth century under the rule of a multitude of quasi-absolute
minor potentates was much weaker than that of the same class living
in larger nation-states, such relative disempowerment resulting in the
need to concentrate much more on the expression of ostensibly private or subjective, rather than public or objective, aspects of individual liberty. It is from such a perspective that the importance accorded
to music by German-speaking composers of the eighteenth and nineteenth centuries in germanophone Europe (and, indeed, across the
world) starts to make sense. It is from the same perspective (the ideological peculiarities of the *Aufklärung*) that the primacy of instrumental music, as advocated by Wackenroder or Tieck before Hegel
and also by Adolf Bernhard Marx, Eduard Hanslick and a host of
others after Hanslick, can be understood as more than the mere metaphysical meanderings of misguided romantics, however much it may
appear that way with historical hindsight. When trying to pinpoint
the historical place and time for the linking of the evaluative notion
of 'musical work' with the aesthetics of absolute music, and when
concluding that location to be German-speaking Europe in the early
nineteenth century, we are therefore positing a conjuncture of ideas
and events which (by definition as conjuncture in the Gramscian
sense) cannot be explained in simple terms of linear causality: rather,
we are dealing with the conflux of a multitude of lengthy, sometimes
contradictory historical processes in dialectical interaction that crys-
tallise into a more easily perceptible whole at a particular historical

der Harmonien und melodischen Verschlingungen und wechselnden Formen; er
wird durch die Musik selbst ganz ausgefüllt.' Note that Hegel placed vocal music
in the category of *Begleitmusik* (translatable as 'accompanimental music').
18. Charles Ford, *Così? Sexual Politics in Mozart's Operas*, Manchester, Manchester
University Press, 1991, pp. 2–4, 31–37.

time and place. In other words, we are in agreement with Lydia Goehr that it was around 1800 – and, it should be added, primarily among intellectuals in German-speaking Europe – that the concept of 'work' (in the sense of musical end product or commodity) started to become more frequently identified with the superior aesthetic values that many keepers of the 'classical' seal have attributed to a certain kind of Central European instrumental music ever since.[19] This point of conjuncture contains many other strands of relevance to the understanding of the term under discussion.

As Carl Dahlhaus has explained, the (then) new romantic aesthetic also prioritised 'texts' rather than 'performances', the latter becoming a function of the former rather than vice-versa, as had been the case previously and as is today the case with much music qualifiable as 'popular'.[20] Two further interrelated problems are associated with this attachment of aesthetic value to the work-concept.

First, attempts to identify what ought to be grasped from the work as a 'text', even if its performance may have been a fiasco, have resulted in such categories as 'overriding formal concept' and 'thematic manipulation' being placed on a pedestal, while notions of affect have been relegated to a much lower level and sometimes even referred to in such derogatory terms as 'stage emotion' or 'histrionics'. The manner in which Beethoven symphonies were subsequently provided with exegeses by such figures as A. B. Marx or Hermann Kretzschmar for the benefit of music students and devotees of cultivated concert music underlines the primacy of the work as the text of an *auteur* and the primacy of a supposedly abstract formal narrative within the work.[21]

19. Lydia Goehr, *The Imaginary Museum of Musical Works: An Essay in the Philosophy of Music*, Oxford, Clarendon Press, 1992, p. 115.
20. Dahlhaus (1989), pp. 9–12.
21. See: Adolf Bernhard Marx, *Ludwig van Beethoven, Leben und Schaffen*, Leipzig, Breitkopf & Härtel, 1902; Hermann Kretzschmar, *Gesammelte Aufsätze aus den Jahrbüchern der Musikbibliotek Peters*, Leipzig, Breitkopf & Härtel and C. F. Peters, 2 vols, 1910–11; id., *Führer durch den Konzertsaal*, Leipzig, Breitkopf & Härtel, 1919. Dahlhaus (1989), p. 9, comments that 'Beethoven's symphonies [came to] represent inviolable musical "texts" whose meaning is to be deciphered with "exegetical" interpretations; a Rossini score, on the other hand [was regarded as] a mere recipe for performance, and it is the performance which forms the crucial aesthetic arbiter as the realisation of a draft rather than an exegesis of a text'. Note also that *Le petit Robert* takes pains to identify *oeuvre* in relation to authorship: 'l'oeuvre d'un écrivain, d'un artiste'.

Second, the tendency to accord pride of place to 'overriding formal concept', as just mentioned, and the need to find convincing arguments for such primacy in the establishment of an 'autonomous' aesthetics of music, have led to a bias for musical parameters operational in the construction of form and in thematic manipulation, i.e. to a concentration on tonal aspects, particularly harmony, with less regard paid to melodic profile or articulation,[22] even less on periodicity, much less still on rhythm or metre, and practically nothing at all on timbre. There has developed an impressive arsenal of terms and theories constituting a conceptual universe relevant to the complexities of harmony and formal construction but of minor relevance to any music whose interest is created primarily through complexities found in other parameters of expression. Such a one-sided understanding of musical complexity is also related to the evaluative concept of the musical work, in that the parameters relevant to the aesthetics of 'absolute' music are notatable – reproducible in the commodity form of sheet music or written score – whereas the others are much less so, if at all.

'Work', Value, Aesthetics and Musical Institutionalisation

The critical reader will surely be aware that the narrative of this essay has now entered the realm of music's institutionalisation upon our continent. Indeed, it is with this institutionalisation, rather than at the cross-roads of the historical conjuncture described above, that the main dangers of aesthetic evaluation in relation to the work-concept are to be found. We are now no longer dealing with intellectual or artistic processes in the making, nor with the historical specificity or logic of those processes, but with the logistics of power. We are dealing with part of the conceptual equivalent to the petrification of composers as those little alabaster busts that classical buffs used to keep (and still keep) on top of their well-polished pianos.[23] The irony of

22. Schumann saw fit to speak of melody as the 'battle cry of dilettantes' (Dahlhaus (1989), p. 12). Compare the aversion of late-nineteenth-century German music aesthetes towards the work of Verdi with the thorough treatment of the topic in Gino Stefani, 'Melody: A Popular Perspective', *Popular Music*, Vol. 4 (1987), pp. 21–36, and in Gino Stefani and Luca Marconi, *La melodia*, Milan, Bompiani, 1992.

23. To illustrate this point, Dahlhaus (1989), p. 79, includes a photograph of a Beethoven statue, the composer clad in a bourgeois coat folded like a Roman toga.

this process is that the dynamic independence that instrumental music once possessed in relation to other, older, forms of music that were felt to be fettered by certain types of extra-musical bonding was stripped of that historicity and, in a new state of sanctity, preserved in conservatories that by 1900 had virtually eradicated anything that might upset the canon, including the ornamentation and improvisation techniques that had once been part of the tradition whose champions the same conservatories professed to be.[24] This left the seemingly supra-social 'music itself' deep-frozen in the shape of sacrosanct works commodified as notation and recruiting a century and a half of 'broiler instrumentalists' to perpetuate it.[25] In short, we need to remember that the proportion of living to dead composers in the concert repertoire in France fell from 3 against 1 in the 1780s to 1 against 3 in the 1870s, and that this process was aided rather than impeded, by the hegemonic notion of a musical work.[26] We need also to remember that over a hundred years later the classical canon still reigns supreme in concert halls, as well in many institutions of higher education and research across Europe. It is when seen in this light that the notion of a 'musical work' becomes highly problematic and appears too pretentious for application in the field of popular music scholarship.

24. Much about classical ornamentation practice has had to be rediscovered in recent years, and the art of improvisation has been continuously practised in the classical tradition only by church organists. It is also worth remembering that improvisation was once one of the most important creative practices of the European classical music tradition: Landini, Sweelinck, Buxtehude, Bach, Handel, Mozart, Beethoven, Liszt and Franck were all renowned not only as composers but also as improvisers; one of Beethoven's bitterest complaints about his deafness was that it impaired his ability to improvise.

25. have to thank Jan Ling (University of Göteborg) for the expression 'piano broiler', which denotes the conservatory student who, neither improvising nor composing, practises scales, Czerny études and the canonic repertoire twelve hours a day in the hope of emerging as an acclaimed virtuoso in a saturated classical music performance labour market. This may seem a harsh caricature, but it is much less severe than what Hindemith, in *A Composer's World* (Cambridge, Mass., Harvard University Press, 1952, pp. 218ff), had to say about the standard conservatory mentality.

26. Ling (1989), p. 173, citing William Weber, 'How Concerts Went Classical in the Nineteenth Century', *Proceedings of the Annual Meeting of the Western Society for French History 1977*, Vol. 5, pp. 161–68.

Que Faire?

I do not intend to raise other problems of terminology relating to musical 'events', 'performances', 'songs', 'pieces' or 'works' that are specific to popular music scholarship, since these issues are eloquently raised and amply discussed by other contributions to this symposium. There is, however, a pressing need to find some kind of solution to the terminological issue raised at the start of this essay. We are faced, I think, with two general alternatives.

The first, and in my view ideal, solution would be to trust (in the hegemonic spirit of market economy) to some sort of terminological self-regulation and to derive our definitions from established practice in the manner adopted by dictionaries. The advantage of such a policy is that terminology can be based on a wide consensus of what is perceived to be a 'work', a 'piece', a 'number', a 'performance', an 'event', etc., the proven validity of any term residing in its general perception, function and usage. However, the disadvantage is as obvious as it is crippling: such consensual practice has yet to become established.

If *a posteriori* terminology, by its very nature descriptive of conceptual practice, is not feasible, and if our need to find satisfactory nomenclature is at all important, then we have no choice but to opt for a prescriptive terminology: 'prescriptive' in the sense of providing adequate terms in advance of concepts in common use, whether or not those common terms subsequently coincide with those we suggest. The main problem with this strategy is similar to that of our predecessors who tried to formulate the aesthetic practices and ideals of instrumental music around the time of the bourgeois revolution in Europe. Just as their attempts, whether with historical hindsight we agree with them or not, to systematise specific aspects of (then) contemporary trends in music were later institutionalised, petrified, falsified, preserved and repeated like litanies for over a hundred years, we need to be acutely aware of our own processes of institutionalisation; of our own canons (however 'subcultural', 'emergent' or 'alternative' they may currently appear to be); of our own subjectivities and their relation to careers, income and success. As popular music scholars, we also need to bear in mind that music produced by speakers of English, often with paratexts using the English language, is now at least as widespread throughout the world as music in the Central European tradition was just over a century ago, and that we ourselves are anglophone academics attempting to understand, and explain the workings of, such music. Without such self-reflection and historical awareness, popular music scholars could end up like the rearguard of the old aesthetic canon, ethnocentrically claiming universal, absolute and other supra-socially transcendent values for one set of musical practices and ignoring the real conditions, functions, contexts and structural complexities of others.

8

The Work-Concept and
Composer-Centredness

Michael Talbot

In her important and provocative book *The Imaginary Museum of Musical Works* Lydia Goehr presents what she calls her 'central claim' in the following terms:

> The claim is that given certain changes in the late eighteenth century, persons who thought, spoke about, or produced music were able for the first time to comprehend and treat the activity of producing music as one primarily involving the composition and performance of works. The work-concept at this point found its regulative rôle. This claim is not committed to the supposition that the work-concept has, since this time, retained its original foundation in the sense that it has come to take on no further meaning. Nor does it imply that composers producing music in centuries prior to the nineteenth were not producing works. Thus, despite the story of its emergence into a regulative concept in the late-eighteenth century, the use of the work-concept is not confined to products only of this and later periods.[1]

Whatever one's initial reaction to this bold statement, the identification of the late eighteenth century as a watershed in the evolution of music coincides with certain other great historical changes that are commonly recognised as having affected music around the same time. All of them have to do with increased autonomy in some shape or form. In the sphere of social conditions, we see the emergence on a mass scale of the fully professional but essentially freelance composer and/or virtuoso performer who, in a way recognisably modern, invents a personal manner of livelihood by 'commuting' between different sources of income (selling compositions to publishers, fulfilling private commissions, giving music lessons, appearing at public concerts as

1. Lydia Goehr, *The Imaginary Museum of Musical Works: An Essay in the Philosophy of Music*, Oxford, Clarendon Press, 1992, p. 113.

director or soloist, etc.). In that of consumption, we observe the rise of music serving as pure recreation, whether in a domestic setting or in the concert hall, and the associated move into a dominant position of 'non-functional' – generally instrumental – music, henceforth freed from dependence on religious or secular ceremony or social activities such as dancing and banqueting. In that of repertoire, we note the formation, for the first time, of a universal musical 'canon': a cumulatively expanding body of performed compositions comprising what are reckoned the best from both past and present. All these developments were, of course, mutually supportive and perhaps even mutually dependent. Without the institutions of commercial music publication and the public concert, both potentially lucrative sources of income, composers would not have been able to break free in such large numbers from their older mode of existence as artisan-functionaries beholden (usually) to a single employer. Conversely, without entrepreneurially minded composers, music publishing and public concerts would never have flourished as they did.

To these developments, all well in train as the nineteenth century succeeded the eighteenth, Lydia Goehr adds a further one: the acquisition by the work-concept of a regulative rôle. There are two interesting components of this formulation that need at the outset to be discussed. One is the manner in which a regulative function operates. The other is how, if at all, a work is affected by being produced according to a specific concept.

Goehr takes pains, in the paragraph quoted earlier, to explain that musical works exist objectively irrespective of the regulative rôle assigned (or not) to the work-concept. She is definitely not claiming that within the Western art-music tradition works, as we understand the term today, did not exist prior to 1800 or a little earlier. A widely held view of musicologists is that Western art music has been, since the days of the first notated plainsong, a tradition distinguished from virtually all other musics by its cultivation in the form of discrete works having (a) a fixed beginning and end, and (b) an identity based on a blueprint for performance (or, if one prefers, silent contemplation) encoded in notation.[2] I find nothing in Goehr's book to

2. Later in her book (pp. 114–15) Goehr argues that although pre-1800 composers produced what we retrospectively call works, which function in today's repertoire exactly as post-1800 works do, the fact that these products were not structured by the work-concept at the time of their composition is important.

contradict this view, which accords with my own belief. Jazz, in contrast, does not normally deal in 'works'. It has 'standards' (such as *Honeysuckle Rose*), but different live or recorded performances based on the same standard are not reducible to a common work. Even a classical theme or short piece treated as a jazz standard thereby forfeits its status as a work (which is not to deny that in its changed rôle it may acquire a new, possibly preferable, status!). However, Goehr is nowhere talking of genuine 'non-works' such as a version of *Night Train* by Oscar Peterson or a *doina* improvised by Klezmer musicians. The only distinction she draws is between works within the Western art-music tradition respectively recognised and not recognised as such by their composers. The problem with this is that the earlier, 'non-recognised' works resemble the later, 'recognised' ones in every way. They possess absolutely no general features (such as a strong reliance on improvisation or an indeterminate ending) that would bring them closer to the class of non-works. Whatever the new-found regulative rôle is, it makes no discernible difference to the product considered in its own right.

Ultimately, what Goehr must be talking about is not works in relation to the work-concept but rather the work-concept in relation to works. In other words, the intended accent falls on the musical culture that brings forth works rather than the physiognomy of the products themselves. But the potential trouble with the term 'work-concept' is that, by including 'work' as the first element in a compound expression, it tends to divert attention from the broader context towards the individual product, as well as implying that if the regulative control of the concept is missing, this product is liable to be different or even deficient in some way.

In the main part of my essay I will describe what I perceive as a further great change that affected music around 1800 and which should be viewed as complementary to those mentioned in my second

Certainly, the fact that early composers preferred to refer to musical compositions by an appropriate genre title (sonata, overture, etc.) rather than a catch-all term such as 'work', which Goehr adduces as prime evidence, cannot be gainsaid as a generalisation. What is at issue, however, is the conclusion that one draws from this. In my opinion, the increased use since 1800 of the term 'work' (including synonyms such as 'composition' and cognates in other languages) points to something much broader than a belated embrace by composers, performers and audiences of declared works. What this is forms the core of my essay.

paragraph. My argument is, at least in part, a reformulation of Lydia Goehr's 'central claim' using a different vocabulary and originating from a non-philosophical background. Perhaps it is less similar to hers than I think it is and merely borrows some of the same evidence to make a different point. Whatever the case, I gladly acknowledge the inspiration I have drawn from *The Imaginary Museum of Musical Works*.

Composers and Works

Let us first examine the implications of Goehr's perceptive observation that prior to 1800 the use of the term 'work' (together with 'composition', *oeuvre, Werk* and all other synonyms and equivalents in foreign languages) to denote a single musical product is very rare.[3] The truth of the observation can best be gauged by studying the incidence, before and after *c.*1800, of the plural form 'works' in relation to individual composers. For the whole point of 'work' as a catch-all term is that it refers indiscriminately to products of any size, specification and purpose. It is as apt for a Beethoven bagatelle as for *Fidelio*. If we therefore speak of the 'works of Beethoven', we place under one roof musical products of widely contrasted types. The only conditions they have to satisfy are that (a) they are musical products of some sort and (b) Beethoven wrote them.

The interesting thing is that, to the best of my knowledge, we have to wait for the collected editions of selected composers issued by Breitkopf & Härtel precisely around 1800 to see 'works' used in the plural with this sense. Samuel Arnold's collected edition of Handel's music (1787–97), the grandfather of such enterprises, eschews the word completely, but we encounter it in 1798, when the Leipzig firm inaugurates its *Oeuvres complettes* [sic] of Mozart, followed in 1800 and 1803 by similarly titled series devoted respectively to the music of Haydn and Clementi. It soon becomes normal to use 'work' and 'composition' in this non-specific sense.[4] As Goehr remarks, the shift

---

3. Goehr (1992), pp. 115–19.
4. In the much narrower sense of 'opus' (applicable only to an item published with the composer's sanction) the term 'work' is applied to music much earlier. For example, Johann Mattheson's treatise *Der musicalische Patriot* (Hamburg, 1728) contains on pp. 373–74 a chronological list of the author's 'Werke', which comprise both literary and musical publications.

of usage brings music into line with literature (originally, 'composition' was understood more as a literary than, as today, a predominantly musical term) and the fine arts.[5] Indeed, it serves to equate music with the other arts and thereby elevate its status, causing the composer (and, in some circumstances, the performer) to be perceived as an artist rather than an artisan. The 'works' of Goethe, Beethoven and Goya are from this point onwards placed on a common level and evaluated according to similar criteria. The steep and rapid rise in the relative importance of instrumental and absolute music after 1800 is predicated on the new-found belief that music need not (more radically formulated: music **should** not) hang on the coat-tails of another practice in order to be accorded the dignity and meaningfulness of high art.

However, the fact that one should suddenly wish, under certain conditions, to lump together under the common denominator of 'work' a bagatelle (or even a set of bagatelles) and *Fidelio* suggests an even more radical shift. My own 'central claim' is this: between 1780 and 1820, approximately, a genre-centred and performer-centred practice became a composer-centred one.[6] Ordinary music-lovers in their mass (we are not talking here of practitioners, patrons and connoisseurs) began to 'sort' music in their minds primarily according to composer, and not, as previously, according to genre (a term broadened here to include medium and style, factors closely intertwined with genre) or performer. I should make it clear that I do not regard my own 'central claim' as antagonistic to Goehr's; indeed, it is complementary, even though my emphases are different.

The result, which has remained basically stable since the middle of the nineteenth century, is evident any time one visits the 'classical' section of a record shop. The largest number of recordings are displayed alphabetically by composer, from Adam to Zemlinsky. Much smaller displays are devoted to music in specific genres or media (e.g., Opera, Choral Music) or performed by specific artists (e.g., Glenn Gould).[7] If one now moves across to the 'popular' or 'jazz' section of the same shop, one will see that very different criteria for organisation, ones

5. Goehr (1992), pp. 148–57 and *passim*.
6. For brevity, I will hereafter use '1800' as shorthand for the whole period both before and after 1800 during which the change occurred.
7. Many of the recordings displayed in these sections are likely to be there only because, being anthologies containing works by several composers, they cannot easily be placed in the alphabetical series.

that would have been more familiar to music-lovers before 1800, are in force. The primary sorting is by genre and/or sub-genre. A second-level sorting groups the recordings by performing artists. Composers (in so far as they are recognised as different from performers in musical practices other than Western art music) come a poor third.

We must be careful here. In Western art music composers themselves, and probably many performers and some patrons along with them, have always 'sorted' music first by composer. But that is really no more significant than to observe that violin-makers take a keen interest in what their colleagues do: understandably, they have a professional bias. Again, some patrons have, well before the nineteenth century, proved their composer-centredness by seeking out and collecting works by their favourite authors. The seventeenth-century Venetian nobleman Polo Michiel collected the works of Alessandro Stradella, while in Vienna Leopold I amassed manuscripts of music by the Bolognese master Giovanni Paolo Colonna. But such emphasis on the composer is quite unusual for its time.[8] We could compare it with the present-day public's awareness of choreographers. Despite their use of sophisticated systems of notation that enable their choreographies (their 'works', as we might in other circumstances choose to call them) to be executed faithfully in their absence – which is no more and no less than musical scores permit – choreographers have not yet made the leap in the public imagination from artisans to artists. How many people look inside their programmes for a ballet performance to discover first of all the identity of the choreographer? How many talk knowledgeably about the qualities of George Balanchine's style in relation to Martha Graham's? How many are even aware that what the dancers do may sometimes be performed from a text almost as binding as that of a musical composition? Thurston Dart's famous dictum (to my knowledge, never written down) that travelling in space is equivalent to travelling in time could, *mutatis mutandis*, serve

---

8. Peter Wright has pointed out to me, in support of this argument, that prior to the single-author collections issued by the printer Ottaviano Petrucci at the beginning of the sixteenth century, such collections are very rare. Where they occur (in connection, for instance, with Guillaume de Machaut), there always seems to be some special additional factor. In the case mentioned, this would be the composer's parallel eminence as a poet – and perhaps also (a not unconnected fact) his high social status. Until the eighteenth century the dominant form of collection in manuscript sources remains the genre-based or medium-based anthology of works by several composers.

here. Choreography, a creative practice in a different sphere, today occupies a small niche in public awareness closely comparable with that of musical composition three hundred years ago.

The importance of genre in earlier times as a mechanism for classifying music emerges very clearly in the writings of the German theorists and music journalists active in the late baroque period, among whom may be mentioned Mattheson, Scheibe, Marpurg and Quantz. Consider, for example, the following extracts from Quantz's celebrated treatise on flute-playing (1752):

> An *overture*, which is played at the beginning of an opera, requires a grave and majestic opening, a brilliant and well-elaborated principal subject, and a good mixture of various instruments such as oboes, flutes, and hunting horns. It owes its origins to the French. *Lully* has provided good models for it; but some German composers, among others, especially Handel and Telemann, have far surpassed him. ... Since the overture produces such a good effect, however, it is a pity that it is no longer in vogue in Germany.
>
> The Italian *sinfonias*, which have the same purpose as overtures, require the same qualities of majesty in their ideas. Since, however, the majority are fashioned by composers who have exercised their talents more fully in vocal than in instrumental music, there are at present very few sinfonias that have all the required attributes, and can serve as good models.[9]

What is interesting here is how Quantz associates intrinsic qualities with each genre, as if to suggest that one successful overture is necessarily much like another. Composers are introduced by name as examples of good practitioners within a genre, but only in the same spirit as one would cite Stradivarius as a good violin-maker or Chippendale as a good chair-maker. Handel and Telemann are praised because they bring out the qualities already prescribed for overtures supremely well, not because they call attention to themselves in a wider context as original artists. There is no suggestion here that an enterprising composer might, of his own volition, transform the nature of an overture for a special artistic (the very word is anachronistic!) purpose.

One reason why Quantz's descriptions read so curiously today is, of course, that genre itself has become progressively enfeebled within

---

9. Johann Joachim Quantz, *On Playing the Flute*, trans. Edward R. Reilly, London, Faber, 1966, p. 316.

Western art music since the nineteenth century.[10] This process has taken many forms. Existing genres have been hybridised, as in Berlioz's 'dramatic symphony' *Roméo et Juliette*. Genre classifications have been 'defamiliarised', playfully or profoundly, as in Stravinsky's *Symphonies of Wind Instruments*. Boundaries of all kinds have been extended beyond their previous limits of tolerance (as in Bartók's *Concerto for Orchestra* and its imitations), and many twentieth-century composers have rejected genre affiliation altogether for their pieces. A latter-day Quantz can no longer say, 'A symphony is …'; at most, he can now say, 'A symphony was …'. The decline of genre as a significant factor in a work's identity has been a natural corollary of the composer's rise over the same period.

What is true for genre applies also to medium (as in the distinction between a solo sonata, a trio sonata or a *quadro*) and to style. Quantz and his contemporaries devote much space to differentiating style according to function and context (the theatrical, ecclesiastical and chamber styles), compositional technique (*stylus phantasticus*, *stylus symphoniacus*), national criteria (the French, Italian, German, Polish and Scottish styles) and surface details (the 'Lombardic' style, the *galant* style). Music is carefully categorised in a number of ways (regarded at the time as very necessary for its appreciation) before one arrives at the stage of evaluating composers comparatively. This situation finds many echoes in today's popular music, where it seems (to an outsider) that as much critical energy is expended on the correct identification and categorisation of genres and sub-genres as on evaluation of the merits and demerits of individual artists and groups. Even within the realm of Western art music, particularly among listeners less familiar with its norms, a few voices will still be heard to say that they do not like chamber music or do like concertos. It is significant, and illustrative of the change that I am describing, that we today regard such 'blanket' approval or disapproval of genres or performance media as very naïve, whereas we happily tolerate other persons' fundamental likes and dislikes of individual composers.

Identifying works primarily with the artists performing them was also much more common before 1800. For a start, the performer is, quite literally, visible in a way that the composer is not. Moreover, any convincing performance is founded on the illusion that the executant

10. John Williamson quotes from Carl Dahlhaus on this subject see Chapter 9, p. 187.

is a creator, if not **the** creator, of the music presented. When we praise
an interpretation for its spontaneity, we pay it the tribute of suggesting that it, and, by extension, the very material to which it is applied,
is newly invented in the act of performance. In Western art music
there is a tolerated (indeed, necessary) contradiction between the
knowledge that a musical performance is an operation dependent for
its existence on an earlier, invisible operation (composition) and the
fiction, in which executants and audiences share, that the performance is itself an act of creation. This is the reason why those relatively few elements that are (or can be presented deceptively as being)
improvised tend to be highlighted in a performance. The resistance by
performers to the idea, proposed by Stravinsky and others, that the
'interpretation' of a musical score should be replaced by its mere
'reproduction' becomes very understandable in this light.

Before 1800, the fiction appears to have been sustained in a purer
form than after. In written discussions of musical performances,
whether in letters, journals or press reports, the accent nearly always
falls on the executant. The eclipse of the composer by the performer
is evident from the extreme rarity with which the quality of a composition and the quality of its execution are distinguished. It is in fact
a mark of the composer-centredness of our musical culture today that
we find it easy to say that a fine new composition by composer X has
been inadequately presented by performer Y. However obvious to us,
such a distinction was foreign to the reception of Western art music
by lay audiences prior to 1800, for whom composition and performance shaded into one another, a confusion abetted by the wider
scope accorded to improvisation.[11] Needless to say, it is even more
foreign to all other musical traditions, past and present.

A performer-centred reception of Western art music still exists in
the margins. We have all met people for whom 'the singer not the
song' is the criterion. However, this mode is increasingly viewed as

11. In his pioneering musical journal *Critica musica* (2 vols, Hamburg, 1722–25),
   Johann Mattheson published an article (supportive of his own views) by the
   composer Johann Krieger, in which the following sentences appear (Vol. 2,
   p. 223): 'It remains certain, however, that one should make a precise distinction
   between the performance and the composition of a piece, for one cannot arrive
   at a fair verdict unless both are taken into account. The worst composition, if
   performed well, always gains more admirers than the very best, if this has the
   misfortune to be played badly.' (trans. MT). That the point needed to be made
   at all speaks volumes for the general state of music reception at the time.

naïve, at least in those countries where musicology impinges on musical life. One sign of this is the falling incidence of single-artist anthologies (of the type 'Singer X in Concert' or 'The Art of pianist Y') in the record catalogues.[12] Today, it is less the singularity of a Horowitz or a Casals that enthuses the average record collector or concert-goer than that of a Satie or a Pärt. This tendency is massively reinforced by musicology, which, in its academic (as in journal articles) and divulgative (as in sleeve notes) modes alike, continually calls attention to the intimate bond between composer and work, thereby tending to squeeze out the performer.[13]

In contrast, the public profile of the pre-1800 composer was low, often astonishingly so. It would have been lower still, had composers not taken the lead in presenting their works before audiences, thereby revealing by their presence as performers what might otherwise have remained hidden in the shadows. For whereas it is nowadays regarded as obligatory to name the composer prominently in those contexts where music is most frequently heard – the concert-hall, the radio or television broadcast and the commercial recording – this was far from being the case in the days when public concerts were the exception and music was encountered most often as a complement to some other activity: religious, ceremonial or social. A person attending a church service with music, entertained by *Tafelmusik* while dining or even (and this, to the modern mind, is incredible) going to the opera might have no opportunity, save by casual word of mouth, to learn the composer's identity. One might have thought that in playbills advertising operas, or at least in the printed librettos that doubled as souvenir programmes, mention of the composer's name, alongside that of the librettist, would be *de rigueur*. True, the situation improved vastly in the eighteenth century in comparison with that during the seventeenth, but there remain many examples of operatic productions that failed – at least, via the medium of the written word – to reveal

12. I have the impression that single-artist anthologies of this kind remain more popular in those countries less thoroughly penetrated by musicological 'enlightenment' – say, Greece or Poland.
13. It is possible to conceive, if only in theory, a musicology of Western art music in which the biography and creative practice of performers occupied minds more than those of composers; indeed, the musicology of jazz provides a ready-made model. Since the rise of modern musicology (as applied to Western art music) post-dates the shift to composer-centredness, this discipline has identified itself *ab initio* with the new outlook and is a powerful force for its perpetuation.

the composer's identity.[14] In cases where the music for an opera was the product of several hands (a *pasticcio*) a certain reticence or vagueness is understandable, but the same casualness also affects operas with a single author, particularly in their later revivals where the composer was not personally present.[15]

The lack of any overriding interest in the authorship of a composition is betrayed, equally, by the general public tolerance extended before 1800 to the appropriation by one composer of the music of another. When plagiarism was publicly unmasked, as in the celebrated scandal of 1731 concerning Giovanni Bononcini's passing off as his own composition a madrigal by Antonio Lotti, the interesting thing to note is that the status of the work in question was rarely jeopardised. Identification of the true composer, whether more or less famous than the presumed composer, made little difference to its popularity. Today, in contrast, it can cause real anguish to a music-lover to be told that the *Adagio in G minor for Organ and Strings* 'by' Albinoni is no such thing, but an entirely modern concoction. Such is the perceived loss of value by a musical composition if the link to a cherished composer is severed that it often falls abruptly out of the repertoire or the unwelcome new attribution is simply ignored.[16]

The low profile of composers vis-à-vis leading performers was often underlined before 1800 by vast disparities in their remuneration, particularly in the heyday of *opera seria*. A series of detailed accounts for one season (1729–30) at a Venetian opera-house (San Giovanni Grisostomo) shows that whereas the four composers from

14. See, for instance, the surviving playbills advertising the operas *La calma fra le tempeste* (Reggio Emilia, 684) and *L'Arsace* (Modena, 1719). Both are reproduced as plates in *Storia dell'opera italiana*, ed. Lorenzo Bianconi and Giorgio Pestelli, Vol. 4: *Il sistema produttivo e le sue competenze*, Turin, EDT, 1987, following p. 64.

15. I suspect that in the case of operas revived in the absence of their composers it was sometimes to the advantage of local *maestri di cappella* not to publicise the name of the composer in order that some of the glory might by default devolve on them. The unqualified acceptance of multi-authored operas in the eighteenth century stands in stark contrast to our reluctance to revive them in modern times. The contrast points up tellingly how dependent our regard for a work has become on its association with a single, identifiable composer.

16. A case in point would be the *Trumpet Voluntary*, which in modern times achieved great popularity in the guise of a work by Purcell but has so far kindled little interest in its true composer, Jeremiah Clarke, whose claim is frequently ignored or played down.

whom new scores were commissioned earned an average of 2,125 *lire*, the eight solo singers employed for a run of 50 performances took home an average of 9,237 *lire* apiece, the amount running from 2,680 (for a bit-part singer) to 22,000 (for the famous Francesca Cuzzoni, one of Handel's *dive*).[17] These figures, which are not untypical for this time, show clearly that the market for good composers was less competitive than that for good singers. It made more difference to the success of a production to have a star singer than a star composer, and the scope for the latter to 'bid up' his price was comparatively limited.

Musical sources, particularly manuscript copies, are hardly more reliable in respect of authorship. Every researcher into early music has had to confront the problem of misattributed, and, even more often, nonattributed, sources. The reasons for these instances of missing or misidentified authorship are many and various, and there is no need to rehearse them again here.[18] What is important for my argument is that in centuries before the nineteenth there was a sufficient tolerance of vagueness about the composer's identity for such a situation to persist uncorrected. From Beethoven onwards, however, all vagueness disappears. Composers regularly append their names to their scores, and copyists or publishers transmit them reliably. No more do we encounter a case such as the so-called Op. 3 Quartets of Haydn (in reality by Romanus Hofstetter). The existence, since the nineteenth century, of effective copyright protection has not only safeguarded composers' financial interests but also validated their claims to authorship.

Are there exceptions to this composer-fixation in post-1800 Western art music? At the margin some remain. So-called 'light' classical music, continuously on the retreat in Britain since the great rise of Rock in the 1960s, places an unusually high value on uninterruptedness and unobtrusiveness, factors that discourage the use of programme notes or spoken introductions to the pieces performed. Thus the old 'Music While You Work' slot on the BBC Light Programme of

17. The budget for this season is analysed in detail in Michael Talbot, *Tomaso Albinoni: The Venetian Composer and His World*, Oxford, Clarendon Press, 1990, pp. 194–205.

18. See my discussion of the problem in 'The Genuine and the Spurious. Some Thoughts on Problems of Authorship Concerning Baroque Composition', in *Vivaldi. Vero e falso. Problemi di attribuzione*, ed. Antonio Fanna and Michael Talbot, Florence, Olschki, 1992, pp. 13–24.

the 1950s, the background music played today in supermarkets or restaurants and a typical performance given by a military band on a seaside pier all observe this convention of wordlessness that places the onus of identifying the composer (which, doubtless, very few listeners wish to do) on the audience.

For the full appreciation of 'serious' classical music, however, the identity of the composer has long been deemed indispensable. It is even possible to argue that the relationship of composer and work has become reversed over the last two centuries. Our focus is no longer on the individual work that we credit to a given composer: it is on the individual composer to whom we ascribe given works. Hence the profoundly disorienting experience of listening to music without prior announcement of its author, as occurred some years ago in 'The Innocent Ear' on the BBC's Radio Three. We feel that we are not ready to assimilate a piece of music unless we can place it in a frame of reference defined first and foremost by its composer. The *Eroica Symphony* is not just a symphony written in the early nineteenth century that happens to be especially good and original because it is by Beethoven: it is one piece of the jigsaw that we assemble in our minds as part of our quest to arrive at the fullest possible picture of Beethoven, the composer of genius. We do not insist that musical works be autobiographical in the direct mode of Smetana's string quartet *Aus meinem Leben* or Richard Strauss's *Sinfonia domestica*. However, we like to think that, consciously or not, a musical composition reflects the state and course of a composer's inner life. Thus we are tempted to believe that Haydn's (misleadingly labelled) *Sturm und Drang* symphonies are connected with his marital problems rather than being the product of a new fashion, not confined to Haydn, for minor-key turbulence. We are nowadays disappointed if a composer's works evidence no 'progress' in the light of their advancing years and the evolution of the musical language as a whole. Considered strictly as a musical artefact, Rakhmaninov's *Third Symphony* is no better and no worse than if it had been composed in 1905 instead of 1935. Even so, some of us feel that its contemporaneity with Schoenberg's *Violin Concerto* and Bartók's *Fifth String Quartet* poses a problem. In the minds of many, originality has been redefined to mean not merely 'difference' but now also 'forward-looking-ness'.

Because it possesses (not by accident, as Lydia Goehr has shown) such an exact equivalence to author-centredness in literature or artist-centredness in painting, composer-centredness in Western art music has, for several generations, seemed to belong to the natural order of things. The metaphor of the jigsaw puzzle introduced in the preceding paragraph suggests a fruitful way to view the rôle of the single product that we call a work. The completed jigsaw represents a composer's oeuvre. The individual work (whether large like *Fidelio* or small like a bagatelle) resembles the single piece that we place in relation to the other pieces. By calling any piece of music indiscriminately a 'work', we insist on its standardised function in relation to the oeuvre of its composer.[19] In its capacity as a 'work', *Fidelio* is something that we associate in the first instance with a composer (Beethoven) rather than with a genre (opera), a sub-genre (*Singspiel*, 'rescue opera'), a performer or performers (conductor X, orchestra Y, singers Z) or any other person or thing. To my mind, that is the real novelty and significance of the work-concept as Goehr describes it. The artefact remains exactly the same; but after 1800 we look at it in a different way (whether as composers, performers or listeners), and so, in that special sense, it 'changes'.

The composer-centredness of musical life has had, finally, a profound effect on the way composers, in the course of their careers, construct an oeuvre. Prior to 1800 the great majority of composers, even the most highly admired, were specialists. Positive feedback from patrons, publishers and audiences caused them to produce more of the same rather than to venture into new territory. A Corelli had no need to write operas, nor a Gluck string quartets. Critical opinion was perfectly content with such specialisation and could on occasion disparage a composer's aspirations towards universality; one recalls Tartini's reported statement, perhaps tinged with a little jealousy, that vocal and instrumental composition were too different to be mastered by the same person (he had Vivaldi in mind).[20] Specialisation also suited a situation in which the musician as performer, or director of a

---

19. Joseph Kerman voices similar thoughts on the relationship between individual works of a composer and his oeuvre as a whole: 'Between the *oeuvre* and the single work a dialectic of appreciation may be said to exist, whereby we can even take pleasure in a quite indifferent piece of music for what it reminds us of the structured integrity of an entire lifework. The sense of the whole depends on all the individual pieces, but it is also true that the sense of the individual piece is illuminated by the cumulative light of the totality.' (*The Beethoven Quartets*, London, Oxford University Press, 1967, p. 90).

20. Charles de Brosses, *Lettres historiques et critiques sur l'Italie*, Paris, Ponthieu, 1799, Vol. 2, p. 316.

performance, was expected to take the lead in promoting the music of the same person as composer.

In the nineteenth century this began to change, though not immediately. While there was still room for such specialist composers as Chopin and Verdi, universality began to be seen as a prime desideratum, perhaps in the light of the inspiring example provided by the great Viennese Classical composers. Success in a given genre was no longer considered a reason for continuing in it, but rather the opposite: having proved himself in one area, a composer was free – indeed, almost obliged – to move on to conquer fresh areas. In the twentieth century a composer has to be versatile to be accepted as great, and it is noteworthy how the more ambitious young composers of today, encouraged by the critics, aim from the start for a broad 'portfolio' of works from which no major area is lacking. Opera, in particular, is a test all have sooner or later to pass. To state the matter paradoxically, works have become the authors of their composers; they are not so much end-products to be assessed on their own terms as the starting points from which the public fashions its image of each creative artist.

Composer-Centredness in Perspective

I end this essay with some reflections on the broader historical significance of the move to composer-centredness after 1800 and on possible future developments within Western art music and other musics.

Extraordinary as this claim may seem, I do not think it unreasonable to trace the history of the Western art-music tradition, with all its peculiarities, back to one apparently unconnected, fortuitous occurrence: the decision of the Universal Church (or of important fractions within it) to have a universally employed musical setting for its liturgy. Uniformity over a wide, and at that time still expanding, area presupposes efficiency of transmission. A system of instructions (notation) with only mnemonic function is no longer good enough: what is now needed is a form of encoding the prescribed music (plainsong) that enables the user to translate what it says into practice both impeccably and entirely unaided.

Although the first notated plainsong 'works' (one may indeed call them that, however unconventionally, since they possess all the essential properties of a work, including a fixed beginning and end) were of a length and complexity that did not preclude memorisation, the efficiency of the notation very soon allowed the dimensions and the complexity of a musical work to exceed the bounds of individual memory. Using notation to plan, as well as to encode, a work became more usual. An apt parallel can be drawn with architecture. One needs no architect's plans to conceive or build an igloo, but the Empire State Building cannot do without them, either at the design stage or in connection with their implementation. It is precisely this use of musical notation as an aid in the process of composition itself that marks out Western art music from other traditions employing it (Chinese, Korean, Japanese, etc.) in the early Middle Ages. It also enables one to compose a piece of any length that makes absolutely no reference to any earlier piece: the *cantus* need no longer be *prius factus*.

The advent of polyphony consolidated the dependence of Western art music on notation. A score (to use this term rather anachronistically) could now expand indefinitely not only along its 'horizontal' axis to make a longer piece but also along its 'vertical' axis to make a more complex and variegated one. The notated form of a composition as large in both these 'dimensions' as a Mahler symphony is not simply the accurate documentary record of a finished product that preceded it: together with its preliminary sketches and drafts, this score incorporates the whole evolutionary process of the work's composition from initial conception to final polishing.

This emancipation of music-making from improvisation and memorisation marks, in embryo, the beginning of the distinction between composer and performer. By definition, whenever a polyphonic vocal piece is performed, not more than one singer can be the composer (who may, in theory, 'remember' his part perfectly): the others, in contrast, have had to learn what they perform from the written page and are therefore non-composers. The irreplaceable and unique rôle of the composer is recognised at least as early as the thirteenth century, when Léonin posthumously earned from the theorist known today as Anonymous IV the epithet of 'best composer of organum' (*optimus organista*).

It is at first sight remarkable for how many centuries a precise understanding of the composer's function continued among practitioners, patrons and connoisseurs without becoming a dominant aspect of the everyday reception of music. Our wonder will perhaps grow less if we consider the world of modern Western popular music. If for no other reason than the orderly distribution of royalties, every 'number' is credited to one or more composers, whose names are clearly marked for those who wish to read them. The point is, however, that few trouble to read them. How many viewers will be clearly aware, as they watch the Eurovision Song Contest, that the contest is theoretically (and, in terms of prize-money, also genuinely) one between song-writers, not between performing artists, let alone nations? This is what makes the comparatively recent (200-years-old) composer-centredness of Western art music so exceptional, even aberrant, in the context of world musics.

Is composer-centredness here to stay? I see no signs of its demise in conventionally notated music, though in some quarters efforts are being made to re-forge the union of composer and performer, as exemplified in the ensembles formed and directed by Steve Reich, Michael Nyman and Steve Martland. Can a band directed by Steve Martland and occupied largely with performances of his music be equated (in the sense that interests us here) with a *Kapelle* directed by J. S. Bach? It is hard to see how it can. The personal involvement of the composer in the performance of his works, far from submerging him, today increases his hegemony by creating a more efficient machine to publicise his music. Nor do ostensible acts of renunciation by composers change much. John Cage never sacrificed an ounce of fame or royalty income by instructing performers to be free: 'freedom' according to Cage is always going to be different from that according to Cornelius Cardew.[21]

Some change is, however, possible in the case of music encoded directly into sound via a recording studio. As in written notation, the facility that will eventually transmit the composition is used also to create it. In contrast, however, the hiatus between encoding and performance is eliminated (to replay a recording hardly counts, in the operational sense, as a separate act!). The result is that the composer-technician is able unaided to realise, from conception right through to performance, a piece of any length or polyphonic-timbral complexity.

We should not necessarily applaud every aspect of this development. The redundancy, at all stages, of the ensemble robs music of a social dimension still considered a precious part of music-making. Music-making via the electro-acoustic studio enters the enclosed

---

21. Goehr (1992), pp. 244 and 260–65, seems to share my scepticism over the extent to which those members of the recent avant-garde who claimed not to compose works have delivered on their promise.

world of the 'personal' stereo, television and TV dinner. Perhaps more importantly, the ability of others to criticise a composition in detail is much reduced, since a recording is not 'readable', i.e. translatable into sound purely in the imagination, in the same way as a score. But for the first time, Western and other musics share a common encoding medium that privileges (and carries the historical baggage of) no single one of them in particular. In such conditions, convergence, fusion and *rapprochement* of every kind are likely to occur. We could soon find (if we do not already have) rock compositions with the tonal architecture of Western art music or art-music compositions employing the long fade-out. The composer will remain paramount, but his or her functions will become much more diverse and inclusive.

However, the easy malleability of recorded sound certainly facilitates the production of alternative versions of pieces (extended, shortened, remixed, etc.). The effect of this will perhaps be to subvert the discrete, fixed identity of the musical work, which has so long been its *conditio sine qua non*. If this happens, we could move into an age rich in composers but poor in definable works.

On the other hand, recorded sound (even of conventional live performance) has the power to turn non-works into real works. Once it has been recorded, improvised music, without in any change in the practice of the musicians themselves, acquires a fixed, infinitely repeatable essence that allows it to be treated, if we so wish, as a quasi-work. Indeed, as the pianist Joanna MacGregor has shown, a fully notated aural transcription of a recorded jazz number (for example, a performance by Thelonious Monk of his *Round Midnight*) is just as capable of orthodox concert presentation as a Gershwin prelude. If a machine were able – perhaps one already is! – to bring onto screen and print out in standard notation whatever recorded music it was playing (with all accidental irregularities smoothed out, as when a scanner interprets visual images), we might acquire the means, without the labour of transcription, to create an unlimited number of quasi-works suited to live presentation. In this rare instance, technology would be used, ironically, to create the conditions for its own future avoidance.

To conclude: as I see it, the conceptual changes affecting Western art music around 1800 – changes to our ideas not only of 'work' but also of 'artist', 'genius', 'fidelity' (in interpretation) and many other things – originated from the radical realignment that I have described as a shift from a genre-centred and performer-centred culture to a composer-centred one. If there is a new and regulative 'work-concept' after 1800, it is a by-product of a new and equally regulative 'composer-concept'. To borrow and extend Lydia Goehr's metaphor: musical works enter their imaginary museum only because composers have already entered their imaginary Pantheon.

9

The Musical Artwork and its Materials in the Music and Aesthetics of Busoni

John Williamson

Any consideration of the history of the musical artwork that attempts to take full account of its weakening in the twentieth century eventually has to confront the apparently marginal case of Ferruccio Busoni. In his writings, which closely follow his compositional practice, the nineteenth-century cult of the genius and the figure of the composer-performer generate a picture of the musical artwork that follows in a Platonic tradition but with bewildering contradictions that point to the progressive weakening of the concept in the twentieth century. On one level, Busoni illustrates in his music and aesthetics the first implications of a general phenomenon best encapsulated by Carl Dahlhaus: '... since the late eighteenth century all genres have rapidly lost substance. ... every genre fades to an abstract generalisation, derived from individual structures after they have accumulated; and finally, in the twentieth century, individual structures submit only under duress to being allocated to any genre'.[1] Hardly less relevant is Busoni's confusion of the roles of editor, transcriber and composer, whereby a 'work' may be a variant, completion or complete rethinking of a pre-existing work. Albrecht Riethmüller illustrates this confounding of categories principally from Busoni's reaction to, and treatment of, the music of J. S. Bach, but transcription and recomposition also overlap with aesthetically indeterminate results in Busoni's attitude to his own music. Both are particular instances of a more fundamental problem perceived by Riethmüller:

> In the understanding of the nineteenth century and of the twentieth until now the first and most essential requirement of a composition is

1. Carl Dahlhaus, *Esthetics of Music*, trans. William Austin, Cambridge, Cambridge University Press, 1982, p. 15.

that it be new and original, further, that it be attributable to a particular author who fulfils this aesthetic postulate of newness and originality. Even these few fundamental requirements begin to totter when one turns to Busoni.[2]

Whether Busoni would have recognised his importance in this generalisation is open to debate. It is arguable that his aesthetic writings brought together a number of strains that taken separately do not seriously fly in the face of common assumptions held in his lifetime. It is only when he placed them thus in somewhat startling juxtaposition that the ideas acquired tension and even discord. As Bojan Bujić has noted, his most substantial aesthetic work, *Entwurf einer neuen Ästhetik der Tonkunst*, 'is an example of a fine artistic intuition rather than of systematic thought'.[3] Busoni's intuition brings together a number of questions about music and its future in a manner 'well-meant and full of peace' (as he commented to Hans Pfitzner) that fails to disguise the often rather provocative features of his musical praxis.[4] But the *Entwurf* is not Busoni's sole contribution to the theory and aesthetics of music. It has a number of satellites that expand on, underline or, on occasion, contradict several of its more important ideas. In this, it is not unlike Busoni's stage works, which have their predominantly instrumental satellites as pre-existing 'sketches' or later transcriptions. Many of these satellites to the *Entwurf* derive from open letters, programme notes and occasional journalistic forays that defend aspects of the author's composition and performance. As a result, they can be, and sometimes have been, used to give substance to the rather enigmatic sequence of ideas in the *Entwurf*.

Not the least striking feature of the *Entwurf* is its turn from praise of a very abstract form of absolute music (and, implicitly, of instrumental music, on which Lydia Goehr assumes most notions of work

---

2. Albrecht Riethmüller, *Ferruccio Busonis Poetik*, Mainz, Schott, 1988, p. 13. All translations from the original German are by the present author unless otherwise stated.
3. Bojan Bujić, *Music in European Thought 1851–1912*, Cambridge, Cambridge University Press, 1988, p. 368.
4. Ferruccio Busoni, *The Essence of Music and other Papers*, trans. Rosamund Ley, New York, Dover, 1957, p. 19 (abbreviated hereafter as *Essence*). This collection contains most of Busoni's important essays, as well as some passages that belong to editions of the *Entwurf* later than that of the standard English translation (see below, note 7).

and *Werktreue* to be founded) to previewing its possible rebirth in the context of musical drama.[5] This argument is worked out further in the essay *Wesen und Einheit der Musik* (*Essence*: 1–16). Lurking behind this shift (it can hardly be called a transition) are other, deeper contradictions. Bujić has noted the tension between two of Busoni's most frequently quoted maxims: '… the musical artwork exists, before its tones resound'; and 'All arts … ever aim at the one end, namely, the imitation of nature and the interpretation of human feelings'.[6] Busoni's view of the relationship of absolute to theatrical music depends at least in part on the working out of the relationship between these two maxims, of which the first offers the more revealing key to his practice as a composer. His famous description of music as a child 'hardly four hundred years old', for which 'we apply laws made for maturity to a child that knows nothing of responsibility', is in its context a declaration that music is as yet a novice in 'the imitation of nature and the interpretation of human feelings'.[7] Music's goal and 'destiny', 'to win freedom' and 'become the most complete of all reflexes of Nature by reason of its untrammelled immateriality', is to be realised by creating an improbable synthesis of music's 'immateriality' and art's capacity for mimesis and interpretation. It is hardly surprising that, in view of such a programme, the *Entwurf* has acquired a reputation for a certain blithe naïveté in its utopian stance (a charge levelled by Hans Pfitzner that still carries force).[8]

In considering the *Entwurf*, it has all too often been the case that

5. Lydia Goehr, *The Imaginary Museum of Musical Works: An Essay in the Philosophy of Music*, Oxford, Oxford University Press, 1992, p. 2.
6. Bujić (1988), p. 368.
7. Ferruccio Busoni, *Entwurf einer neuen Ästhetik der Tonkunst*, Hamburg, Karl Dieter Wagner, 1973, p. 11; I have used this edition of the 1916 text throughout but followed the English translation of Dr. Th[eodore] Baker in 'Sketch of a New Esthetic of Music', *Three Classics in the Aesthetic of Music*, New York, Dover, 1962; here pp. 76–77. This standard translation, however, follows the edition of 1911 and does not correspond exactly with the text and layout of 1916. Further references in the present essay will be given in the form *Entwurf*, followed by the relevant page numbers in the German edition and the English translation.
8. Hans Pfitzner, 'Futuristengefahr', in *Gesammelte Schriften*, vol. 1, Augsburg, Filser, 1926, pp. 185–223; see also Peter Franklin, *The Idea of Music*, London, Macmillan, 1985, pp. 124–30, and Fedele D'Amico, 'L'utopia di Ferruccio Busoni e il *Doktor Faust*', in *Il flusso del tempo. Scritti su Ferruccio Busoni*, ed. Sergio Sablich and Rossana Dalmonte, Milan, Unicopli, 1985, pp. 267–71.

comment has focused on the controversy that it engendered. Yet the arguments have a historical interest within the sphere of ideas, given their numerous echoes from Busoni's wide reading. Riethmüller has observed that the picture of music as child is almost plagiarised from Wackenroder, and that other features (notably the composer's idea of the 'oneness of music') may have been borrowed from Croce's *Estetica come scienza dell'espressione e linguistica generale* of 1902.[9] Bujić has detected elements resembling 'Dilthey's and Nietzsche's philosophy of life and Dessoir's notion of the study of art detached from a philosophical system'.[10] The echoes of Nietzsche are hardly surprising, in view of the extensive quotation from *Jenseits von Gut und Böse* with which Busoni launches the peroration to the *Entwurf* (*Entwurf*: 42–43/95–96). Yet the example of Nietzsche illustrates the extent to which Busoni avoids acknowledging specific intellectual forebears. In an open letter to Paul Bekker of 1920, usually reprinted under the title 'Young Classicism', Busoni declared that 'Neither Beethoven's wry smile nor Zarathustra's "liberating laugh" but the smile of wisdom, of divinity and absolute music' was to be music's declared goal (*Essence*: 21–22). Even when quoting Nietzsche's famous evocation of a 'super-German music' from *Jenseits von Gut und Böse*, he takes care to balance it with a quotation from Tolstoy that draws some of the sting of Nietzsche's words. Above all, Busoni's curious style, with its tendency towards the lapidary at one extreme and the rhapsodic at the other, is remarkably effective at hiding his sources.

In this unsystematic and eclectic music aesthetic it is perhaps unrealistic to look for concrete definitions and sustained lines of argument. Yet in the tensions and inconsistencies some of the problems of the concept of the musical artwork for the twentieth century are clearly indicated. What it might stand for or mean is far from clear in Busoni's writings, which tend first to speak of music in the abstract and then to proceed to forms and genres in particular, leaving a hole where the category 'work' should be. But it is possible to supply, by inference, a picture of the artwork in Busoni that, if it tends to any fixed standpoint, may be said to be Platonic, in a sense related at least in part to Jerrold Levinson's definition, albeit with certain qualifications.[11]

---

9. Riethmüller (1988), pp. 159 and 185.
10. Bujić (1988), p. 368.
11. Jerrold Levinson, 'What a Musical Work is', *Journal of Philosophy*, Vol. 77 (1980), pp. 5–28, at pp. 9, 14, 19 and 26.

Busoni's *Entwurf* begins by separating the 'ageless' qualities of the artwork (spirit, emotion and humanity) from those that 'age rapidly' (form, manner of expression, flavour of epoch; *Entwurf*: 9–10/75–76). His argument is directed towards artworks in general and distinguishes between the various art-forms and species only by noting that their durability is in direct proportion to the purity of 'their essential means and ends' (*Entwurf*: 10/76). This is a first pass at the (as yet unspoken) notion of absolute music, which is then approached from a slightly different direction: music's 'one radiant attribute', its incorporeality (*Entwurf*: 11/77). This lends music a freedom with which, in Busoni's eyes, mankind finds it hard to cope. Weighed down by the chains of man's imposed rules, music aims 'to win freedom as its destiny' and to realise its 'untrammelled immateriality' independently of the 'idea' (which Busoni himself sets in quotation marks; *Entwurf*: 12/77). By rejecting illustration and programmes as aspects of the 'idea', he prepares the way directly for 'absolute music', which is only a stage on the path to the deeper notion of 'die Ur-Musik'. The standard English translation renders this term as 'infinite music', which is not inappropriate, since it is presumably that free essence that music originally possessed and aims to regain (*Entwurf*: 15/79). 'Absolute music' is thus essentially a flawed stage to be associated with the lawgivers and chains of humanity. To illuminate Busoni's estimate of it, we might adapt Riethmüller's definition of *Tonkunst* in relation to 'Ur-Musik': that it was 'no longer the higher, artistically formed and over-formed music, but, in direct inversion, was to be thought below that highest music as, so to speak, its deficient mode'.[12] But the encompassing 'Ur-Musik' reminds us that Bujić unapologetically claims Busoni as a Pythagorean, presumably on the strength of that very concept.[13] That composers can recover elements of such an 'Ur-Musik' is the message of the examples chosen by Busoni of passages that escape from the genres and 'architectonic' forms of human lawgivers. These examples, however, which include the introductions to the finales of Beethoven's '*Hammerklavier*' *Sonata* and Schumann's *Fourth Symphony*, are mostly of episodes rather than works. Further, they include introductions in which self-sufficient genres such as fantasy and two-part invention survive as fragments (as in the '*Hammerklavier*'), adding another strand to Dahlhaus's melancholy

12. Riethmüller (1988), p. 157.
13. Bujic (1988), p. 368.

depiction of the decay of genres in the twentieth century: the generic fragment as *topos*.[14] Bach's organ fantasias are singled out by Busoni as examples of a genre that seems to fulfil the two functions of generating self-contained works (albeit allowed a greater measure of fantasy than others) and approaching the condition of 'die Ur-Musik'.

In this fallen state works are barely to be distinguished from transcriptions. 'Every notation is, in itself, the transcription of an abstract idea' (*Entwurf*: 24/85). This drastic statement is made with full acceptance of the consequences: that in writing down a musical idea (and by intention a musical work), the original form is lost. Intention, form, agency 'still more closely define the way and the limits' (*Entwurf*: 23/85). As a result, the idea 'is depressed to the type of a class. That is, an Arrangement [*sic*] of the original. From this first transcription to a second the step is comparatively short and unimportant' (*Entwurf*: 24/85). But once this step towards notation is taken, a further dimension of transcription is revealed: '… the performance of a work is also a transcription, and still, whatever liberties it may take, it can never annihilate the original' (*Entwurf*: 24/85).[15] It is difficult to grasp here exactly what Busoni means by 'das Original', since he had already distinguished between 'die Originalgestalt' and 'die Originalfassung' – the former clearly the property of the idea before the compulsion to write it down, the latter probably the first full written version or a work (in which case the standard translation probably errs in giving 'archetype' for 'Originalfassung'). Either version would fit into Busoni's sentence for 'das Original' without seriously damaging his meaning, although 'die Originalgestalt' is probably the sense intended.   It is here that Busoni makes his famous statement: '… the musical artwork exists, before its tones resound and after they die away, *complete and intact*. It exists both within and outside of time, and through its nature we can obtain a definite conception of the otherwise intangible notion of the Ideality of Time' (*Entwurf*: 24/85). Arguably, this clarifies the status of the various 'originals' with which he has been wrestling in the preceding

14. A somewhat different perspective on this theme in Busoni is found elsewhere in Dahlhaus: *Foundations of Music History*, trans. J. B. Robinson, Cambridge, Cambridge University Press, 1982, pp. 7–8.

15. That 'an impromptu performance' might also be a transcription is conceded by Stephen Davies in a disclaimer whose implications he leaves aside: 'Transcription, Authenticity and Performance', *British Journal of Aesthetics*, Vol. 28 (1988), 216–27, at p. 216.

paragraphs, in that it might be imagined that the work 'outside time' is the 'Originalgestalt', and that the work 'within time' takes as its first transcription 'die Originalfassung'. But, more importantly, Busoni now comes face to face with the concrete artwork that he has largely skirted in the previous pages. Characteristically, he first allows himself a tendentious digression on musicality before introducing the figure of the creator, whose very presence gives a certain context to the artwork. Its continuing existence (even outside time) would seem to be a matter of the unplayed score rather than of that 'discovered' artwork from the pages of Wolterstorff.[16] In as much as there is space for a creator in Busoni's view of the musical artwork, he would seem to subscribe to Levinson's principal definition ('Works ... do not exist prior to the composer's compositional activity'); equally, his picture of music as a work 'outside time' is not intended to portray music as a pure sound structure of the kind dismissed by Levinson.[17] Works, at least, are created, not discovered, in Busoni's view as expressed in the *Entwurf*. But his comments on the creator's role are as enigmatic as other passages of the *Entwurf* and must be subjected to one of the minor qualifications mentioned earlier.

The creator turns out to be yet another lawgiver, whose duties involve the annulment of his own laws from work to work in a constant search for the exact form appropriate to the original idea. As with more than a few moments in Busoni's writings, the spirit of Nietzsche seems to hang over this section; but it is written in such general terms as to defy any exact intellectual parentage. By comparison, the later quotation of the words from *Jenseits von Gut und Böse* is almost vulgarly explicit and perhaps misleading in suggesting what sort of 'Ur-Musik' Busoni might have had in mind. But the image of Zarathustra in Part III of Nietzsche's book, sitting surrounded by broken law-tables and half-written new tables, serves rather well, if only as a curious commentary on Busoni's career as a composer.[18] As ever, he treads a precarious path between traditionalist and revolutionary, turning aside from 'intentional avoidance of rules' masquerading 'as creative power' (*Entwurf*: 30/88).

16. Nicholas Wolterstorff, *Works and Worlds of Art*, Oxford, Oxford University Press, 1980.
17. Goehr (1992), p. 45, paraphrasing Levinson (1980), p. 9; see also Levinson, ibid., p. 7.
18. Friedrich Nietzsche, *Also sprach Zarathustra*, Munich, Goldmann, 1979, pp. 160–76.

Towards the end of his life Busoni discovered a text that helped him to become more specific about the musical artwork. In Anatole France's *Histoire comique* he came across the sentence 'For the content of a piece of music existed and exists complete and unalterable before and after it has sounded', which is close enough to his own formulation in the *Entwurf* (*Essence*: 194). A Nietzschean parentage for this idea seems to be indirectly revealed in a further quotation from France ('Do you not believe that everything that is to happen has already and for all time happened?'), in which we almost catch an echo (conscious or otherwise) of Zarathustra intuiting the doctrine of the Eternal Recurrence.[19] Busoni took the trouble, in 'Vom Wesen der Musik' (an essay of 1924), to write out the whole passage with which this sentence begins, and appended a commentary. France's text plays with the problem of succession by using metaphors taken from cosmology:

> The universe appears to us continuously incomplete and we have the illusion that it is continuously completing itself. So, as we become aware of the phenomena successively, we believe that they do in fact come into effect successively. We have the idea that those we no longer see are in the past and those we do not yet see are in the future.

The coming point is obvious. Like a disciple of Einstein, France argues for a perspective of relativity (though still free from any thoroughgoing principle of uncertainty; in Busoni's aesthetic, neither God nor the composer as yet throws dice). Ignorant of true order, we 'only know the order of our perception of them'. France's conceit, witty or otherwise, is meant to calm an author anxiously awaiting the end of the first performance of his play, who asks the Zarathustrian question quoted above. According to the astronomical metaphors of his respondent, his play may, from the viewpoint of another galaxy, have indeed been performed before (*Essence*: 194–96).

In response, Busoni imagines a musical cosmos imbued 'with all forms, motives and combinations of past and future music' (*Essence*: 197–200). In this fantasy music threatens to become that closed system that Renée Cox refutes in her essay against Wolterstorff (even if we cannot speak even here of the set rules of a true closed system as in Cox's recurring comparator, chess).[20] Each composer is a

19. Nietzsche (1979), p. 128.
20. Renée Cox, 'Are Musical Works Discovered?', *Journal of Aesthetics and Art Criticism*, Vol. 43 (1984–85), pp. 369–73.

cultivator of one small area of this musical atmosphere: a person who collects, forms, surveys, manipulates and, implicitly, discovers. Composers do not invent 'new resources' but build on the discoveries of others. They reveal models of the whole infinity of music; they bring an element of the eternal through the human consciousness into the piece of music, which 'is frozen as soon as it is drawn through the darkness of our mentality'. The act of creation is in reality a process of discovery that becomes concrete in the mere intention of transcribing and notating it. It is hardly surprising that Busoni in his last year should have turned to this subtly different picture of the composer, since it chimes well with the problem of the final scene of *Doktor Faust*: how to demonstrate to a new generation the continuity of the hero's 'unconquerable will'.

Busoni's picture of the musical work thus allows for creation, but in a sense that also drifts towards discovery of some pre-existing type that renders all notations transcriptions. This is the major point on which he fails to live up to Levinson's picture of the musical artwork. For Levinson, the act of transcription implies that a new work has been created, so closely is he tied to the notion of an inseparable notation for each musical work.[21] Busoni, in contrast, subordinates the musical work to the abstract idea. Whereas Levinson sees all transcriptions as works, Busoni comes close to seeing all works as transcriptions, which suggests that they have arrived at essentially the same practical position from opposite directions. The status of transcription in relation to Levinson's position is also a point raised by Lydia Goehr.[22] Examples mentioned by her include 'Busoni's and Kreisler's arrangements of music originally composed by Bach'. Her extension of this, the statement that Kreisler '"composed" almost exclusively by arrangement', takes us to the heart of those many compositions of Busoni that are 'completions' of, or 'studies for', other works by Bach or by himself. It is therefore doubtful whether Busoni would have subscribed to Stephen Davies's distinction between versions that arise in the course of the composition process (which he illustrates with the various forms of Stravinsky's *The Wedding*) and true transcriptions exhibiting an intention to transcribe. Busoni's conception of notation takes much of the sting out of Davies's apparently unanswerable contention that 'the final version' of an arduous

21. Levinson (1980), pp. 27–28.
22. Goehr (1992), pp. 60–63.

composition process 'could not be a transcription because there was at the time it was written no independently existing work to which it could stand as a transcription'.[23]

Goehr's suggestion that 'perhaps a transcription, an arrangement, or an orchestration of a work is itself a work in its own right' seems close to Busoni's own practice. Drawing back from this extreme conclusion, Goehr wonders whether transcriptions might after all 'not yield new works, even though orchestrations and arrangements do'. In this context she cites a distinction between paraphrase and transcription offered by Alan Walker in his biography of Liszt: 'The paraphrase, as its name implies, is a free variation of the original. The transcription, on the other hand, is strict, literal, objective'.[24]

This is a difficult area, since Walker's definitions, alarmingly strewn with implicit value judgements, actually ride roughshod over a bewildering diversity of titles, genres and compositions. His two categories overlap in Liszt's practice to a considerable extent. There are paraphrases – for instance, those on *Ernani* and *Rigoletto*, or on Isolde's 'Liebestod' – that ingeniously combine fidelity to a composer's sequence of events (albeit with startling alterations to detail, such as the famous augmented fourth smuggled into 'Bella figlia dell'amore') with additional 'virtuoso' figuration in such a way as to satisfy Davies's definition of a transcription without being 'strict, literal, objective'.[25] Indeed, part of the point of the transcription in Liszt's hands was to paraphrase orchestral and vocal colours in pianistic terms, as well as the reverse. But Busoni himself also had some thoughts on the question of variation that can be applied to Walker's use of the term. In the *Entwurf* he noted that even 'Worshippers of the Letter' admired variation form, even though it produced arrangements 'least respectful when most ingenious ... So the arrangement is not good, because it *varies* the original; and the variation *is* good, although it '*arranges*' the original' (*Entwurf*: 24/86). Given the vagueness of the problem, it is legitimate to wish to have a clear distinction such as Walker proposes, but, in practice, his definitions are well-nigh unworkable in the face of an attitude such as Busoni's, which comes

---

23. Davies (1988), p. 217.
24. Alan Walker, *Franz Liszt*, vol. 1: *The Virtuoso Years 1811–1847*, London, Faber, 1983, p. 167.
25. Davies (1988), p. 217.

close to the 'gloriously romantic conception of composers' that Goehr ascribes to Levinson.[26]

It is a striking facet of Busoni's continuation of the Lisztian tradition of transcription and paraphrase that he seldom subscribed to literal rendition of one composition in another medium. A transcription by Busoni was almost unthinkable without some degree of variation or 'arrangement'. The relationship of the chorus for Turandot's attendants in Act II of Busoni's opera and the Elegy for piano entitled *Turandots Frauengemach* shows how far transcription implied extensive reworking. The additional counterpoints supplied to the more literal Bachian sections in the *Fantasia contrappuntistica* are illustrations at the lower end of the scale. For Riethmüller, analysis of the act of transformation in the musical work is almost enough in itself; that transformation might actually be the essence and justification of the musical artwork in Busoni, however, goes beyond analysis.[27] By extension, a performance conceived as an act of transcription must presumably also have a sense of 'arrangement' or variation. But in reality Busoni's aesthetic was far from being simply performance-based. One should not minimise the enormous reserves of technique and virtuosity required to perform such acts of transcription in performance; these raise the act of performance into the realms of a 'transcendental' virtuosity (in Liszt's sense) that makes every individual performance a kind of 'artwork'. Busoni's aesthetic presupposed the intelligence and technique to deal with a species of super-artwork that touched on the eternal. It is difficult to know, in such a context, whether the concept of the musical artwork was weakened by its increasing divorce from form and genre through the endless possibility of transformation, or whether performance was correspondingly strengthened by placing the possibility in the performer's hands.

When considering the status of transcription in an essay that is slightly later than the first edition of the *Entwurf*, Busoni restated a number of his main points, in places virtually reproducing the original text. In addition, he noted that transcriptions were an essential stage in the education of both composer and executant. Busoni's own transcription for orchestra and piano of Liszt's *Spanish Rhapsody* was, on one level, part of his education as a player, part of the encounter which reshaped his technique. Essentially, Busoni subscribed to

26. Goehr (1992), p. 62.
27. Riethmüller (1988), p. 165.

Davies's view that 'transcription may have a pedagogical use', though he could have stated this more strongly; one suspects that, for Busoni, life bore a strong resemblance to a *Bildungsroman*.[28] On another level, this transcription solved a problem of Liszt's original, which refused the pianist the possibility 'of moving to the climaxes in a sufficiently brilliant light'. Transcription was here an aid both to the composer's conception and to the individuality of the performer. The relationship between the two personalities is part of the key to Busoni's notion that any performance is, in a sense, also a transcription. It is a matching of minds suited to an era in which the nineteenth-century identity between composer and executant was no longer guaranteed (*Essence*: 86). Such a meeting of minds appeared to Busoni to transcend the sometimes tawdry origins of the transcription. Thus he was aware that Liszt's *Réminiscences de Don Juan* (which is essentially a paraphrase with elements of transcription, in Walker's terms) sprang 'from the ground of salon music and of opera pot-pourris', and was likely to give offence to 'the strict purists', with whom he had a degree of sympathy. But the 'symbolic significance' of the work as a kind of technical touchstone for pianists required, in turn, aesthetic study: a defining choice of adjective for the Busonian transcription (and also for Liszt; *Essence*: 92–93). Busoni's own commentary is too short for the full implications to be worked out, but it stresses that Liszt's decorative figuration is used essentially for characterisation, which is a general feature of the more elaborate and structurally ambitious of Liszt's transcriptions. In general terms, Busoni might have agreed with Davies's theory of transcription in accepting that there was some underlying authenticity at work in the act of transcribing, a form of being faithful to the spirit of the musical content rather than its letter. But, in practice, Busoni's delight in the multiple possibilities of transcription tended to blur the line between transcribing and editing, since the footnotes to his edition of *Réminiscences de Don Juan* present alternatives deriving from Liszt's version for two pianos that impress him as coming closer to the spirit of Mozart's original. The performer with finely developed aesthetic sensibilities is presumably at liberty to work these into his 'transcription'.

Busoni also had some thoughts, written in 1905, on the subject of Goehr's other problematic category, orchestration, where he

---

28. Davies (1988), p. 220.

proposes a distinction as troublesome as Walker's view of transcriptions and paraphrases. Expressing the hope that Richard Strauss's forthcoming revision of Berlioz's *Grand Traité d'instrumentation et d'orchestration modernes* 'will avoid the fundamental defects of all instruction books on instrumentation up to the present', he locates the most important rule in a distinction between 'absolute orchestration' and the orchestration 'of what was originally only an abstract musical composition, or one conceived for another instrument. The first is the only genuine one, the second belongs to "arrangements" ...' (*Essence*: 34–36). This is clearly a minefield, and one rendered no less problematic by the quotation marks round 'arrangements'; one might agree that these are necessary in view of the doubt that Busoni's whole aesthetic throws on the status of the work. Furthermore, the subsequent comments make it quite clear that claims to 'absolute orchestration' are not to be taken at face value but conceal many examples of mere 'arrangement' or even 'transcription' of abstract compositions. Thus Busoni's ear detects 'arrangement' rather than 'absolute orchestration' in parts of the prelude to *Die Meistersinger* and in most of Beethoven, for whom 'the musical idea and the poetic human value' transcend other matters. To confuse the picture further, he notes in the *Entwurf* that 'most of Beethoven's piano compositions sound like transcriptions of orchestral works' (*Entwurf*: 24/86). Thus Beethoven's music tends, as a whole, to the abstract; but his orchestral works are 'arrangements', and his keyboard works sound (at least to Busoni's imagination) as if they should perhaps have been orchestrated. In Busoni's picture of the musical work instrumentation's status veers alarmingly between an ideal of the orchestra as a 'connected organism' (which seems to him to be but spasmodically, even childishly, present in works within the nineteenth-century repertoire) and an implicitly lifeless but not unskilful procedure that supports a certain type of musical abstraction. There is reason here to suppose that this abstraction is not the 'Ur-Musik' glimpsed in patches of Beethoven and Schumann, but the 'architectonic music' associated (in the *Entwurf*) with traditional formal schemata. But 'absolute orchestration' would seem in Busoni's own compositional praxis to be something of an ideal that tolerates a certain flexibility. The interesting case of the *Sonatina secunda* comes to mind: presented as 'absolute music', and then 'arranged' to form much of the music for the First Prologue of *Doktor Faust*. But which is the work, and which the arrangement? Busoni effectively muddies the waters by describing the *Sonatina* as a sketch for the opera, as if it took on its proper form only in the latter (*Essence*: 72–73). Whether we are to imagine the orchestrated version of what is after all only part of the *Sonatina* as having some precedence depends ultimately on how we relate Busoni's concept of the musical artwork to the stage.

In general, Busoni's picture of the work of music depends more on the idea of an 'Ur-Musik' than on the nineteenth century's idea of 'absolute music'. It is the concept of an 'Ur-Musik' that enables him to waive notions of *Werktreue* and to insist on transcription and composition as essentially the same activity. When Jim Samson refers to Busoni's 'fetish' of performance, he expresses another facet of 'Ur-Musik': that the dividing line between composition and performance is also blurred.[29]

There is a further anomaly here: that Busoni verged on a performance-led musical culture, while seeming to subscribe implicitly to the nineteenth-century cult of the musical genius, with its concomitant emphasis on the sanctity of the work. Alongside the downgrading of forms and genres went a belief in high art that, in Busoni's picture, is as emphatic as anything in the writings of his nineteenth-century predecessors, though it seems most deeply wedded to opera:

> *Arlecchino* is less than a challenge and more than a jest. To feel it as a challenge is putting it at a disadvantage, and to represent it as something not to be taken seriously is to belittle it. In the end it stands almost 'jenseits von Gut und Böse' ... (with an inclination towards the good). And finally, it is an independent work of art.
>
> Its incidental content of confession and instruction is not important enough to cross the path of what is artistic or to turn it away from that path. As a work of art it is sufficiently aristocratic to be able to claim a line of ancestors which makes it legitimate. As a handicraft it belongs to the scores that are made carefully and fastidiously. Is it pleasing? Has it significance? It endeavours to unite both excellences in the way proposed by the director of the theatre in the prologue to [Goethe's] *Faust* (*Essence*: 68).

In this essay on his comic opera some of Busoni's objectives for a stage work at least become clear. Although the reference to the opera's 'content of confession and instruction' is presented half-apologetically, there is often a strong hint of the didactic when Busoni talks

---

29. In this volume, p. 126.

about music and the stage: partly as if opera were an initiation into an *arcanum*; partly as if it were a species of moralising, or at least a means of avoiding the sensual. Pedigree is important, both in the musical and the literary sense (where E. T. A. Hoffmann is the most obvious ancestor in this case, besides the *commedia dell'arte*). Pedigree implies tradition, although this is a pedigree of the spirit, a subscription to the aristocracy of art. And fastidiousness of workmanship is a virtue, possibly incidental but not to be despised.

After this, it is hardly surprising that the performer is also bound by certain requirements that limit the experience of performance in a comparably severe way. In addition to technique, 'the great artist must necessarily have an unusual intelligence and culture'. Education must be a matter of more than just musicianship, and to this must be added a list of requirements that include Schumann's 'poetry' and a good taste that may be interpreted as the performer's equivalent to the composer's fastidiousness of craftsmanship (*Essence*: 80–81).

Even if individual works did not, or could not, approach the 'Ur-Musik', they were conditioned by its essential 'oneness', on which Busoni repeatedly laid stress. In this idea he reclaimed absolute music for himself, purged of the 'architectonic'; for its essential quality was that 'Music remains, wherever and in whatever form it appears, exclusively music and nothing else' (*Essence*: 1). It was characterised only by content, i.e. invention and atmosphere, and quality, i.e. form and shape. This served to downgrade such transient factors as form, purpose and sound medium. It may be objected that in this classification form leads a charmed life, being expelled from one list only to reappear in another, but this is another example of Busoni's distinction between 'architectonic forms' and the 'form' that is appropriate and unique to each composition. It is clear that Busoni is here thinking historically and expressing a hope for a future in which it would no longer be necessary to insist on the distinctness of church music, programme music and theatre music. As in Bach's works, there would only be small fluctuations in style dependent on the instrument chosen for the realisation.

It is impossible, in this context, to submit a full study of the path that leads from the individual musical work to the super-work of the musical stage envisaged by Busoni, in which forms and genres would be reborn in the context of a curiously austere and chaste form of drama from which Beethovenian rhetoric and Wagnerian 'lasciviousness' had been purged. But a question that ought to be addressed is:

why were the various studies for such works as *Arlecchino* and *Doktor Faust* necessary to Busoni? They seem to have been, essentially, rehearsals of 'themes and styles' appropriate to 'stimulation, compass and atmosphere'. Busoni also acknowledged the need to 'mould musically independent forms'; but a significant point is that most of the pieces that provided thematic material cannot truly be said to have pointed the way to complete formal structures in the opera (*Essence*: 72–73). In Walker's terms, the relationship between study and stage-work is more akin to paraphrase than to transcription. Even the *Sarabande* that provides the summation of the mystical-magical side of the work was shorn of a substantial episode, as if Busoni were making a sharp distinction between what was appropriate for the concert-hall, where the thematic and tonal implications of various kinds of thirds-chains could be worked out in greater detail, and the 'Symphonic Intermezzo' of an opera. The accompanying *Cortège*, too, was radically transformed from a continuous piece into framing and continuity music for a scene. Busoni's studies, however much their designation and purpose may seem subservient to the grand constellation of *Doktor Faust*, sustain the rôle of independent, self-contained and creatively original concert pieces rather well.

At the very least, Busoni worshipped (his own word) form, if not architectonics and genres, and his aesthetic of stage music was dominated by the need to restore forms and individual numbers, albeit of a newly created or recreated kind. Yet critical appreciation of form in Busoni's stage work has usually hinged on a kind of degenerate form, in which the true essential was style. Dent makes the point succinctly when paraphrasing Busoni to the effect that opera could accommodate all styles as necessary.[30] Accordingly, such compositional studies as the *Second Sonatina*, the *Sarabande und Cortège*, and the *Nocturne symphonique* are attempts to find musical styles appropriate to certain types of dramatic situation. Thus, for Busoni, form was an aspect of quality, but forms became aspects of atmosphere and, by extension, content, following his schema in *Wesen und Einheit der Musik*. In this essay Busoni subscribes in tentative fashion to what was later to be Dahlhaus's view: that history becomes the substance of works. Even where compositional studies do not exist to help us define scenes and episodes, it is usually possible to discern in Busoni's structuring of *Doktor Faust* a stylistic or generic fingerprint that operates as a

---

30. Edward J. Dent, *Ferruccio Busoni*, reprint, London, Eulenburg, 1974, p. 305.

musical-dramatic signifier. In a sense, Busoni's view that music was essentially one, so that such categories as 'court music' and 'church music' were meaningless, was a preparation for the subservient role that forms were to play in the super-form of *Doktor Faust*.

In Busoni's aesthetic some of the properties of the musical artwork would seem to become its material, a conclusion that some analysts have confirmed. Céléstin Deliège has made this point in a suitably concise way by suggesting that, while Busoni's music as a whole tends towards the rhapsodic, in *Doktor Faust* we are presented not with a thematic rhapsody but a 'rhapsody of styles'.[31] In this analysis the ambiguous Phrygian modality of the opening *Symphonia* may suggest 'the metaphysical colour' of the whole work; and this is the first of a series of stylistic parallels offered by Deliège that contain examples plucked from Busoni's contemporaries (including composers of the Second Viennese School) and assorted predecessors, such as (unnamed) sacred polyphonists of the sixteenth century. Analysis of Busoni has, in general, subscribed to the investigation of signs and *topoi*, while avoiding the immense problems of generalising about style and structure in a composer with a pronounced scorn for law-givers and a unique attitude to tonality; Riethmüller's concern with the chorale is symptomatic of this.[32] But analysis is inevitably still conditioned by the concept of the musical artwork, which Busoni weakened but did not abandon. In Dahlhaus's picture of the decline of genres and structures a notable element is the category of the work-in-progress, in which 'the goal ... is of virtually no importance compared with the manner in which it is pursued.'[33] Just as Busoni, at the end of his life, tended to move towards the notion of creation as discovery, so his goals grew larger. In the *Entwurf* he came to the conclusion that, in order to realise an aesthetic of liberty, it might be necessary to leave Earth; but in defiance of this seeming impossibility he noted that such a pilgrim alone might perhaps succeed (*Entwurf*: 44/97). This is also one sense of the ending of *Doktor Faust*. But *Doktor Faust* was still intended to be finished as a witness to the

31. Céléstin Deliège, 'Limiti razionali di un'estetica della libertà', in *Il flusso del tempo. Scritti su Ferruccio Busoni*, p. 273.
32. Riethmüller (1988), pp. 127–65.
33. Carl Dahlhaus, 'Plea for a Romantic Category: The Concept of the Work of Art in the Newest Music', in id., *Schoenberg and the New Music*, trans. Derrick Puffett and Alfred Clayton, Cambridge, Cambridge University Press, 1987, p. 211.

pilgrimage. If the work-in-progress emerges from its composition history, this was not through Busoni's desire or intention. The various
studies that it generated remained 'works as transcriptions', even
though, contrary to Davies's prescription, the work that they transcribe was not yet complete – and achieved completion only through
the work of editors.

10

Re-composing Schubert

James Wishart

Approaches to Existing Works

It should almost be self-evident that the integrity of a musical work is something of supreme concern to composers. This can sometimes result in extreme over-reaction if a composer suspects that his or her artistic vision is in jeopardy. Perhaps, in this regard, the behaviour of Kaikhosru Sorabji in withdrawing his works from performance for decades, because he could not trust any interpreter to perform them as he wished, can be partially understood. Other composers have prefaced scores, or instructed publishers, with specific prohibitions against unauthorised 'tampering' with their works. The more purist generation of composers in the twentieth century might be expected to be more clearly antagonistic towards the business of arrangement and transcription of their scores. Paradoxical as it may seem, this is not completely so, for not only have several composers wished to set out their own works in multiple forms – Ravel's orchestrations of his own piano music constitute one example here, and a more extreme manifestation would perhaps be the type of musical democratisation evident in the multiple dispositions of Percy Grainger's works – but composers have also continued to take up works of others, usually of previous generations, in order to produce new compositions.

Before embarking on the scrutiny of one short operatic excerpt and two self-contained works that are all in some way 'based' on pre-existent music of Schubert, I want to spend a short time addressing selectively the variety of approaches and methodologies that some twentieth-century composers have adopted when confronting a musical work by another composer.

The Sympathetic Completion?

Poor Mozart, poor Schubert: if only they had had more time, what other masterpieces they could have composed! Such uncritical non-sense is sometimes heard from commentators, providing a context in which the compulsive score-finisher can flourish. There are limitless temptations in this musical world: the intriguing torso of the final *Contrapunctus* of Bach's *Art of Fugue* ; several works of Mozart (including the thorny issue of the *Requiem*); certain operas (Puccini's *Turandot* and Berg's *Lulu*, to name but two); and, eponymously, Schubert's *'Unfinished' Symphony*. One cannot entirely blame the completers, who have sometimes been connected to the composers as pupils (Tibor Serly sympathetically filling in 17 bars in Bartók's *Third Piano Concerto*, but doing something a little more radical and questionable with the *Viola Concerto*), or have sometimes (supposedly) reconstructed existing manuscript short scores or sketches to make a piece totally performable, which could conceivably be said to be the case with Franco Alfano (*Turandot*) and Friedrich Cerha (*Lulu*).

But does the world need yet more completed works that Mozart (or others) laid aside, perhaps for very good reasons? And when sketches exist, should we resist the temptation to try to 'make sense' of them? The most recent example, familiar in many people's minds, will be Elgar's *Third Symphony*, or, as the official description of the work runs, the sketches for Elgar's *Third Symphony* 'elaborated by Anthony Payne'. The choice of words adopted by agreement with Elgar's descendants is surely significant: 'elaborated' being used in order to avoid such words as 'completed', 'composed', 'arranged' or 'orchestrated'.

The Compulsive Orchestrator

In an era when some concert-goers, and not a few critics as well, seem to acknowledge a hierarchy of relative importance in classical music, where opera and orchestral music sit somewhere near the top and many other valuable and important genres remain further down the scale, there is a sense in which a work may seem to have gained extra 'significance' by being presented in orchestral clothing. Maybe the original work was denied regular hearings by being written for a fairly 'lowly' combination, as in Debussy's *Six Epigraphes antiques* for piano duet. In a pragmatic spirit, Debussy himself recycled them (not wholly convincingly) for piano solo. This minor work has also been orchestrated twice, by Ernest Ansermet and Rudolf Escher.

Perhaps an even clearer example is that of Mussorgsky: a composer seemingly beloved by many others in terms of their making new versions of his works. Two major song-cycles, *The Nursery* and *Songs and Dances of Death*, have been orchestrated by later Russian composers within a few years of one another, Shostakovich and Edison Denisov. No doubt, both composers wished to pay homage in their own terms to Mussorgsky and felt that they could create the necessary orchestral colours to provide what the original composer never managed to create.

The Ultra-pragmatic Composer

Most composers have a personal vision of some kind: revisiting an old work (of their own) is a not uncommon operation, but multiple reworking of a composition is a much less usual phenomenon. One example of the latter would be the Estonian composer Arvo Pärt, who has configured his *Fratres* in many different ways: for an ensemble of 12 cellos; a string quartet; violin and piano; strings and percussion; wind octet and percussion. Paul Hillier, in his recent study of the composer, dryly points out that 'the underlying musical substance remains the same'.[1] Clearly, the material, although seemingly typical of Pärt's general style, holds some special significance for the composer, prompting him to try to create new contexts for the work in these manifold versions.

My own, somewhat humbler experience with a small three-minute piece, initially written for piano solo and bearing the somewhat unprepossessing title of *Og*, suggests that other motivations are possible. *Og* now exists in additional versions for flute and piano, oboe and piano, clarinet and piano, trumpet and piano, violin and piano, and viola and piano.[2] Certainly, there are changes in each piece to suit the requirements of the instruments, and these entail (occasionally) more than just range-tweakings or the avoidance of impracticalities, but the essence of the piece stays the same. If someone wished to look through these six refractions of the original piano miniature, perhaps the word 'essence' would define itself rather more sharply, encompassing the observation that the registers change only minutely. Perhaps this is the reason why (as yet) there is no *Og* for cello and piano (or, even more definitively) for double-bass and piano. A version of

1. Paul Hillier, *Arvo Pärt*, Oxford, Oxford University Press, 1997, p. 106.
2. James Wishart, *Og (Songs and Ironies)*, Liverpool, 1996.

Og with significantly changed registers would perhaps constitute a more radical new expression of the material.

My own starting-point for this trifle was the desire to write something that could be used in music education terms as a learning piece at the level of UK Associated Board Grade VIII. Thus my motivation for creating a plurality of *Ogs* could be seen to be pragmatic, even potentially 'commercially minded' (composers are known sometimes to yield to subtle pressure from publishers to produce alternative versions of works aimed at increasing the saleability of the composition and spreading the composer's reputation).

Distancing Through Quotation

When one musical work refers to another (sometimes in the form of short quotations), there is nearly always a subtext that can explain the choice of source-work. A composer may sometimes truthfully suggest that the source-work came to mind by a process of allusion, i.e. the immediate musical context suggested a familiar or parallel moment from a pre-existing work, but the majority of cases of quotation involve a deeper level of connection. It might be hard to find an overall logic in the choice of Skryabin's *Le Poème de l'extase*, Bach's *Brandenburg Concerto no. 1*, the *Veni Creator Spiritus* plainchant and Tchaikovsky's *Dance of the Sugar-Plum Fairy* as near-neighbours in an orchestral work, but perhaps the very zaniness of the stylistic incongruity was what attracted Bernd Alois Zimmermann to put them side by side and sometimes on top of each other in his late orchestral work *Photoptosis*.[3]

There is a more immediate logic underpinning the choice of quotations in the famous middle movement of Berio's *Sinfonia* of 1968: not the circumstance that found him on holiday in Sicily with only the resources of the Catania public library to augment his (presumably prodigious) musical memory while writing this movement, but the connections sometimes brought about by the musical glue that binds the movement together (the *Scherzo* from Mahler's *Resurrection Symphony*) and, even more, the constant narrative text that draws on Samuel Beckett's *The Unnameable*, alongside more contemporary street-references and musical in-jokes.[4]

3. Bernd Alois Zimmermann, *Photoptosis (Prelude for Large Orchestra)*, Mainz, Schott, 1970
4. Luciano Berio, *Sinfonia*, Vienna, Universal Edition, 1972.

Quotation, when the concentration falls on a single musical excerpt rather than the collage-type approach that characterises the Zimmermann and Berio instances, exaggerates stylistic distance and incongruity. Countless examples bear this out: the childish strains of an early Mozart piano sonata heard amid a welter of complex atonal orchestral counterpoint in Schnittke's *Third Symphony*;[5] the dissonant orchestral fanfare from Beethoven's *Choral Symphony* in Tippett's *Third Symphony*;[6] the use of 'repertoire standard' moments from Chopin and Beethoven, significantly blurred by pedal markings, in the two *Makrokosmos* cycles (nos. 1 and 2) for solo piano by George Crumb.[7]

In each of these examples there is a disturbance of the equilibrium, something more than parading the composer's knowledge of other composers or challenging the audience to follow the argument. Perhaps these examples (significantly, all the pieces mentioned above except that of Schnittke were written between 1968 and 1973) represent an attempt to create moments of shock by juxtaposing the complex atonal textures with consonant moments, in the way that composers of an earlier generation might suddenly have interpolated more strongly dissonant moments to achieve a similar effect.[8]

Composers may indeed wish to refer to music of very distant times in their own music. This can perhaps be seen most clearly in the pre-1970 works of Peter Maxwell Davies, including *Worldes Blis*, *Missa super l'homme armé* and *St Thomas Wake*. Does this, paradoxically, make it easier for the composer to absorb the source-works into his musical style? The distortion principles applied in Maxwell Davies's work around the time when he was writing the opera *Taverner* mean that the original material is hardly ever glimpsed in its original

5. Alfred Schnittke, *Symphony no. 3*, Hamburg, Sikorski, 1985.
6. Michael Tippett, *Symphony no. 3*, London, Schott, 1974.
7. George Crumb, *Makrokosmos I: Twelve Fantasy-Pieces after the Zodiac for Amplified Piano*, New York, Edition Peters, 1972, p. 18 (excerpt from Chopin *Fantaisie-impromptu* in movement 11, entitled: *Dream Image (Love-Death Music), Gemini*); id., *Makrokosmos II: Twelve Fantasy-Pieces after the Zodiac for Amplified Piano*, New York, Edition Peters, 1973, p. 18 (excerpt from Beethoven's *'Hammerklavier' Sonata* in movement 11, entitled: *Litany of the Galactic Bells, Leo*).
8. This is almost a musical *topos*; the tradition encompasses both the unfunny conclusion to Mozart's *Ein musikalischer Spass* and the bathetic conclusion of Ives's *Symphony no. 2*.

colours. In *Taverner*, the final curtain falls on the music of the six-teenth-century composer John Taverner played by four recorders, but, significantly, it is left incomplete and unresolved. Elsewhere in the opera, the *Taverner* source-music is always presented in highly distorted fashion.[9] In *St Thomas Wake*, the Bull pavan is reprised on the harp, and is very soon heard 'camped up' by the on-stage jazz band.[10] Of course the composer is under no obligation at all to respect his sources unduly, and the inclusion of an alien artefact can often be employed more as a means to an end than for its intrinsic qualities.

Relishing the Discomfort Factor
Just as punk bands in the 1970s gained gratification from their dis-tortions and nose-thumbing at establishments of all kinds, 'serious' composers are capable of juvenile behaviour as well. Making their audience shift uneasily in its seats is one of the small pleasures that sometimes appeal to them. One way of disconcerting an audience is to be seemingly indifferent to the manner of presentation of the source work or quotation, or, more precisely, to be indifferent to the effect produced on the listener. This kind of grotesquerie is perhaps well exemplified in the final movement of Lukas Foss's *Baroque Variations* (Phorion), where a movement from a solo violin partita by Bach is subjected to all manner of degrading and distorting treat-ment.[11]

Franz Schubert Revisited

Tippett
So many issues today are in part driven by the pressure of anniver-saries and celebrations. Schubert's bicentenary (1997) occasioned many tributes from composers and arrangers, in the same way that Purcell's tercentenary in 1995 had done two years previously. In fact, all three pieces discussed in this essay were written well in advance of the bicentenary celebrations and have nothing to do with them. The bicentenary has perhaps merely brought them all to mind. I begin

9. Peter Maxwell Davies, *Taverner*, full score, London, Boosey & Hawkes, 1984, p. 379.
10. Id., *St Thomas Wake: Foxtrot for Orchestra*, London, Boosey & Hawkes, 1972.
11. Lukas Foss, *Baroque Variations*, New York, Carl Fischer, 1967.

with Tippett and his third opera, *The Knot Garden* (1970).[12] The opera is exceptionally concise, its central act lasting no more than 25 minutes, despite having nine scenes. Subtitled *Labyrinth*, the act is a furious cross-cutting of confrontational situations between the principal characters, some of which last only a couple of minutes. The penultimate scene is the most fast-moving of all, whirling characters violently away in turn, in what Tippett describes as 'dissolves'. A relaxation in atmosphere ensues, and the stage instruction reads: 'As the sense of nightmare clears away, Dov comes to life first. He sees the plight of Flora and goes to comfort her'.[13] Dov, the gay musician, who is apparently so impervious to the hurt felt by his partner Mel, can nonetheless empathise with the somewhat alarmed young Flora. The scene that follows becomes the longest of this short central act. Comforting the vulnerable Flora in his arms, Dov sings the following:

Flora, do you like music?
(Music that's bitter-sweet.)
Do you ever sing?[14]

It might occur to us that generally, in opera, characters do not refer to 'talking' or 'singing', composers and their librettists perhaps being fearful that this would prick the bubble of collective suspended disbelief that allows us all (or most of us) to accept the artifice of sung discourse in the medium of opera. In fact, a careful look at (especially) the nineteenth-century operatic repertoire reveals that this is not quite so. Much turns on the paradox lucidly stated by Carolyn Abbate: 'In opera, the characters pacing the stage often suffer from deafness; they do not *hear* the music that is the ambient fluid of their music-drowned world'.[15] This is the normality against which the operatic narrative unfolds. Specific exceptions are mentioned by Abbate elsewhere in her book. They include *Senta's Ballad* (Wagner, *Der fliegende Holländer*) and the *Bell Song* (Delibes, *Lakmé*), in both of which there is evident on-stage awareness that the narrative mode is continued in song.[16]

12. Michael Tippett, *The Knot Garden*, full score, London, Schott, 1970.
13. Id., *The Knot Garden*, libretto, in *The Operas of Michael Tippett*, ed. Nicholas John, London, John Calder, 1985, p. 107.
14. Loc. cit.
15. Carolyn Abbate, *Unsung Voices: Opera and Musical Narrative in the Nineteenth Century*, Princeton, Princeton University Press, 1991, p. 119.
16. Ibid., pp. 96–118 (Wagner) and 4–10 (Delibes).

Flora now responds to Dov by sitting up on her own and plunging straight into a Schubert song. One might expect this kind of song to be placed inside some kind of musical 'quotation marks' in the opera, allowing the places where Tippett's own music stops and the quoted Schubert song begins and ends to be clearly delineated. Tippett certainly provides a sort of initial musical throat-clearing: a harp glissando. Flora then sings *Die liebe Farbe* from Schubert's song-cycle 'Die schöne Müllerin' in the original German, in the 'soprano' key of B minor and with the piano accompaniment very 'correctly' transferred to wind. At the end of the first half-stanza Dov begins to sing (as Tippett describes it: 'translating musingly'), but in English.[17] The song continues (the first half-stanza being repeated instead of moving forward to the second half) 'in the background'; the original melody is now transferred to a solo oboe. The translation acts as a kind of gloss on the song: the new vocal line is Tippett's, but it relates audibly to Schubert's own melodic model. Just as the voice glosses the tune, the accompaniment is glossed or ornamented by chromatic coruscations in the high register of the piano.

The song is not completed; there is a short hesitation before the resolution of the V-I cadence, and a new chord (a Janus-like 'Ib' in G that retains B as the bass-note) is interposed. This acts as both an interrupted cadence concluding the song and the beginning of a new musical statement. Dov has ceased musing and comments: 'But that's a boy's song'.[18] The world of Schubert vanishes, and Dov promises to sing his song – 'a different song' (by which he means a more modern song: one with supposedly greater relevance to his own world and which turns away from empathy for Flora's plight to embrace narcissism and self-justification).[19] This song is indeed vastly different from Schubert's; although it is also strophic, its vocal style, scoring and harmony are far removed from the classicism of *Die liebe Farbe*. But perhaps the tonality and restraint of Schubert has the last word. Dov's disgruntled partner Mel, who observes part of his extended song, attempts to debunk it: 'Come: I taught you that'.[20] This leads to a final line delivered by a somewhat petulant Dov: 'It is false'.[21] The orchestral postlude that accompanies the scene-fade ends (via the retrograde

17. Tippett, *The Knot Garden*, libretto, p. 107.
18. Loc. cit.
19. Loc. cit.
20. Ibid., p. 108.
21. Loc. cit.

of the series that Tippett uses intermittently during the opera) on the note B (the keynote associated with *Die liebe Farbe*). There are other ways in which Schubertian tonal features link into the surrounding Tippett context: the insistent repeated dominant pedal of the song (F sharp, heard during Flora's half-stanza on the horn) that forms a connection with the F sharp basis of the introduction to Flora's song, and also with the tonality at the beginning and end of each stanza of Dov's subsequent song.

A number of interesting aspects emerge from this song-scene. Previously, I described the song as unfolding within quotation marks, provided by a harp glissando at the beginning and an interrupting piano chord at the end. I also commented that the two quotation marks helped to delineate the boundary between Tippett and Schubert. The problem with this description is that, while the opening half-stanza is pure Schubert, the second half-stanza, sung by Dov in English, is a hybrid: still an imported artefact, with the Schubertian melodic line continuing under Dov's musical-textual paraphrase. The new elements, Dov's 'commentary' and the treble-register embellishments, take the music for a while into a genuine merger of Schubert and Tippett styles. This proves unsustainable for more than a brief moment: its very fragility is confirmed when the piano chord cuts the episode short. As well as being highly expressive in its own right, this chord acts a kind of gear-shift, moving the music out of this combination-style, and also shifting from aria to recitative – from a lingering in an artificial, rarefied world of archaisms to the tougher world of contemporary reality.

It might be argued that, by withholding the final chord of the song, Tippett is reproducing a somewhat cliché-ridden approach to an imported source. I would contend, however, that the solution that Tippett adopts to make the connection to Dov's personal song-testament, i.e. what I have described as a Janus-like chord, is exceptional in its simplicity, expressivity and conciseness, carrying with it considerable significance. The hiatus between the V and the delayed I creates a sense of anticipation, and the chord, when it arrives, is simple, and can immediately be perceived as concluding the musical argument of the Schubertian original by virtue of being an interruption. The use of solo piano in this register and voicing is 'new' within the context of this scene, but the piano has already been heard playing the most significant rôle in the hybridised second half-stanza. In this sense, the choice of piano as a timbre is a significant gesture. The

harmony used is still markedly tonal, indeed classical: it could easily
be mistaken (similar register, very slightly different voicing, different
bass-note) for the opening chord of Beethoven's *Fourth Piano Concerto*, an extremely familiar work in the repertory. The connection
with the Beethoven work is slightly strengthened by the presentation
of the chord. In Beethoven, the first sound we hear is this quiet chord
from the solo pianist – which may, or may not, surprise us, depending on our familiarity with not just this work but also the normal
archetypes and expectations of concerto first-movement form. The
separateness of this chord in the Tippett scene momentarily ushers us
into this world, as well as providing a context for an interrupting gesture that is perfectly consistent with Schubert's own style, and a harmonic and gestural device which happens also to be totally congruent
with that of Tippett.

Conceivably, I am placing a significance on one specific musical element that was not necessarily envisaged by Tippett in quite this
manner; but this does not necessarily devalue the observations. In this
short scene, and by the specific manner in which he uses the Schubert
song, Tippett not only fills out the dramatic development of his characters and provides an element of stability after the maelstrom of
complex confrontational relationships that has occurred earlier in the
act: he also brings about a brief moment of integration between two
radically different styles across the divide of some 150 years of musical development, achieving an expressive and intelligent transition
from Schubert to himself.

Berio[22]

Luciano Berio's own compositional aesthetic has always left room for
revisiting older works, most often the same composer's own: witness
the way in which some of the works in the series of highly virtuosic
Sequenze for solo instruments have been recomposed to form part of
another series of compositions that Berio names *Chemins* (these
include several works under that title and also the *Corale*, which takes
as its starting point the eighth *Sequenza*, which is for solo violin). In
each of these instances, Berio elaborates the original work, often
extending its scale and length but also articulating implicit harmonies
and counterpoints found in the original *Sequenza*. Berio has also

---

22. Franz Schubert-Luciano Berio, *Rendering for Orchestra (1988–1990)*, Vienna,
     Universal Edition, 1989.

turned at fairly regular intervals to the transcription and arrangement of works by other composers, partly as light relief and partly as a way of paying homage to those figures he particularly admires. This would seem to be the rationale behind his versions of Brecht-Weill songs and the two sets of early Mahler songs. Fidelity to stylistic norms seems the predominant approach in all of these works.

Berio has maintained an interest in the works of Schubert for a considerable length of time. Specifically, he has been interested in the sketches for the final (tenth) symphony which have been in the public domain since their publication over twenty years ago.[23] Not entirely certain what to do with this material, Berio nonetheless decisively rejected the musicological reconstruction for full orchestra made by Brian Newbould.[24] When his composition *Rendering* emerged in 1990, it became clear that Berio's approach was far removed from the musically 'pure' point of view represented by enlightened scholarship. *Rendering* unfolds in a single span but clearly and audibly encompasses the three partially sketched movements: an *Allegro*, followed by a slow movement and a *Scherzo-Finale* hybrid. The scoring of Berio's work is consistent with that of a late Schubert orchestral work, leaving aside the addition of a celesta, whose specific role is discussed below.

The printed score reproduces the sketches (mostly in two-stave format, which is in the main conceived for, and playable on, a keyboard instrument) at the foot of the page, complete with blanks, mistakes and all the original marks of tempo and expression. It is immediately obvious which bars of the score are intended as genuine Schubert and which are Berio (the sketches disappear intermittently from the foot of the page). The way that some sketches are relatively extended, while others are more truncated, is also represented in the score; we can therefore see the points at which Berio placed sketches next to one another. Without a detailed examination of all the published sketches (which would exceed the scope of this essay), it is not possible to determine the significance lying behind the selection of some sketches and the rejection of others. No editorial commentary is provided: this is first and foremost to be considered as a completed version of Schubert sketches 'elaborated' by Berio (this was, we remember, the term used to describe Anthony Payne's reworking of

23. Franz Schubert, *Drei Symphonie-Fragmente*, Kassel, Bärenreiter, 1978.
24. Ibid., *Symphony no. 10 in D major*, realised by Brian Newbould, London, 1995.

Elgar's *Third Symphony* sketches, but it is one that might be thought equally appropriate for the Berio work under discussion).

Essentially, Berio is providing us with one creative individual's interpretation of what Schubert might conceivably have expected to be performed by an orchestra under the title of *Tenth Symphony*. But, in contrast to Newbould's version and other familiar examples of the completion of fragmentary works, Berio has chosen to fill the gaps between the available sketches in a personal, highly idiosyncratic manner. Taking a distinctly non-musicological approach, Berio wishes, almost, to emphasise the moments that are **not** present in the sketch. Each time that a gap in the movement's structure emerges before the re-entry of another sketch fragment, Berio fills it in with material that is audibly not Schubert's. But this is not the full story. The trigger, the signifier, the aural cue, is the entry of the celesta, an instrument not available to Schubert, but one which, given careful scoring, can be singled out atop an orchestral texture otherwise *anno* 1828. Equipped with this knowledge, a listener can identify with absolute precision the places where the sketches break off and where they recommence.

What happens in these moments of absence? Berio has produced textures that are often radically non-Schubertian, with their reliance on more complex counterpoint and solo colours, and, in addition, their copious recourse to intra-Schubertian reference. The non-sketch material employed comes from late Schubert works: principally the *Piano Trio no. 1*, D 898 (1827), the *Piano Sonata no. 21*, D 960 (1828) and the song-cycle 'Winterreise', D 911 (1827). Fragments of these major late works, sometimes rhythmically distorted and often wrenched from their original surroundings, provide the recognisable framework for these linking episodes.

The analogy that Berio chooses to invoke is one taken from the world of art: specifically, the manner in which important early wall frescoes are today often preserved and exhibited. When frescoes are uncovered, it is almost inevitable that the picture will not be revealed in its entirety. However painstaking the restoration process, there will be gaps left in the whole. One modern approach is to smooth out these gaps and make them as unremarkable and inconspicuous as possible. This process, sometimes called 'rendering', effectively brings about an absence of meaningful visual data in each gap. The intention is to encourage the viewer's eyes to range across the full dimensions of the restored fresco, taking in the various fragments that have been successfully salvaged but ignoring the intervening gaps. In this way, while being clearly aware that a fresco is damaged, one can effectively suppress this information and appreciate the work of art, blanking out the missing areas. The point of rendering is precisely to make these void areas visually neutral in such a way that a viewer does not become consciously aware of how the damaged areas have been dealt with. Giotto's frescoes in Assisi, before the catastrophic earthquakes of 1997, were examples of this type of restorative approach.[25] Some Italian approaches to art restoration differ slightly from the more generally accepted European normative methods, and there are some instances of frescoes in which the gaps have been filled in with material featuring clearly discernible cross-hatched markings, whose purpose is to ensure that there is no confusion between what is original fresco and what is restorative in-fill.[26]

Does this analogy stand up in relation to this orchestral work of Berio? There must be some doubt about this. The provision of an aural signal, here conveyed by the entrance of the celesta, would appear to contradict the fundamental idea of the neutral nature, the anonymity, of the rendering material. The textures and harmonies are so instantly foreign to the familiar Schubertian world that there is a sense of alienation and distancing, which is perhaps at variance with the intention to supply extra material that will not draw attention to itself. But if we consider the particular restorative technique that employs cross-hatching, we may perhaps have found a more appropriate analogy. In interviews, and in introductions to the work, Berio has always stressed the element of neutrality and plainness, but this could be somewhat disingenuous.

Here are two excerpts from his own introduction to the score:

> *Rendering* with its dual authorship is intended as a restoration of these sketches, it is not a completion nor a reconstruction. This restoration is made along the lines of the modern restoration of frescoes that aims at reviving the old colours without however trying to disguise the damage that time has caused, often leaving inevitable empty patches in the composition, for instance as in the case of Giotto in Assisi ...

25. It is unclear at the time of writing whether any of the Giotto frescoes in Assisi are irretrievably lost as a result of earthquake damage or whether all can be at least partially restored. The process of restoration is, understandably, extremely protracted.
26. Information kindly supplied verbally by Anne Compton, Curator of Art Collections at the University of Liverpool (September, 1998).

In the empty places between one sketch and the next there is a kind of connective tissue which is constantly different and changing, always 'pianissimo' and 'distant', intermingled with reminiscences of late Schubert ... and crossed by polyphonic textures based on fragments of the same sketches. This musical 'cement' comments on the discontinuities and the gaps which exist between one sketch and another and is always announced by the sound of a celesta, and must be performed 'quasi senza suono' and without expression'.[27]

A few significant words leap from the page – the comparison of the newly composed Berio sections with 'connective tissue', and the description of this musical 'cement', which comments on the discontinuities and gaps between successive sketches. Berio clearly does expect the listener to perceive the Schubertian strands in his newly composed 'cement' and not be unduly disconcerted by stylistic dissonance. The analogy of emptiness and neutrality is enhanced by Berio's injunction for these episodes to be played 'without expression'. One thing the listener perceives is a radical change in harmonic rhythm. If we take the very first Berio interpolation, beginning at score reference number 6, the majority of the sequence (lasting about 90 seconds) is harmonically static on either A (the dominant of the first movement of Schubert's original, reached at the end of the first sketch fragment) or D (the tonic), or an inverted pedal F sharp (used to make the transition to the next sketch, which is now firmly back in the tonic region).[28] Short, mostly chromatic, linking passages connect these moments of stasis.

It is important to clarify the position concerning the interpretation of the sketch material. Berio has taken the sketches and scored them sympathetically with regard to stylistic considerations, filled out their missing harmonies, supplied convincing accompanimental textures, corrected obvious mistakes and, generally speaking, produced a very faithful series of glimpses of Schubertian orchestral writing in 1828. No doubt, from a strictly musicological point of view, his decision, in the slow movement, to admit short counterpoint exercises that 'happen' to appear on the same sheets of manuscript paper (they are even dated precisely, in the sketches, to November 1828) would be considered egregious, but these elements are contained within the Berio musical 'cement' that looms somewhat larger in this central panel of the work.

27. Schubert-Berio (1989), Berio's preface on p. i.
28. Ibid., pp. 7–15.

Even after repeated hearings, this work retains its ability to disconcert. The idea of 'Polystylism' as frequently applied to the work of Alfred Schnittke, in which the composer's own style coexists with those of earlier masters, comes to mind. But in the present case, the stylistic diversity is so extreme that it is difficult to accept that the sections newly composed by Berio genuinely assume a neutral role, as implied by the title. Although the beginning and the end of the work are convincing enough in their tonal substance (and the emphatic resolution in D does indeed seem final!), a curious question-mark hangs over the entire enterprise. This observation is not in any way intended as a criticism of Berio's sincerity or competence, but merely makes the point that the concepts underlying this work are complex and not easily grasped.

Zender

Hans Zender's composition, described on the cover of the score as 'a composed interpretation', is scored for solo tenor and small orchestra. It was completed in 1993.[29] There is a small element of staging in this version, some entries and exits of musicians being specified in the score. The keys chosen for the songs accord with those found in the new Schubert collected edition, and all 24 songs appear in their familiar order in Zender's work.[30]

Some movements are extremely faithful in intention and leave Schubert relatively untransformed, except for the transition from piano accompaniment to that of a small chamber orchestra. For example, the third song, *Gefrorne Tränen*, has no notes changed at all, relying for its effect on the constant alternation of accompanying timbres: *col legno* strings giving way to clarinets and bassoons, to marimba, to guitar, and so on.[31] This fragmentation suits, in part, the stylised frozen imagery of the text, as well as the deliberation and 'separateness' manifested in the articulation markings of the original piano accompaniment. The only eccentric moment occurs during the second quatrain, when the imagery of cold – 'dass ihr erstarrt zu Eise' – occasions an overt pictorial reference immediately after the word 'Eise': a buzzing sound on harp usually obtained by jarring the pedal mechanism between 'slots'.

29. Hans Zender, *Schuberts 'Winterreise'*, Wiesbaden, Breitkopf & Härtel, 1996.
30. Franz Schubert, 'Winterreise', D 911, in *Neue Schubert-Ausgabe, Serie IV (Lieder), Bd IVa*, Kassel, Bärenreiter, 1979.
31. Zender (1996), no. 3, *Gefrorne Tränen*, pp. 27–32.

Other movements introduce further compositional interventions from Zender. The fourth song, *Erstarrung*, faithfully expands the uneasy piano triplet figurations into an ensemble context and heightens the cold and unease already present in Schubert.[32] But the most palpable change concerns the use of what might be termed 'false starts' in the accompanying ritornello: prefacing the Schubert song (and parallel points occurring later in the song) with five crotchet beats of additional Schubertian texture that serve to throw askew the rhythmic clarity of the music each time they are heard. The seventh song, *Auf dem Flusse*, also includes a prefatory section by Zender, here derived from four minor triads, E minor (the key of the song), D sharp minor (the region used half-way through the second quatrain), G sharp minor (that used during the final, fourth quatrain) and (only once) G minor, which does not appear in the song at all.[33] These triads are presented and overlapped alongside motivic references to the initial melodic phrase of the solo voice. On the entry of the voice in the song 'proper', the accompaniment reverts first to pizzicato strings, then to solo guitar. This scoring enhances the intimacy and points up the contrast of scale between this opening section and the viciousness of the treatment near the end of the song. In Schubert's original, the second half of the last quatrain is repeated in order to intensify the experience, allowing a more extravagant, higher-lying vocal line to bring the song to an end. Zender repeats more than this, the first time almost drowning out the voice by referring back to those 'foreign' triads that were 'trailed' in his new introduction. The voice even seems to give up the struggle in the middle of a phrase, keeping back the last syllable of 'ob's wohl auch so reissend schwillt' until – after a seven-bar icy blast from an exceedingly shrilly scored tutti, heavily reliant on distorting flutter-tonguing and tremolando – the final note and syllable return suddenly to the uneasy calm and quiet of the guitar and string pizzicato textures encountered earlier. The repeated quatrain is not quite so violently treated, but the impact of the intrusive and threatening G sharp minor episode cannot, for Zender, be so easily reconciled, since he chooses to superimpose this triad (albeit in harmonics) over Schubert's E minor final chord.

This kind of treatment exemplifies Zender's approach during most of the work. There are several movements marked by further

32. Ibid., no. 4, *Erstarrung*, pp. 33–45.
33. Ibid., no. 7, *Auf dem Flusse*, pp. 65–73.

extraordinary treatments, but I must inevitably be selective in my discussion. The opening *Gute Nacht* is enormously extended vis-à-vis the original, with a long introduction only gradually establishing the tonal basis (repeated D minor chords) and admitting some canonic imitation of the song's 'head-motive'.[34] Vocal and rhythmic distortions are also present; the song's extended duration is perhaps intended to create a more overt link forward to the final song of the cycle, *Der Leiermann*, which I will discuss later.

Der stürmische Morgen is elevated to hyper-realism not only by the use of percussive simulations of storm conditions (side drum rolls, rainsticks, etc.) but also by its discontinuities: beats or whole bars are interpolated as evident interruptions, engendering a constant sense of hesitation and uncertainty.[35] *Mut* makes even more of a virtue out of the 'false start' principle, with three wind machines filling in the unexpected gaps as the texture is progressively raised (and eventually lowered) through a series of chromatic steps.[36] Two songs, *Die Nebensonnen* and *Die Post*, use a plurality of tempi and pulses to enliven the accompanying texture. In *Die Nebensonnen*, the justification for this approach comes, presumably, from the imagery of twin suns.[37]

Die Post finds Zender in a more radical frame of mind.[38] Not content with the comparatively modest eight-bar introduction provided by Schubert, he provides a much longer one that features an additional 21 bars of fragmentary fanfare-like motifs, sometimes overlapping with one another, before the full-textured version is heard. The rhythm that dominates the song – dotted quaver, semiquaver, quaver – is presented effectively in multiple tempi, but for notational convenience Zender writes these all within the prevailing metre of (mainly) 6/8. For a clarification of Zender's approach, see Fig. 1. The principal rhythmic cell (with its relative proportions of 3–1–2) has five alternative presentations, two of which are augmentations, two diminutions, and one a kind of deformed augmentation that changes the proportions to 2–1–2). One must imagine that Schubert intended the main rhythmic shape to be emblematic in some way of the manner in which the post was delivered (on horseback) at a breathless gallop. Zender allows this metaphor of purposeful activity to proliferate. In

34. Ibid., no. 1, *Gute Nacht*, pp. 1–19.
35. Ibid., no. 18, *Der stürmische Morgen*, pp. 142–49.
36. Ibid., no. 22, *Mut*, pp. 164–78.
37. Ibid., no. 23, *Die Nebensonnen*, pp. 179–86.
38. Ibid., no. 13, *Die Post*, pp. 106–19.

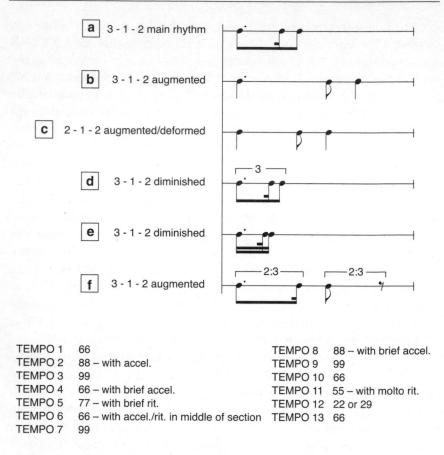

TEMPO 1	66
TEMPO 2	88 – with accel.
TEMPO 3	99
TEMPO 4	66 – with brief accel.
TEMPO 5	77 – with brief rit.
TEMPO 6	66 – with accel./rit. in middle of section
TEMPO 7	99

TEMPO 8	88 – with brief accel.
TEMPO 9	99
TEMPO 10	66
TEMPO 11	55 – with molto rit.
TEMPO 12	22 or 29
TEMPO 13	66

All metronome markings are based on a durational value of dotted crotchet

Figure 1   Schubert/Zender, *Die Post*: manipulation of pulse/tempo

the eight-bar 'introduction' to the first verse, the head-motive (whose rhythm is labelled 'a' in Fig. 1) is subjected to parodistic distortion and imitation, to the commentary of rhythms 'd' and 'e', which are often so placed within the bar as to maximise rhythmic proliferation and a general sense of dislocation. Once the vocal line enters, these diminutions of the main rhythm 'a', which are heard as accelerating imitations, reappear near the end of selected vocal phrases, other phrases being left largely as composed by Schubert.

Without access to a score, it would sometimes be difficult for a listener to discern whether the changing pace of rhythm 'a' was due to a notational change or to a tempo fluctuation. The second half of

Fig. 1 reveals the profusion of tempo changes in Zender's version of this song. All the *ritardando* or *accelerando* episodes coincide with repetitions of the text 'Mein Herz, mein Herz!', as if this phrase cued an increase in emotional momentum. Wilhelm Müller's last two lines of text are repeated only once by Schubert but twice by Zender, the second and third times at a deliberately pedestrian tempo, shown in the score as 'quaver = 66 or 88', which could thus mean a tempo three times slower than the main reference tempo of 'dotted crotchet = 66'.

On the first time that this couplet is heard (at the core tempo), the rhythmic proliferations are silenced, as if the onset of the minor key and the protagonist's pessimism has rendered this element superfluous. The second setting of the couplet (Schubert's first, but now repeated at a funereal tempo) occasions a use of vocal amplification, not with the prime purpose of ensuring audibility over the orchestra, which is largely marked down to *piano* or *pianissimo* during the vocal phrases, but for the sake of sonority alone. On the commercial recording conducted by the composer there seems also to be an increase in ambient reverberation (which is not indicated in the score).[39] The postlude, when eventually reached, reverts suddenly to the main tempo, making fresh recourse to the technique of rhythmic proliferation until the last two bars.

The super-slow minor key episode is probably the most shocking of Zender's accretions and alterations to Schubert. It perhaps owes something to those images of slowed-down time familiar to us from cinematic models (which sometimes also entail intensified ambient reverberation on the accompanying soundtrack). Our immediate impression is of something very deliberately 'wrong', a calculated gesture of impropriety towards the source. A comparison that seems appropriate, however, is with the well-known recording, by the Canadian pianist Glenn Gould, of the Theme and Variations opening Mozart's *A major piano sonata*, K 331, which has been derided by most commentators for its deliberately funereal pace.[40] Gould makes

39. Hans Zender, *Schuberts 'Winterreise'*, performed by Hans Peter Blochwitz (tenor) with Ensemble Modern, conducted by the composer on RCA Victor, Red Seal 09026 68067 2 (2-CD set), 1995.

40. Wolfgang Amadeus Mozart, *Piano Sonata no. 11 in A major*, K 331, played by Glenn Gould (piano) on Sony SM4K52627 (4-CD set). This is a re-issue of the original recording of 1970.

a case, through his performance, for an exceptionally slow beginning to this movement in order that the tempi of subsequent variations may relate to one another in a specific fashion. In the case of Zender's recomposition of *Die Post*, the relative simplicity and starkness of the exaggeratedly slow episode causes the listener to reflect a little more on the heartache expressed by the singer without being in any way deflected by the largely positive signification of the *Hauptrhythmus* and its concomitant alternative guises. When we snap out of this reflection into the postlude, we experience a sense of pent-up fervour that erupts briefly as the first two bars of the postlude present rhythmic motives 'a', 'b', 'd', 'e' and 'f' simultaneously.

The repeated bare fifths in the left hand of the piano part of Schubert's accompaniment to *Der Leiermann* are iconic, coming as close to the wheezing, frozen sonority of a barrel-organ drone as one is able without escaping from a pianistic timbre.[41] With the resources of a chamber orchestra at his disposal, Zender can inevitably be more graphic in his representation, employing mistuned open strings, combinations of wind sonorities, guitar, harp and brass, not forgetting the strains of the accordion, which perhaps provides the closest timbral analogue. The bare fifths alone, heard in accumulated aggregates, provide the opening and closing frame of this movement. If Fig. 2 is consulted, one can see how the opening seven-pitch aggregate returns at the end of the song, before cross-fading into a more complex chord that is most simply rationalised as an aggregate of piled-up thirds, but in which a strong element of fifths is also evident. The fifths element predominates as the chord's energy is dissipated into the concluding bare fifths formed from the notes A, D, G and C, which perhaps portray absence, bareness, indifference, non-being.

Each vocal phrase is delivered without textual, melodic or rhythmic alteration in the home key of B minor, but intervening accompanimental phrases move gradually away from this key, taking in six other drone-dyads, which act as the base/bass for minor-key episodes. Recalling the techniques used in *Die Post*, the melodic 'head-motive' of the accompaniment is subjected to rhythmic variants, two of which are shown at the bottom of Fig. 2. The Schubert original comes, perhaps rather lamely, to a consonant conclusion (the emphasis having earlier been placed on the often dissonant simultaneity of I and V brought about by the omnipresent fifths-drone). No doubt, Schubert

---

41. Zender (1996), no. 24, *Der Leiermann*, pp. 187–96.

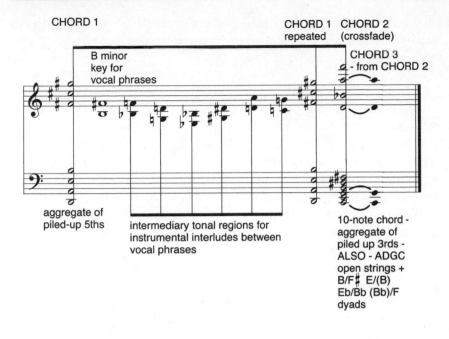

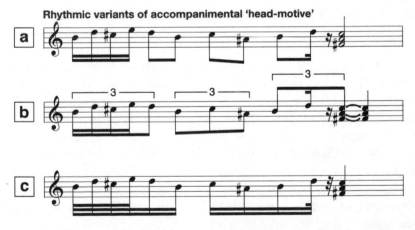

Figure 2 Schubert/Zender *Der Leiermann*: manipulation of interval, tonality and melodic line

had his own reasons for resolving the song in that manner, not just the pressure of stylistic conventions but perhaps the very effect of inadequacy and weakness that such a resolution causes. Zender, predictably, finds this solution inappropriate. Instead, he conjures up an alternative aura of inadequacy and emptiness with a bare-fifths string chord. Both solutions, his and Schubert's, are poignant and despairing, finding simple, almost elegant means with which to round off this cycle.

Reconsidering the Starting-point

How do these three Schubertian excursions fit into my earlier selective description of categories, if at all? Tippett's brief quotation of Schubert's song must partly be seen in its dramatic context as a moment of suspended time, floating outside the immediate context of the characters in the 'Labyrinth'. By using the immediately familiar archaism of Schubert, Tippett is telling us something about Flora's innocence and naïveté, is concentrating our attention on the imminent contrast which will be perceived between this song and Dov's 'showy' song, his brash moment of self-aggrandisement; the difference is perhaps that between the culture of Europe, represented by *Die liebe Farbe*, and that of California represented in the cod-Americanisms of 'play it cool'.[42] Could this be one of the cases, of which other examples are discussed in Abbate's *Unsung Voices*, where the subject-matter and/or mode of delivery are a reflection of the central narrative impulses of the operatic drama? The Schubert song is strophic (as in many nineteenth-century operatic examples discussed by Abbate), but is in no sense is a ballad or an emblem of dramatic or heroic action. The song therefore serves only to reinforce the image already established of Flora as waif-like and innocent. The conjunction of two radically different songs in this scene possibly suggests that the characters are completely conscious of their 'music-positioned' situation as described in Edward Cone's *The Composer's Voice*: 'When characters subsist by virtue of the operatic medium, the musically communicable aspects of their personalities have been brought to full consciousness, so that the characters naturally express themselves in song – song of which, in the peculiar operatic world they inhabit, they are fully aware'.[43]

Musically speaking, Tippett is momentarily suspending his own style and yet showing how the two styles are not as distantly separated as might have been thought. The decision to ornament the second

42. Tippett, *The Knot Garden*, libretto, p. 107.
43. Edward T. Cone, *The Composer's Voice*, Berkeley and Los Angeles, University of California Press, 1974, p. 133.

half-stanza and introduce Dov (together with the English language and a new melodic line) into the closed world of the Schubert song is a risky one. There is a precedent earlier within Act 2 (in Scene 7) for this kind of approach: briefly, at the height of an emotional duet for Mel and Denise, the protest song *We Shall Overcome* enters subtly within the orchestra, albeit with more complex harmony than could ever be imagined on any street protest! As the song reaches its pitch and emotional height ('Deep in my heart ...'), Mel joins in the song, articulating the 'thoughts' of the orchestra and twinning the closed world of the protest song with the 'original' Tippett style of Denise's coloratura vocal line.[44] Here, too, the moment passes quickly, and, as in Flora's and Dov's Schubert song, the song cannot be completed. It is not so much that the allusion is false, more that it cannot, by its nature, be sustained for too long. The Tippett/Schubert episode in *The Knot Garden* is arguably a successful example of the way in which quotation can bring out extra levels of subtext; it also introduces welcome relief and variety.

Luciano Berio's approach in *Rendering* might initially seem to fit better into the category of 'sympathetic completion'. But one must concede that Berio attempts rather more than this term by itself would suggest, since his approach is partly scholarly. He attempts to make some formal sense out of the heterogeneous sketches and does his best to extract convincing textures from what are sometimes only skeletal suggestions made by Schubert. The fact that he resists – and, indeed, is actively hostile towards – what he terms a 'musicological' approach is probably connected most of all with his self-image as a composer.

Berio finds himself, perhaps, caught between two stools. The metaphor of the frescoes is a good one, but one that does not take sufficient account of the enormous perceptual difference between the plastic and temporal arts. Simply put, it is very hard to manufacture an inconspicuous 'musical cement', as he sets out to do! Whether the few 'strains' of the late piano sonata, the piano trio or 'Winterreise' that waft across the orchestra in these 'Berio' moments can be recognised is one consideration to ponder. Intellectually speaking, these fragments may provide a link between the compositionally distinct worlds of Schubert and Berio, but, taken as a whole, the musical 'cross-hatching' is simply too prominent, and yet, paradoxically, also

44. Tippett, *The Knot Garden*, libretto, p. 107.

too self-effacing in a different way. By the standards of Berio's own works of the 1980s and 1990s, the textures in these moments of 'infill' are insufficiently characterised: more a case of 'waiting for something to happen'. In saying this, I may, of course, have provided Berio with a justification, since what does certainly 'happen' is the re-entry of a 'Schubert' moment that. at least for a while, brushes away the memory of the 'Berio' interventions.

When conceiving the central movement of *Sinfonia*, a work which already been mentioned, Berio went in search of the appropriate classical piece that could not only run through the entire movement and accept the juxtaposition and superimposition of stylistic entities from Bach to Stockhausen, but also possessed stylistic characteristics that were not too enormously distant from his own. Before alighting on the Mahler *Scherzo* as the musical river that was to flow through the movement, Berio was considering:

> harmonically 'exploding' the last three movements of Beethoven's Quartet in C sharp minor op. 131 – though without quotations and with 'little flags' composed by me instead. The vocal parts would have had a more instrumental character and the text would naturally have been quite different. I finally opted for Mahler not only because his music proliferates spontaneously, but also because it allowed me to extend, transform and comment on all of its aspects: including that of orchestration. ... Translating Beethoven's Op. 131 into orchestral terms would have been a very risky operation and, in view of the task in hand, not an entirely justified one'.[45]

Berio does not state in so many words that Mahler's music was stylistically nearer his own, but he shows awareness of the cultural context and of the relationships that could be created with Mahler, but which could not so simply or convincingly be attempted with Beethoven. With *Rendering*, composed some 20 years later, Berio has possibly undertaken a similar 'very risky operation', the outcome of which cannot easily be measured. This piece is very hard to categorise, and the fact of its homage to Schubert (the score places Schubert's name before Berio's in a hyphenated joint attribution) has perhaps led Berio into a relationship with Schubert's style and language that simply cannot stand. An alternative view might be that we need to develop

45. Luciano Berio and Rossana Dalmonte, 'Interview 5', in *Luciano Berio: Two Interviews with Rossana Dalmonte and Bálint András Varga*, trans. and ed. David Osmond-Smith, London, Marion Boyars, 1985, pp. 107–8.

some new criteria for listening and appreciation that are sufficiently responsive to this changed environment of stylistic co-existence.

Hans Zender's 'composed interpretation' of 'Winterreise' in a way 'risks all'. There are elements of this that could almost conform to my slightly tongue-in-cheek heading 'Relishing the Discomfort Factor'. Zender's work is in no way orchestrated in Schubertian style, and the world of late-twentieth-century modernism is everywhere on view: in the instrumentation, the timbral sophistication, the composer's attitude to rhythm, the use of polytonality, the adventurous manipulation of pulse and tempo, and many other dimensions. A Schubertian purist might well be horrified at the extent of the changes which are made to the letter of the score. However, if one steps slightly further back and re-evaluates the emotional journey taken by Schubert in this work, one must acknowledge that Zender has chronicled many of the same stages of spiritual and emotional turbulence as Schubert, but he has done so, in part, with the aid of more modern means. Zender has clearly understood deeply not only Müller's text but also Schubert's compositional approach. The portrayal of emptiness and desolation that Zender achieves, not only in *Der Leiermann* but even in the cycle's first song, *Gute Nacht*, is very consistent, and it justifies the radically new approach taken to the source. Just as Verdi's *Macbeth* or *Otello* can be evaluated as wholly independent works (although these operas have the advantage of belonging to an art-form very different from that of their immediate source, Shakespeare's plays), so Zender, too, now asks us to view his 'interpretation' of 'Winterreise' on its own terms. The two cycles (Schubert's and Zender's) can co-exist. One is not necessarily 'better' than the other: Zender's 'Winterreise' is not a pale imitation of Schubert's but a separate and **original** work that happens to take its starting-point from the earlier cycle. If we can accept (and many musicians do) the notion of the equality of significance of transcriptions of works, irrespective of the circumstances in which they were originally conceived or performed – so that Liszt's virtuosic version of *Der Erlkönig* has as much right to be programmed and appreciated for itself as Schubert's original – then we have to accept Zender's reworking as a valid composition on its own terms.[46]

46. Franz Liszt-Franz Schubert, *Der Erlkönig*, S. 558 no. 4, in Franz Liszt, '12 Lieder (1837–38)', reprinted in id., *Schubert Song Transcriptions*, Vol. 1, New York, Dover Publications, 1995.

It takes only a glance down most composers' work-lists as given in publishers' brochures to establish that the interest of composers in music from the past, both recent and distant, is very much a continuing one. Sometimes, it is true, these 'derived' pieces are mere *pièces d'occasion*, fill-ups for concert programmes. More often, however, they represent something far deeper that arises out of the composer's own desire to confront his or her own musical heritage and make sense of it. The listener may understandably feel uncomfortable with the very notion of 'recomposition', the idea that a Robin Holloway can take a Schumann song-cycle and surround it with his own ensemble 'commentaries'.[47] But one should not too quickly draw the inference that this kind of association arises from mere arrogance or from a wish to assert one's own importance against a reputable figure culled from musical history. It comes, more simply, from an individual's desire to create new works out of old.

47. Robin Holloway, *Fantasy-Pieces on 'Liederkreis' for 13 Instruments*, op. 16 (1970–71), London, Oxford University Press, 1971. This work, also known more simply as *Liederkreis*, uses material from Schumann's 'Liederkreis', Op. 24, on texts by Heine.

11

'On the Problems of Dating' or 'Looking Backward and Forward with Strohm'

Lydia Goehr

What happens when philosophers and historians quarrel over a date? The most favourable outcome is that each learns something from and about the other. This essay is a response to Reinhard Strohm's 'Looking Back at Ourselves: The Problem with the Musical Work-Concept' (pp. 128–52). I agree with Strohm that we reveal something about our modern selves when we interpret our desire to date this troublesome concept. But that agreement belies a tension between us that he already begins to make explicit in his title. His title refers to a looking back, when the argument of his text tells us to look forward. Whereas I chose in my *Imaginary Museum* to look back at the emergence of the work-concept from the perspective of 1800, Strohm urges me (and others) to look forward to 1800 from a historical juncture situated at least three centuries earlier. What turns on this difference of direction and starting point? Strohm likes to articulate this difference by drawing a contrast between the historian's **real** data and the philosopher's **invented** data. Let us see how far this articulation gets us.

The articulation is strange, not least because Strohm begins his essay precisely by objecting to the distinction between reality and invention that Michael Talbot employed in his title for the symposium in which this collection of essays originated. Though surely recognising the age-old philosophical debate that has given so much import to this distinction, and upon which Talbot was drawing, Strohm balks at the thought that if one speaks of concepts as 'invented' or 'fabricated', one is forced by the distinction to deny them their reality. To sustain this provocation, Strohm alters the traditional meaning of 'real' that motivated the (philosophical) distinction in the first place. He moves away from the metaphysical claim that 'real' means 'given', 'natural', perhaps 'unchanging' and 'essential', and makes it stand for something like 'having lived a life', 'having existed' or 'having played a rôle in a practice'. His move is skilful: by shifting our attention away from the old metaphysical dilemma to the straightforward idea that the work-concept has existed, he also shifts the topic from the philosophical to the historical. When, he now can ask, did the work-concept exist, and when did it originate? One might think that Strohm would propose his own date for the origination of the work-concept. But he does not – although he does like to draw on a fifteenth-century, Tinctorian, point of reference. Again it is a skilful step, because in not providing a definite thesis of origin, he is able to remain neutral, philosophically speaking, between the work-concept's reality and/or invention. In any event, for Strohm to counter his chosen opposition, it suffices only to show that the work-concept existed before 1800, a thesis that does not require a commitment to origin.

In each step of his critique against the '1800-theorists', i.e. the proponents of a 'watershed' or 'paradigm shift' associated with that date, Strohm claims to have history on his side. He accuses his opposition, by contrast, of investigating and treating the work-concept, and of making assertions about its status as regulative etc., from 'meta-historical', 'philosophical' and 'a priori' perspectives. He argues against two different positions. First, he claims that some theorists (notably myself) have adopted *a priori* a definition of the work-concept borrowed from an Anglo-American tradition of philosophical thinking, and then simply looked for a period in history that best supports it. This period turns out to be around 1800. Second, he accuses theorists – mostly German, philosophically inclined musicologists such as Carl Dahlhaus, but once again I find myself included – of taking their preferred work-concept, thickened in this instance by the profound philosophical currents of German Idealism and Romanticism (again, around 1800), and of then identifying its origin there. But why, Strohm asks quite reasonably, do theorists find the origin of the concept there, and not just a particularly well developed expression of a given stage of the concept's life?

Strohm's answer to this question is telling. To wish to find the 'origins' of our concepts around 1800 reflects, he argues (p. 133–34), a desire to identify and even actively to promote a 'crisis' in modernity (a period likewise marked by 1800 'origins'). To expose the contingency of modernity's reigning myths or 'hallowed concepts' is to begin to demythify them. But why are we concerned to do this now, he asks, and why do we go about it as if from an external, philosophically imposed perspective?

Strohm remarks (p. 130) on the tendency amongst 1800-theorists to ignore the historical fact that the attempted destruction of the work-concept is already part of the history of modernity. It did not begin just with the twentieth-century avant-garde, but originated among the very theorists and practitioners in the nineteenth century who also helped give to the concept its modern, mythic power. Strohm's point is not simply cultural 'self-diagnosis'. To show that the seeds of a myth's destruction were sown in the same period that sustained that myth serves his more general argument aimed at undercutting the exaggerated status of the work-concept. The power of the work-concept has been overstated in the modern period, he argues, and (conversely) understated in previous ones. Or if the work-concept was only one of a number of concepts governing modern musical practice, even when that concept was at the height of its power, then the same is arguably true of practice before 1800, when the power relations between the relevant concepts were different. Remember that Strohm has only to show that the work-concept existed in earlier periods, not that it had the equivalent power.

Strohm continues his argument. The fact, he laments (p. 137), that theorists have focused on one period more than any other reveals more about how the scholars in question have imposed their *a priori* determinations on history than it says about historical reality. In so imposing their determinations, they have created the impression that a great 'watershed' occurred around 1800. Identifying that watershed with the emergence of the work-concept has then allowed these theorists to speak of periods prior to 1800 as being different in 'hard and fast' ways. But these ways have been too 'hard and fast'. Strohm accordingly reminds his opposition that there is at least as much continuity as discontinuity across musical periods, a fact that, even if we grant that something significant happened in 1800, might suffice to sustain reasonable scepticism that the work-concept could have originated at this precise point.

Again, Strohm's argument is doubly directed: he is arguing against exaggerating watershed moments or paradigm changes in the history of music, and he is also arguing against identifying conceptual origins with these large moments of change. Has Strohm exaggerated his opposition's position? He has some textual evidence (if read in a most literal way) on his side. He points to those many instances in the literature where theorists say that 'for the first time, musicians did or were able to do such and such', or that 'the concept emerged at this time', or that 'the practice prior to 1800 survived and even thrived without a work-concept'. All these ways of speaking suggest that theorists have imposed too radical a separation between the time 'before' and the time 'after'.

In advancing this objection, Strohm is more correct than even he himself knows when he voices a specific complaint against my version of the 1800-thesis, as distinct from that (or those) of the German musicologists (p. 140). For, when I was formulating my version, I remember being struck by an ambiguity in Dahlhaus's account, one that Strohm should appreciate but one that I tried to highlight and resolve. Although Dahlhaus described the emergence of the work-concept as part of the late-eighteenth-century development of autonomy, bourgeois practice, and so on, he was nonetheless content to continue to use the concept when speaking of music from earlier periods. I remember deciding to try to describe earlier music practice without reference to the work-concept to bring home the strong ramifications of the 1800-thesis. My thought was that, if it were true that the work-concept emerged only around 1800, then the conceptual apparatus of the practice must have been interestingly different before that time. I decided to stress the differences overtly, a decision that made my story conceptually selective (Strohm says 'generalised').

I took all the factors that entered into the 1800 work-concept and tried to show either that these (same or similar) factors previously operated within a different conceptual scheme or that they were not present at all. Again, I tried less to be faithful to the historical complexity of musical practice than to engage in a sort of conceptual or imaginative experiment on the practice. Part of my purpose was to see both how different and how similar practice could be with and without the work-concept. That it could be extremely similar allowed the retroactive imposition of the concept on periods prior to its existence (thus justifying Dahlhaus's extended use of the concept after all). But, at the same time, the fact that the practice could be so different allowed one to see that it could actually operate without a work-concept. And if this was true, then the basic claim that had initiated my interest in this topic was also true: that not all music had necessarily to be packaged in terms of works.

This initiating interest had been born out of reaction to philosophers who took as unproblematic the idea that all objects fall under their respective concepts in exactly the same way: that when we package music by Tartini, Beethoven or Cage in terms of works, we do so for exactly the same reasons. On traditional ontological grounds the assumption was fairly unproblematic, but as soon as one began to adopt a (later) Wittgensteinian position, as I had decided to do, then one could see that concepts or names acquire their meaning in the complex contexts of their use(s). I had come to realise that to call a bit of music a 'work' could carry an enormous amount of philosophical, aesthetic, ideological, contextual, political and/or social baggage. It did not have to (perhaps), but so often it did; and precisely this baggage contributed to how we understood and packaged the music in question. This was true, as Strohm himself acknowledges (p. 132), of the 'anti-work' works of many avant-garde composers. But it was also true, I believed, of how we had come to treat the so-called works of 'early' music. Indeed, many of the devilish problems of 'authenticity' that so occupied musicians and musicologists in the 1980s had arisen through an easy, careless or imperialistic use of the 'Werktreue' concept. Being true to music, to performance, to history (if one could be so true), I argued, did not necessarily imply that one had to be true to a work. (Incidentally, Strohm complains that the term 'Werktreue' is a coinage of modernism, not of Romanticism (though he is vague on the dating); but could it not be, by his own argument, that the concept existed before this particular term was invented?).

Furthermore, I was quite familiar with the traditional philosophers' platform: that to describe a concept purely ontologically was not a descriptive mode that needed to accommodate historical (contingent?) differences. But I saw another way to account for this generic use of the work-concept: one that derived from a historical investigation into how the work-concept came, after 1800, to be used willy-nilly to describe the items of many musical practices, classical, popular, European and otherwise. I wanted to show that the most generic of our cultural concepts, despite the appearance of neutrality, givenness or pure ontological content, are often the most historically laden. To use a concept generically was to employ it as if it carried no historical baggage. This 'as if' employment tended to belie all manner of assumptive import. At the minimum, I wanted to say, 'Let's be aware of this import, even if we decide thereafter to use the concept in a generic way.' The more courageous, destructive argument was that, by becoming aware of this import, the generic employment would be undermined, and that that might bring about a change (perhaps a paradigm change!) in our practice. I think I meant by this, in my more ambitious moments, both musical and philosophical practice.

The use of history I made in my philosophical account of open and emergent concepts was not designed to reduce ontology to history or history to ontology (reductions that rightly puzzle Strohm). Rather, I wanted to see how far ontology could be made sensitive to the historical life of a concept. Contrary to Strohm's assumption, I do not remember being especially influenced by Lissa's objections to Ingarden, though I was aware of them. I was far more influenced at that time by Wittgenstein. (Here, I am trying less to give special weight to my intentions than to enter them into the record.) My ontology, admittedly, moved from the domain of objects to that of concepts, from the world of objects to conceptual schemes; but this was by no means an unfamiliar or particularly radical move in philosophical method. I did, however, try to show that **pure** ontology cannot (and perhaps should not) be made sensitive to historical variation, something I thought only Nelson Goodman fully acknowledged. And I did also think that Anglo-American ontologists too often fell into rather unstimulating disputes over which bits of history they did, and did not, wish to accommodate in their philosophical accounts. In place of that method, I offered a rather more adaptive, impure and complex ontological picture that tallied well with my historical account.

However, Strohm thinks that I unreasonably reduced both my ontology and my history to an overly convenient history of concepts. When I was writing my book, I remember being thoroughly intrigued by the way in which theorists who wished to challenge a given definition of the work-concept hardly ever drew their counter-examples from the period or part of practice that was being used to guide their theory. Strohm is more annoyed than intrigued. He charges me, first, with developing my 1800-theory on the basis of the paradigm of Beethoven's *Fifth Symphony*, and, second, with ignoring, suppressing or twisting the condition of any piece of music that does not conform to my model. I, by contrast, was fascinated by the fact that ontologists almost always began with the paradigmatic example of Beethoven's *Fifth Symphony* and then proceeded to draw counter-examples from a period in which the work-concept was either absent or had a different function (say, in the early history of Western art music or in jazz or popular practices), or else to take them from concurrent or later periods when the work-concept was being explicitly challenged. I thought that the ontologists chose their examples to confirm their theories. Strohm levels the same reproach at me and articulates the charge as one of circular or tautological argument.

To strengthen the charge, Strohm himself proposes, albeit sketchily, counter-examples to my view of 'works' that are taken from a different period, the 'Tinctorian' period (p. 142–44). He asks how I knew, or could be so firmly convinced, that my examples counted as *bona fide* works, whereas his did not. I say with some reservation that I thought I had some history on my side. I had looked hard at all the uses of noun-terms in musical writings – such terms as composition, song, piece, oeuvre, *ouvrage*, work, opus and opera – in different musical periods and, further, at many of the associated concepts, including notation, performance, composition, listening, repeatability, audience, concert practice, copyright and plagiarism. I never denied that musicians produced music, songs, overtures, oratorios and symphonies, or pieces, compositions, opera, etc. I just did not think that every time musicians produced these items, they thereby produced works. From a modern standpoint, I argued, we could retroactively say that they did, simply because the modern use of the work-concept allowed a generic use. But this did not mean that the generic use was always part of the character of an always existing work-concept. I thought that even when the word 'work' (and its equivalents or close approximations in other languages) or words conceptually very close to 'work', e.g. 'composition', 'opus', 'piece', were used in early musical practices, they often had very specific and limited uses and did not pick out exactly the same individuated items. Often, they invested elements in the practice with an importance that overshadowed that of the constellation of elements that would have been picked out by the modern work-concept. But, Strohm is right to ask, what counts as 'picking out the same item'?

I treated the work-concept as very thick, as carrying a lot of baggage. I also claimed that the work-concept emerged in 1800 with a regulative use. Strohm again poses the right challenge: even if the work-concept achieved a certain kind of thickness in 1800, and even a regulative status (though he does not like the way in which I use the terminology; of this more below), why could I not allow that there was perhaps a thinner and less assertive notion of the work prior to that? I did not allow it, because I did not see the historical evidence for it. I saw lots of hints of it in hindsight, but I believed that the noun-terms of musical practice, and the objects produced, fell under a conceptual scheme that did not require a work-concept either to make sense of the scheme or to allow the practice to function as admirably as it did, and with the same degree of richness. Musical practice could function, and it could function very well, without a work-concept.

On the other hand, had I allowed that a thinner and less assertive work-concept was present in musical practice prior to 1800, I would have been obliged to conclude either that the work-concept existed prior to 1800 or that another concept, going for all intents and purposes by the same or a similar name, was not the same as the one I claimed emerged around 1800. For Strohm, the former option is philosophically more plausible and historically more accurate. Indeed, why would anyone decide that a concept that was similar to another was actually a different concept, especially when there seemed to be sufficient historical continuity between the two?

In the rest of my response, I want to suggest a range of answers to this last question; together, they show that there is good reason why relations of similarity have to sustain not only assertions of identities but also assertions of difference. My answers permit a more nuanced version of the stronger 1800-thesis that Strohm attributes to me (and others). The claim remains that the work-concept **emerged** with its full regulative force around 1800; it merely avoids the assumption that the concept **originated** then. On the contrary, it allows that the origins of the concept are to be found in periods long before; but it also insists that we can identify them as origins only after the concept has fully emerged. I happen to believe that the separation between claims of emergence and origin is already present in existing versions of the 1800-thesis, even despite some rhetorical expressions to the contrary.[1]

Strohm does not acknowledge this separation. Perhaps he is right not to, given the potentially dangerous consequence he sees. The trouble with engaging in retroactive history – looking backward for origins of a fully developed concept – is that it encourages the tendency to read ideological and aesthetic baggage backward as well. What 'backward'-looking historians tend to do is to read past history as if it is rationally or naturally developing into the state from which they begin their inquiry. To avoid this tendency, Strohm recommends that we start at an earlier point. Let us, he suggests (p. 144), first admit that much of the development of the work-concept had already taken place by, say, the fifteenth century and then trace its development into

---

1.   See *The Imaginary Museum of Musical Works: An Essay in the Philosophy of Music*, Oxford, Clarendon Press, 1992, pp. 107–8.

its full Romantic form by looking forward. For Strohm, his forward-directed description has certain advantages: it releases the work-concept from its Romantic baggage; it undermines the commitment to grand paradigmatic changes or conceptual watersheds; finally, it is more faithful to historical fact.

Wherein lies the difference between looking backward and looking forward? What are we assuming when we speak of looking forward from the fifteenth century, or backward from 1800? I am not asking the classic epistemological question confronted by all historians: how, from the perspective of the present, our 'now' moment, can we think within and through any temporal direction inside history at all? Rather, I am asking about the terms of our interpretative discourse in the classical music tradition that allows us, with sense, to speak of looking forward from the Tinctorian perspective or backward from Beethoven. However, I need to motivate this question further before answering it.

I supported the Beethoven watershed because of its explanatory force. I was interested in understanding the changes I observed in how theorists and practitioners around 1800 treated and spoke about music. I did not think that everything changed around this time, but I was struck by how much did. I thought the best explanation of these changes involved reference to the work-concept, as well as to the many elements of musical practice (highly theoretical and highly practical) that were now conceived in relation to this concept. Of course the account was circular here, but not, as philosophers say, viciously so. It was circular because it was non-reductionist. In its thickness, I had to describe the work-concept by reference to all associated factors, and all associated factors in relation to it. I showed how the new emphasis on the work gave sense to compositional, performance and audience behaviour; how it governed the terms of copyright law, notational determination, etc. I never believed that notational determination, or any other single element or condition of musical practice, was sufficient by itself to prove the existence of the work-concept. I did not even claim that each was *a priori* necessary. However, I did think that to describe the thick content of the work-concept required one to look back and explain in hindsight what kind of changes supported its emergence. I was careful here. I did not want to deny *a priori* the existence or independent histories and functions of any or all of these factors or conditions prior to 1800. I merely suggested that at the point when they came to be related to one another through their shared relation to each other and to the work-concept, they gave a new structure and conceptual scheme to musical practice as a whole. In other words, I argued that the internal dynamic of practice prior to 1800 looked as if it had given rise to a concept, that of a work: a concept that then acquired its strength or authority of regulation precisely by standing in rejection of its past. (Of course, I did not imagine that these things happened overnight.)

To have reduced the work-concept to the totality of these associated factors would not have accommodated the history of how the concept obtained the independent meaning or power it did over the course of the next two centuries. One would not have been able to explain its soon-to-become generic use or how (some of) the associated factors started to work against, or in resistance to, the existence of the work-concept. Think of the battle fought between the formalists and expression theorists, between those who came to see the work as utterly self-sufficient and those who came to see the work as expressive of compositional self. Given these kinds of war, I did not choose, as Talbot does, to attribute to the concept of 'the composer' a paramount significance in the story of modern musical practice, preferring instead to focus on the central and regulative status of the work-concept. I thought my choice had broader explanatory scope.

Moreover, to grant the work-concept regulative status was not necessarily to give it a constitutive status prior to that. I did not see the emergence of the work-concept in terms of a transition from constitutive to regulative use, as Strohm suggests (p. 147). Nor did I, as he also infers (p. 144), have Kant technically in mind in developing the theme of regulation. My use of regulation was more modern and less exact. (I was influenced, rather, by Rawls' adaptation of Kant.) I wanted merely to capture how, around 1800, the musical work-concept became the concept that regulated – dictated or governed – the terms of musical practice. (As Strohm rightly insists, regulation can be a historical matter, pure and simple.) We compose works, score works, perform works, listen to works, criticise works, programme works, own works, etc. In so far as I was drawing on themes of transcendental critique, I was asking only, 'What must be true of the practice, what ideals regulate it, if we are to clarify the dominant discourse and mode of functioning that it has?' The circularity of transcendental critique, of this question, is of course part of its very nature.

My story had another nuance. I did not describe the emergence of the work-concept alone, but also, and more particularly, that of the musical work-concept. There were different work-concepts functioning in the other types of practice. As Strohm remarks, texted music had been dominant for centuries before 1800 and continued after 1800 to be so. Many dramas with music, operas and oratorios had been composed and continued to be composed. However, I argued that around 1800 texted music changed in the matter of text-note priority, and even in its conception, after music came to be defined primarily as the symphonic art of purely instrumental tone. (Even that definition was 'thick'.) The quarrel over priority had raged for centuries, but the terms of the quarrel changed around 1800. Strohm is also correct to say that purely instrumental music caught up around 1800 with the expressive potential of texted music. But, in my view, this truth did not automatically belie the fact that the musical work-concept was fully distinguished from the dramatic work-concept with the rise of purely instrumental or absolute music. To put the point differently: one might have had a work-concept before 1800, but was it a purely musical work-concept? And if it was not, I asked, how different was it?

Strohm raises the issues of continuity and discontinuity, of sameness and difference, and of individuating concepts, in relation to my reading of Listenius (which, contrary to Strohm's assertion, only partially depended on Seidel's reading: I was influenced more by Aristotle's conceptions of 'work' and 'labour', completing one's work, etc.). Strohm asks why 1800-theorists think that the work-concept does not have legitimate identification in Listenius's phrase 'opus absolutum et perfectum'? I read this phrase to refer to something different from that to which the work-concept refers. However, even if Strohm liked my reading (which he does not), he could still ask why, even given the (contingent?) differences, I did not judge the two concepts to be sufficiently similar? And, if there was sufficiently similarity, why is it that 1800-theorists always give priority to their modern concept and judge all other (arguable) uses of the work-concept by it? In other terms, throughout his critique, Strohm has been posing this complex question: why do we choose as our paradigmatic examples of works those produced around 1800? And has not this choice led us simply to beg the question of sameness and difference every time it arose?

Earlier, I posed this question in relation to another. I asked, 'With what justification have we adopted the standpoint of 1800 and looked backward, while Strohm adopts the Tinctorian standpoint of 1470 and looks forward?' Let me now address this question by asking, first, whether Strohm's worry about the 1800 date is a worry about just this date or one about any attempt to date the work-concept? Suppose that Strohm succeeded in convincing us that the work-concept existed in 1470 (in the Tinctorian period), could we not, by his own argument, continue to trace family resemblance relations and find that a concept sufficiently similar existed in 1370, and then in 1270 and so on *ad infinitum*? In other words, Strohm's argument threatens to produce the Sorites Paradox (see his Thesis 2 on p. 151). If resemblance relations are sufficient to certify or guarantee the existence of the work-concept, we might have to conclude that the work-concept existed from the first day of musical practice (whenever that was) by simple virtue of the continuity relations that constitute that practice. And, worse, we might also have to conclude that the concept is, by tracing back all similarity relations, identical to all other concepts. (Each thing is similar in some respect to another thing.)

Recall Goodman's fear that one conclusion we might have to draw from the Sorites Paradox is that Beethoven's *Fifth Symphony* is identical to *Three Blind Mice*. To avoid the unwanted identity, Goodman specified the condition of perfect compliance of performance to score as a way to sharply individuate between 'different' works. This specification was designed precisely to provide a sharp cut-off point between similarity relations, and to be sharp enough to avoid any vagueness. My response now to Strohm's perpetual question is this: whether we are philosophers or historians, we have to provide cut-off points. Strohm disagrees, writing in Thesis 2 that 'the problem of "infinite regression" cannot be solved by throwing a spanner into the works'. But surely the solution depends on what kind of impact the spanner has. The critical question, I think, is this: how sharp do we want to make our cut-off points, and upon what basis do we decide them?

The more rigid or traditional view in philosophy is that cut-off points require a determination of essential features or of necessary and sufficient conditions for the use of concepts. On a less extreme view, cut-off points are given with the appearance and dissemination of the first prototype(s). The prototypes or paradigmatic examples that we pick – at least, according to cognitivists – are grounded in human nature and mental hard wiring. On this view, we can distinguish prototypical instances from a penumbra of non-standard or derivative instances. Prototypes are learned first and remembered most easily. Derivative instances are then conceptualised in terms of, or in relation to, the prototypes. Thus the prototypes are not imposed upon practice according to some philosophical decision. Rather, they are chosen because they strike us as most familiar. Theorists, other than those working in cognitive psychology, have grounded the feeling of familiarity in more or less conservative, or more or less critical, theories of convention, practice, society, ideological formation, stipulation or learned habits (in my book I developed a view of paradigmatic examples as part of a Wittgensteinian theory of open concepts.)

We may reasonably claim that when the 1800-theorists took as their prototype Beethoven's *Fifth Symphony*, it was not because they were adopting an arbitrary standpoint in the history of music. It was, rather, that, even in the contemporary practice of concert-hall music, this work still served as the paradigm. The Beethoven prototype felt most familiar. Why it did has been written about most often under the rubric of the Beethoven myth. This description has revealed less the 'real' circumstances of Beethoven's life and work than the idealising and idealised circumstances of work-production 'mythically' associated with Beethoven – associations that began to be made in Beethoven's lifetime and even, to an extent, by Beethoven himself.

Do we have the same feeling of familiarity in relation to Strohm's Tinctorian time-slice? This is an unfair question (it is too easy). Anyway, it only obscures the harder question, namely, whose feeling of familiarity, or whose choice of prototypes, should we trust? Do not the 1800-theorists feel so familiar with Beethoven because he symbolises our preferred period, our heritage and our contemporary German-orientated anxieties? Perhaps Strohm feels equally familiar with his period? Or perhaps we should not appeal to the feelings of musicologists or philosophers, the experts, at all but should instead canvass the listener's feelings, naïve feelings (as philosophers like to call them)? But which listeners? Which feelings? How does one decide with whose concept and with whose prototypes to begin?

I want to suggest that the choice of starting point does not, indeed, always matter, that is, from a philosophical point of view. I actually did not begin with a feeling of familiarity, a fixed prototype at all (Beethoven was not the prototype in my musical education!). I began more obscurely with theories about the ontological status of musical works offered first by Ingarden and then by several Anglo-American philosophers. It was from them that I first learned about the power of the Beethoven prototype. I then found the same prototype employed similarly by the German musicologists. Influenced by the latter theorists, I began to seek an explanation for the fact that the onto-logical theorists started with the Beethoven prototype. By the end of my enquiry I believed I had one. With it in hand, I did not challenge the prototype. Instead, I challenged the idea that one could produce an ontological theory as if it were free from the commitment to a pro-totype.

Surely Strohm does not really object to my taking a prototype employed by Anglo-American philosophers of music on the grounds that this choice is part of musical practice, too. The philosophy of music is not an imposition on musical practice, although often it feels that way. It is part of it, and shapes and guides it, however indirectly. It helps to constitute its discourse, just as music history does – just as both always have done. Strohm cannot believe that philosophers impose on the facts, while historians merely discover them. He cannot really think it wrong that theorists take a prototype undeni-ably dominant in the discourse, even if it is a philosophical discourse, as a starting point for critical reflection and attempt to work out a better theory of the musical work in reaction to this peculiar discur-sive phenomenon.

Let us now ask what an ontological theory of the work-concept would have looked like, had the theorists started with fifteenth-cen-tury musical composition? Would it – could it – have depended upon the exact same conditions of content, form, notation, compositional authority, performance, reception, repeatability, etc.? Let us ask Strohm the same question. Taking Tinctoris as the starting point, and confronted by the very same historical data, does he find the same or a different constellation of important features? Judged as different or the same, his description could neither prove nor disprove my philo-sophical thesis. That thesis, remember, was that the work-concept does not pick out an essence, nor is it fixed or closed; it is, rather, an open concept that corresponds to perhaps different patterns of salience determined by background cultural practice and choice of prototypes. For the philosophical thesis, more than historical descrip-tion is required.

Yet his description could demonstrate the historical thesis that music practice either did, or did not, change nearly as much as some of us (1800-theorists) like to think. But if, as Strohm suggests, musi-cal practice did not change significantly or paradigmatically, why did he argue so strongly against our taking the starting point that we did? His argument could not have been philosophical, for if there is no significant difference to be shown in the history, no significant difference should be shown by our different starting points. He did not have an argument against our taking a starting point *per se* (despite claims to the contrary). He had an argument against our taking the particular starting point that we did only because it had misled us into miswriting our music history.

The burden on Strohm is to produce a better description (a tactic well adopted, for example, by Harry White in a recent article).[2] What would it show? Well, it would not by itself exclude the possibility that a conflicting description be offered from another starting point. In my view, we have the option to cut up history differently without our necessarily having to conclude that the two descriptions mark an 'essential' (philosophical) difference. (Here, I take issue with Strohm's articulation of the burden in his Thesis 1.) An ideal theory of the musical work could admit varying descriptions differing in their starting points. They would each be adequate to the demands of history and of philosophy. But once they were all before us, what would we do with them? Either we would seek a work-concept so thin that it could accommodate all descriptions given of it, or we would allow that descriptions could conflict, given our choice of very different prototypes. Again, I prefer, and have tried to argue for, the latter route, not least because it shows so well that how we think about music, how our musical discourses develop, depends in very interesting ways on the prototypes we employ and on the myths we construct. On the purest philosophical plane, our choice of examples perhaps does not matter. But I chose the route of philosophical impurity where our choices matter a great deal. That impurity symbolises, as Strohm perceived so well, the intersection between philosophy and cultural diagnosis.

I have tried in my response to Strohm's criticisms to separate out the philosophical arguments from the historical. At no point have I claimed that in my book I got all the history right. Perhaps Strohm is correct to say that I did not. But I was careful to produce credible philosophical arguments that Strohm has not succeeded in undermining. Once more: if there were a work-concept existing before 1800, I would like to see it described independently from the Romantic and

2. Harry White, "'If it's Baroque, Don't Fix It'": Reflections on Lydia Goehr's "Work-Concept" and the Historical Integrity of Musical Composition', *Acta musicologica*, Vol. 69 (1997), pp. 94–104.

modern baggage the concept seems always to carry. Of course, if we find that critics of the 1800-thesis always seem to assume the 1800-concept even as they criticise it, perhaps this is because they are describing the same concept. But then reference to the 1800 standpoint is not necessary in their description at all, unless they concur, which I think they do, that in 1800 something happened that made the concept more explicit or self-conscious than it had ever been before. Perhaps this is all the 1800-theorists have ever wanted to claim. Nonetheless, an independent description would provide the strongest antidote to theorists too comfortably committed to Beethoven. Or, to follow Strohm's cultural diagnosis, for those who stay comfortably committed to their Beethoven prototype, even though they feel post-modern anxiety about it, a genuinely competing description might just be the medicine they most need.

Index of Musical Compositions
and Collections

Editor's note
This index lists the individual musical compositions and collections mentioned in this book. 'Popular' items are indexed by title only. 'Classical' items are indexed first by composer's surname, then by title or equivalent description (unless the surname of the composer appears in the title itself, in which case the title alone is given). Individual compositions are printed in italics; sets, cycles and albums appear in roman type within quotation marks. (In order to retain more of the original flavour, the use of initial capitals for words belonging to the titles of popular songs and albums has not been normalised.) The editor cannot forbear to add that whoever likes to browse in indexes will discover the most amusing juxtapositions in what follows. The letter 'n.' after a page reference indicates the number of a footnote occurring on that page.

Index of Personal Names

Editor's note

This index lists the personal names and the names of musical ensembles mentioned in this book. The names of publishers and companies are excluded. The letter 'n.' after a page reference indicates the number of a footnote occurring on that page.